Monopoly Politics

Monopoly Politics

Competition and Learning in the Evolution of Policy Regimes

ERIK PEINERT

OXFORD
UNIVERSITY PRESS

OXFORD
UNIVERSITY PRESS

Oxford University Press is a department of the University of Oxford. It furthers the University's objective of excellence in research, scholarship, and education by publishing worldwide. Oxford is a registered trademark of Oxford University Press in the United Kingdom and in certain other countries.

Published in the United States of America by Oxford University Press
198 Madison Avenue, New York, NY 10016, United States of America.

CIP data is on file at the Library of Congress.

ISBN 9780197789513

ISBN 9780197789506 (hbk.)

DOI: 10.1093/oso/9780197789506.001.0001

Paperback printed by Marquis Book Printing, Canada
Hardback printed by Bridgeport National Bindery, Inc., United States of America

The manufacturer's authorized representative in the EU for product safety is Oxford University Press España S.A., Parque Empresarial San Fernando de Henares, Avenida de Castilla, 2 – 28830 Madrid (www.oup.es/en).

Contents

List of Figures

List of Table

Preface

This is a book about how states regulate markets: about how states decide who gets to be powerful in the market, how powerful they can become, and correspondingly who is less powerful. In politics, we often frame such questions in terms of ideology, normative values, or sheer political power, but by contrast most states today have come to mediate these power relationships in markets through the mechanism of *competition*. Ensuring that powerful companies face market competition also limits the political power that those companies have, relative to the state itself or in comparison to other interests. After all, arguably, a monopoly is politically powerful precisely because it does not face competition in the market.

Yet competition and monopoly are also core mechanisms through which modern economies grow, innovate, improve living standards, and become more efficient. By exposing a company to more competition, it is at once made less powerful and also pressured to make new products, reduce costs, and grow. Conversely, by protecting a company, that company is at once made more politically powerful and also given resources and space to invest in new technologies, new practices, and new ideas. These technical questions of economic efficiency or growth are not separable from the human and normative questions of political power. The two are one and the same.

For this and other reasons, the core premise of this book is that states struggle to maintain a stable regulatory arrangement for competition and monopoly, unable to mediate the normative stakes of competition against the intrinsic complexities of antitrust policy, intellectual property rights, industrial policies, and trade policy, to name a few. This has led many governments to shift policy back and forth between competition and monopoly, almost mechanically as a pendulum might swing. And the implication, when I began this project in the mid-2010s, was that after decades of policy favoring powerful companies, the United States was facing a crisis of concentration, monopoly, and economic stagnation, and it was likely that the United States would shift policy back toward competition in the near future.

When I first presented this research in 2018 and 2019, I often saw quizzical looks from the back of a seminar room, seeing clear skepticism at the notion that the American government would turn on Silicon Valley, or any other key industry, anytime soon. After all, in the face of the 2008 financial crisis, economic and geopolitical competition from China, unprecedented levels of inequality, and the looming threat of climate change, governments mostly continued with the same political and policy solutions they had for decades. That meant limited economic regulation and stronger protections for multinational corporations, in the form of bailouts, stronger legal rights, favorable trade agreements, and the like. The argument that a real economic problem—a lack of competition—would lead to a policy change seemed naïve at best and functionalist at worst, particularly when powerful business interests would oppose that change.

Yet policy change has come to pass. Following the Trump administration's filing of multiple antitrust cases against Silicon Valley giants in 2020, the Biden administration embraced a whole-of-government competition agenda. And as I was finishing this book, I worked outside academia in a policy role at a Washington, DC, think tank, working with policymakers to implement and support this competition agenda. The course of policy on the ground is far more unpredictable, personal, and haphazard than social scientists would often like to admit, but I watched as many of the basic premises of this argument played out.

That being said, I am writing this preface mere days after President Biden dropped out of the 2024 American presidential election. The political and economic future of the country, and the world, is deeply indeterminate at this moment, and in far more important ways than questions of competition.

Will these competition policies continue under a second Trump presidency? Would they continue under a Harris presidency, should Kamala Harris become president? With so much in question, and democracy itself on the ballot in many ways, I admit I have no idea. While the argument of this book has appeared to play out thus far, I have limited confidence it will continue to do so. New leadership, and the policymakers they appoint, can make different decisions. And as in all of the instances of policy change examined in this book, other choices were and are possible, and those choices depend on cadres of mid-level policymakers, and all of their preexisting commitments to various causes. What I can say is that regardless of decisions in the near term, the American government will need to come to terms with its monopoly problem, in one way or another.

Erik Peinert
July 2024
Washington, DC

Acknowledgments

So many people have helped me along in this process, and it is difficult to fully give each their due, and writing it out is a reminder of how much even a sole-authored work is a collective endeavor.

Mark Blyth has been a constant source of support throughout my entire academic career, from the moment I was even considering pursuing a PhD up to this very day. Whether I knew where I was going with a set of ideas or was completely lost, Mark always guided me in productive directions and pushed me to see the bigger picture. Richard Locke has steadfastly supported my research interests and pursuits, reliably urging me to hammer down conceptual points and to frame the larger message of the project, my work, and what they say about politics generally. Having never stepped in an archive before beginning the research for this project, I was guided by Nitsan Chorev through this process at nearly every step: what to look for, how to look for it, what to do with it, and how to know what something means. Nitsan helped me appreciate the intellectual work needed to build an original historical narrative that still retains its analytical power.

For feedback, comments, conversations, and suggestions—large and small—I want to thank Rawi Abdelal, Melike Arslan, Philippe Bèzes, Sébastian Billows, Brian Callaci, Alain Chatriot, Brett Christophers, Pepper Culpepper, Chase Foster, Patrick le Galès, Eric Helleiner, Anselm Küsters, Tina Li, Kathleen McNamara, Fréderique Marty, Rose McDermott, Eric Monnet, Sanjukta Paul, Sigfrido Ramírez Pérez, Jonas Pontusson, Sabeel Rahman, Vivien Schmidt, Herman Mark Schwartz, Andy Smith, Marshall Steinbaum, Matt Stoller, Kathleen Thelen, Matthias Thiemann, Sanne Verschuren, Gauri Wagle, Spencer Waller, Laurent Warlouzet, and Cornelia Woll.

For support and an intellectual home during this process, I want to thank the *Centre d'études européenne* at Sciences Po for hosting me in the fall of 2018, and I want to thank the Max Planck Institute for European Legal History in Cologne for hosting me in May 2019. I also want to thank the American Economic Liberties Project for the flexibility in finishing the research for this project, and the Economic Security Project for research funding that supported the completion of this book.

Many helped on a day-to-day basis while I was in the archives, but I want like to particularly thank Dara Baker at the Roosevelt Presidential Library, Carla Braswell at the Nixon Presidential Library, and Haley Maynard at the National Archives in College Park for helping me navigate the opaque organization of mid-20th-century Department of Justice records. Additionally, I want to thank Jennifer Newby at the Reagan Presidential Library, Stacy Davis at the Ford Presidential Library, Keith Shuler of the Carter Presidential Library, and Vivien Richard of the *Archives Nationales* in Pierrefitte-sur-Seine for allowing me early access to the records of Georges Pompidou. I could not have even started much of this work without their assistance.

Lastly, I want to recognize the significant intellectual debts I owe to Brett Christophers and Herman Mark Schwartz, whose work greatly inspired the foundational ideas behind this research.

Archival Sources

The following abbreviations are used to refer to the sites where archival records were consulted:

AN	*Archives Nationales* in Pierrefitte-sur-Seine, France
CAEF	*Centre des archives économiques et financières* (Ministry of Finance Archives) in Savigny-le-Temple, France
CNPF	Archives of the *Conseil national du patronat français* in Roubaix, France
FDR	Franklin D. Roosevelt Presidential Library in Hyde Park, NY
GF	Gerald Ford Presidential Library in Ann Arbor, MI
JC	Jimmy Carter Presidential Library in Atlanta, FL
JFK	John F. Kennedy Presidential Library in Boston, MA
LC	Library of Congress, Manuscript Division in Washington, DC
NARA	National Archives and Records Administration in College Park, MD
RN	Richard Nixon Presidential Library in Yorba Linda, CA
RR	Ronald Reagan Presidential Library in Simi Valley, CA

Portions of this book first appeared in *World Politics*, Volume 75, Number 3, 2023. Published with permission by Johns Hopkins University Press.

Chapter 3 is derived, in part, from an article published in the *Review of International Political Economy* on July 8, 2020, available online: https://www.tandfonline.com/doi/abs/10.1080/09692290.2020.1788971.

1
Introduction: The Monopoly Problem in the Long Run

In 2021, President Biden selected Lina Khan, a prominent critic of technology giant Amazon, and more generally an advocate of reinvigorating American antitrust law and enforcement, as chair of the Federal Trade Commission (FTC), one of the United States' main antitrust enforcers. Khan was confirmed by a surprisingly bipartisan 69 to 28 Senate vote. Khan quickly signaled her intent to significantly change the status quo at the FTC, pulling back policies designed to constrain the FTC's legal powers, altering decision-making procedures, and committing to reform the corporate-friendly principles that had guided American antitrust for decades. This prompted a number of longstanding FTC attorneys to seek employment elsewhere, with one commentator noting that "the new chair is telling staff attorneys that she's going to change antitrust enforcement and the way the agency does things to be more vigorous and vigilant . . . and for many, it feels like they're being told that the mission they've pursued and the policies they've implemented—they've been doing it all wrong."[1] So rather than go with the new direction and reverse previous positions and commitments, many staff are looking to leave. Of those that remain, many continue to voice their dissatisfaction with the new leadership.[2]

This blend of bureaucratic politics, staffing, and previous policy commitments can make this appear as a dispute between personalities, but such a view disguises a broader policy shift underway. In December 2020, a number of American states filed a major antitrust action against technology giant Google, alleging that Google attained its monopoly over digital advertising markets through, among other things, anticompetitive tying arrangements

[1] "'A Real Disquiet': FTC Staff Attorneys Are Job Hunting," *The National Law Journal*, July 13, 2021, https://www.law.com/nationallawjournal/2021/07/13/a-real-disquiet-ftc-staff-attorneys-are-job-hunting/.

[2] "Sinking FTC Workplace Rankings Threaten Chair Lina Khan's Agenda," *The Washington Post*, July 13, 2022, https://www.washingtonpost.com/technology/2022/07/13/ftc-lina-khan-rankings/.

Monopoly Politics. Erik Peinert, Oxford University Press. © Oxford University Press (2025).
DOI: 10.1093/oso/9780197789506.003.0001

and acquisitions,[3] following a similar action by the Department of Justice (DOJ).[4] The same month, forty-eight states and the FTC filed against Facebook, alleging that Facebook eliminated potential competitors via an illegal "buy-or-bury" strategy.[5] Khan's appointment was not an isolated staffing choice of the Biden administration. Jonathan Kanter, a longtime critic of Silicon Valley tech giants and an experienced litigator, was chosen as assistant attorney general for antitrust, the country's other main antitrust enforcer.[6] Then in July 2021, Biden signed a broad executive order to expand competition in the American economy,[7] signaling a "whole of government" approach to restoring competition in American markets. Recent years have also seen a slew of bills introduced in Congress to update antitrust law. Compared to a decade ago, when such actions against the United States' most successful firms would have been unthinkable, all of these together amount to a dramatic reversal in policy regarding antitrust and competition.

What Monopoly Problem?

This policy shift is arguably in response to a series of economic problems. Bolstered by policy for decades, monopoly power in the United States has grown to extreme levels in recent years. Following significant deregulation of merger control and antitrust policies in the 1980s, 75% of American industries became more concentrated from the 1990s through the 2010s (Grullon, Larkin, and Michaely 2019). Guided by a "consumer welfare standard," antitrust policy in the United States for forty years now has systematically assumed that large, vertically integrated companies are more efficient, that the risks from increased corporate concentration are minimal, and that a number of anticompetitive restraints by large firms are efficient. Intellectual property (IP) rights—which bestow temporary monopolies—have been greatly bolstered from the 1980s to today. This lack of competition characterizes markets across the technological spectrum,

[3] *State of Texas v. Google, LLC*, Complaint filed December 16, 2020.

[4] *U.S. Department of Justice v. Google, LLC*, Complaint filed October 20, 2020.

[5] *State of New York v. Facebook, Inc.*, Complaint filed December 9, 2020. *Federal Trade Commission v. Facebook, Inc.*, Complaint filed December 9, 2020.

[6] Lauren Hirsch and David McCabe, "Biden to Name a Critic of Big Tech as the Top Antitrust Cop," *New York Times*, July 24, 2021, https://www.nytimes.com/2021/07/20/business/kanter-doj-antitrust.html.

[7] "Executive Order on Promoting Competition in the American Economy," *The White House*, July 9, 2021, https://bidenwhitehouse.archives.gov/briefing-room/presidential-actions/2021/07/09/executive-order-on-promoting-competition-in-the-american-economy/.

where the agricultural, airline, and food-service industries are consolidated with limited competition. Recent research and popular discussion have identified this anticompetitive trend as a key driver of many of today's broader economic and political maladies. For the past decade, profits have been hitting all-time highs in the United States, in a time of somewhat stagnant growth, where most consumers find prices for medication, insurance, transit, and many other essential goods and services rising year after year.

First, and perhaps most expected, monopolies are not good for consumers. The defining feature of market power—the technical, economic term for monopoly—is the ability for a producer to increase prices without substantially losing sales, and as such firms that face little competition tend to charge consumers more than is justified by the costs of production. De Loecker, Eeckhout, and Unger (2020) have shown that the average markups (the difference between sales price and the costs of goods sold) have increased dramatically in the United States since 1980.[8] Philippon (2019) estimates that the average American household is paying $5,000 more per year for standard goods and services than they would be if American markets were as competitive as they were forty years ago.

Beyond these obvious harms, the new era of monopoly power comes in a particular form. New "platform" business models operate as intermediaries connecting a range of buyers and sellers (Rahman and Thelen 2019), giving them access to large amounts of data to enter and dominate adjacent markets. At the same time, whether in software, hardware, pharmaceuticals, retail, or manufacturing, the consolidation of industry and profits has been closely associated with the consolidation of IP like patents, trademarks, and copyright (Autor et al. 2020; Kurz 2023; Schwartz 2016, 2021). For example, Amazon, an online retail platform and cloud computing firm with a vast IP portfolio, uses its control over its platform and intangible data to maintain its position (Rikap 2022).

Accordingly, this form of monopoly power has contributed to the rise in income inequality over the past several decades. With their core profits protected by enhanced IP rights and limited competition, lead firms have increasingly chosen to unbundle production and outsource a large

[8] Kurz (2017) finds similar results with different methodologies, and both Kurz and De Loecker et al. connect this trend to stagnant growth.

fraction of their labor to subcontractors—a "workplace fissuring" made possible through anticompetitive reforms to antitrust, trade, and IP law (Callaci 2018; Paul 2020; Schwartz 2020; Weil 2014). And as profitable firms tend to pay much better wages, as firms have outsourced the less-profitable portions of production, profit differentials between these highly profitable firms and others are among the core drivers of income inequality (Barth et al. 2016; Furman and Orszag 2018; Song et al. 2019). In addition to these effects on labor income inequality, the skyrocketing equity values of the most profitable firms have boosted the wealth of existing asset owners and have created a plethora of new multi-billion-dollar fortunes along the way. The founders or early investors of technology companies have ended up with wealth on the scale of the first gilded age in the early 20th century.

These monopoly protections, and the associated unbundling of production, have a series of negative macroeconomic effects, including depressed investment and lower growth rates. Firms with market power tend to invest less than firms facing competition, for a monopoly investing in R&D or productive capacity will possibly *reduce* profits (Arrow 1962). Moreover, the unbundling of production by IP-heavy monopolies has also meant that profits have been allocated away from investment-heavy sectors (integrated manufacturing, telecommunications, and chemicals), to IP-intensive sectors that invest less (finance, pharmaceuticals, and software) (Schwartz 2020). Accordingly, the largest firms in the United States today have a lower marginal propensity to invest than firms in more competitive markets (Philippon 2019; Schwartz 2021). Gutiérrez and Philippon (2019) show a lagging rate of new business creation in recent decades in the United States, largely driven by anticompetitive regulations and policy, while the contribution of large firms to productivity growth in recent decades has actually been *falling* (Gutiérrez and Philippon 2020). Gutiérrez and Philippon (2018) link this "investment gap" in the United States to declining competition since 2000.

The policy conflict over antitrust, competition, and monopoly is happening in the shadow of this economic context. While there is dispute over exactly which outcomes are attributable to this rise in market power, there is little dispute that corporate concentration has increased in recent years, profits for the largest firms have grown in comparison to others, and income and wealth inequality have increased over the same time period.

What Long Run?

Although the current situation is important in its own right, this book focuses on a broader historical phenomenon, of which current circumstances are merely the latest iteration: there is a pattern of long-term alternations between policy favoring competition and policy favoring market power. Specifically, a number of governments continuously push for policies that enhance commercial competition for decades, only to switch and then for decades implement policies that favor the market power of lead firms, or vice versa.

A few examples help to illustrate. The United States introduced its first antitrust laws in the late 19th century, only to weaken those laws beginning in the late 1910s and strengthen industrial protections for decades through to the mid-1930s (Freyer 2006; Himmelberg 1976; Wells 2002). Turning back toward competition, the United States adopted strict antitrust and liberal trade policies during and after World War II. Then, since the 1970s and 1980s, the United States has strengthened IP protections and weakened antitrust policies (Christophers 2016; Eisner 1991; Philippon 2019), leading to an overall policy approach favoring market power (Khan 2018). And American policy now appears to be turning back toward competition. Britain followed a similar trajectory of pro-competition free trade in the late 19th century, then encouraged cartels during the interwar years—like much of Europe at the time—only to implement American-style antitrust shortly after World War II (Christophers 2016; Freyer 1992), only to then weaken its competition policies again in recent decades (Christophers 2020).

Other countries follow different timelines but a similar pattern. France, having followed similar cartel policies in the interwar years, moved swiftly to crush private cartels after World War II and removed price regulations inherited from the Vichy and occupation government (Didry and Marty 2016; Kipping 2002). But then by the mid-1960s France was directing investment and reworking the very same price controls to protect its "national champion" firms (Adams 1989; Berger 1981; Hall 1986; Kipping 2001). France, decades later, then turned to enhance standard competition policies in the 1980s (Gerber 1998; Schmidt 1996). In Japan, antitrust laws were imposed by the American occupation, but within a few years Japan turned toward anticompetitive industrial management under the aegis of the Ministry of International Trade and Industry (MITI) (Haley 2001; Johnson 1982; Wells 2002). Like in other cases, however, within several decades Japan's

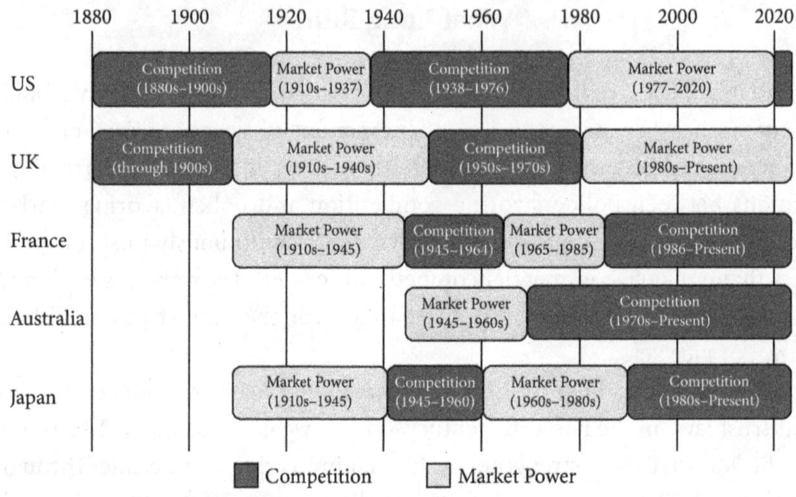

Figure 1.1 Policy Regimes over Time

competition regulators had reasserted themselves and MITI's influence was subdued (Freyer 2006, 160–244). In Australia, cartels and industrial combinations were legal and encouraged for most of the postwar era, but beginning in the 1960s and 1970s the government changed course and adopted stronger competition rules against cartels and concentration (Freyer 2006, 315–392). Figure 1.1 provides a simplified representation of this pattern across countries.

There has long been a recognition that the politics of antitrust and competition, particularly in the United States, have a cyclical, periodic nature.[9] While these broad shifts at points included some conflicting policy goals, there nonetheless is a common tendency of alternations between overall approaches to economic policy—what I call *policy regimes*—in favor of either competition or market power. These regimes can take on historically specific forms but nonetheless, I argue, adhere to this characterization. For example, the United States' policy regime, since the 1970s until very recently, has been systematically in favor of market power built around the "consumer welfare standard" (Khan 2018). France had a market power policy regime based on the defense of "national champion" firms in the 1960s

[9] Hovenkamp (1985, 213) notes "that antitrust is both political and cyclical." Sanders (1999, 267) says that "American enthusiasm for antitrust has shown a marked periodicity." And Sanders (1999, 267) explicitly argues that American and British markets have alternated between competition and monopoly over time.

and the 1970s. Postwar America's policy regime favoring competition was organized loosely around the structure-conduct-performance (SCP) framework. Despite these differences, there is a consistent alternation in the long run between policy regimes favoring competition and those favoring market power.

With many countries seeing similar common shifts over time, this pattern is in contrast to many political economy perspectives that see different countries as representing different "national models" or "varieties of capitalism" uniquely inherited from the past (Esping-Andersen 1990; Hall and Soskice 2001; Iversen and Wren 1998; Thelen 2014). Such perspectives, common in comparative political economy and political science generally, view different countries as representing their own stable and enduring form of capitalism with, for example, France as a "statist" model, the United States and United Kingdom as "liberal" models, and Germany and other northern European states as "coordinated" models in some form (Dobbin 1994; Esping-Andersen 1990; Hall and Soskice 2001). Such views frequently see these national models as "locked-in" or "path-dependent" institutional equilibria (Hall 1986; Mahoney 2000; Pierson 2000), indicating that they are self-reinforcing politically and economically over time and are expected to endure through all but the most severe economic or political shocks. This pattern of alternations, however, suggests a great deal of common institutional fluidity and instability, even given varied historical origins.

An alternating pattern like this cannot easily be explained according to more general theories of politics. While electoral politics experiences swings in policy as the party in power changes, these shifts in policy regimes usually occur when one party or government reverses its own previous policy position, with most of the shifts in policy occurring under the same party and often the same executive leadership. Additionally, while business is generally influential in areas of corporate regulation, such as antitrust, an account of business lobbying would struggle to explain the political losses faced by concentrated business interests during policy regimes favoring competition, such as today. Accounts that focus on the effects of technological change, likewise, have difficulty in explaining why the shifts in policy span many industries that do not use similar technologies or that rely on quite old technologies. New economic ideas, such as the Chicago school of antitrust, are usually not hypothesized to have such consistent back-and-forth patterns.

In contrast to these more conventional views, I argue that this pattern of long-term policy alternations implies something different: a more systemic dynamic internal to the regulation of modern capitalist economies that pushes them to change themselves over time, alternating between modalities of competition and monopoly power. What explains this pattern? Why does policy in a number of advanced industrial states alternate back and forth in the long run between support for competition and the defense of market power?

The Argument in Brief

Borrowing insights from microeconomics, bureaucratic politics, sociology, psychology, and law, this book contends that policy change is an interaction between (a) the self-undermining effects of economic policies over time and (b) the organizational patterns of staff turnover, policy commitment, and learning within policymaking circles. The core of the argument is that policy regimes that consistently favor competition or market power over time intrinsically generate large *diminishing returns*—economic costs that come in the form of economic stagnation, lower employment, and low investment, among others. However, because the policy regime had already endured for so long, policymakers who had spent their political or bureaucratic careers in favor of the policy regime are effectively *committed* to it, unwilling to recognize the costs of the policy regime and change their mind about the appropriate goals of policy. Yet through mundane processes of staff and political turnover, uncommitted policymakers are introduced into policy circles, and these uncommitted actors are willing to learn, change their mind about policy, and push others to do so, eventually shifting to a different policy regime in the opposite direction. Figure 1.2 provides a simplified representation of this sequence.

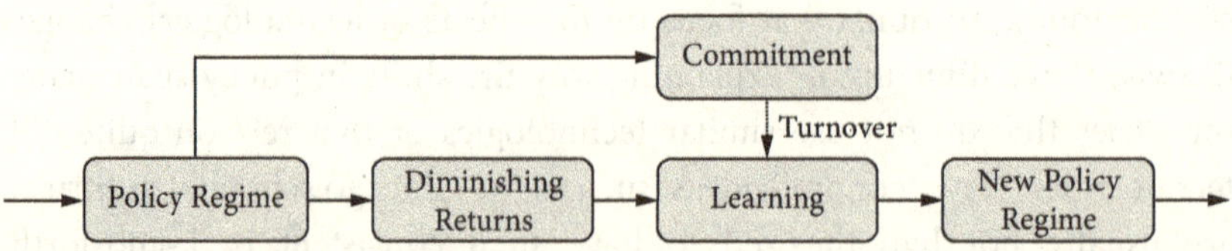

Figure 1.2 Summary of Argument

A *policy regime* refers to a pattern of policy changes consistently in favor of either competition or market power, built around a coherent understanding of how competition and market power should be regulated. By *competition*, I refer to a narrow definition of price competition derived from classic microeconomic models: with a large number of both sellers and buyers, producers face profit-maximizing incentives to increase output and lower prices toward marginal cost. Conversely, market power means that firms, whether producers or buyers, are able to set prices independently of the market, whether that is because of trade barriers, capital requirements, technological limitations, cartelization, or any other mechanism that allows firms to set prices independently. Competition can take on broader meanings—competition for quality, competition for corporate control, and so on—but for the purposes of this book, it is narrowly defined in these terms of prices and relative to marginal cost.

While it is easy to reduce issues of competition and monopoly to recognizable policy arenas like antitrust, governments can promote market power or competition in a variety of ways. Policy areas such as trade openness (to expose domestic firms to international competition), access to credit (to either favor certain firms to provide a level playing field for others), or regulatory restrictions (to add barriers to entry) can be and have been used by governments to the same effect. Likewise, despite rhetorical connotations in which competition is considered "good" and protectionism or other policies that favor market power are considered "bad," there is no normative judgment in favor of or opposed to these general groupings of policies. Both competition and market power have a range of normatively defensible justifications.

These sorts of generalized policy regimes are adopted at a basic level because humans, including policymakers, have a deep distaste for ambiguity or uncertainty (Blyth 2002; Tetlock 2005) that is greatly exacerbated in circumstances where there is a large amount of complex information (Kruglanski and Webster 1996; Webster and Kruglanski 1994), such as the regulation of market competition and industrial organization. This means that policymakers search for ways to simplify complex policy questions into manageable decision-making processes, searching for a simplifying frame to distill large amounts of ambiguous information into conclusions that can guide policy decisions. Policymakers therefore turn to simple *mental models* that close off ambiguity. For example, the simplicity of the Chicago school version of antitrust policy was arguably adopted precisely because it provided an easy decision-making process for judges frustrated by the complexities of antitrust law (Lancieri, Posner, and Zingales 2024; Leslie 2014), giving a range of reasons to generally side with a corporate defendant in litigation.

Whether the consumer welfare standard or any of the others discussed in this book, these mental models nonetheless systematically reach conclusions that favor either competition or market power. Mental models of competition describe unambiguously how competition lowers prices, spurs efficiency, benefits consumers, and increases output. Mental models in favor of market power often invoke understandings of efficiently managed investment, business coordination, or ideal-typical notions of how patent incentives spur innovation, and how overzealous antitrust enforcement threatens this process. In adopting a set of simple frameworks, and correspondingly institutionalizing those mental models into policy and law, the complexity of policy problems is greatly reduced. However, by adopting a simple framework with assumptions about the relative risks from competition or market power, policymakers push policy to systematically favor one or the other.

Policy regimes reflect coherent understandings and assumptions that systematically favor competition or market power, despite coming in a variety of historically specific forms that would not necessarily relate to contemporary definitions of competition, market power, or monopoly. For example, for the past forty years, the consumer welfare standard has dominated antitrust policy in the United States, systematically favoring market power, but it does so not by facially opposing competition but rather by maintaining assumptions that the existence of larger firms is evidence of efficient economies of scale and thus consumer benefits, that all "vertical" mergers increase efficiency, and that barriers to entry are low (Khan 2018).

However, markets depend on a balance between competition and market power (Christophers 2016), and as a result policies that consistently support one or the other are self-limiting in the long run, generating economic and political costs the longer they are pursued. If consistently favoring price competition with the aim of improving efficiency, lowering prices, and ensuring a level playing field, the resulting economy would eventually see depressed profits, price wars, bankruptcies, and uncertain investment prospects. It is these circumstances that motivated the debates over "ruinous" or "destructive" competition in the late 19th and early 20th centuries in America (Berk 2009; Eddy 1912). Key, however, is the relationship between profits and investment. At such competitive extremes, and not knowing when another price war or downturn will come, firms do not have profits to fund further investment, nor do they have the confidence that such investments will pay off.

Alternatively, by consistently favoring market power in hopes of gaining economies of scale, providing companies with the incentives and resources for innovation and investment, stabilizing markets from price wars, or protecting the competitiveness of domestic firms, the eventual result will be dominant market giants able to dictate prices to consumers and squeeze the profit margins of other market actors. Again, key is the relationship between profits and investment: dominant firms will have a great deal of market power and resources to make investments, but isolated from competitive pressures they have limited incentive to continue innovating or expanding themselves (Gutiérrez and Philippon 2017; Christophers 2016). This is more akin to the world we live in today.

Yet in addition to the distaste for uncertainty, policy regimes are further held in place because individuals who have expended significant resources, political capital, time, or energy to a certain position are *committed* to that position (Arkes and Blumer 1985; Jervis 1976; Kuhn 1962). They are unlikely to ever reconsider either their conclusions or the underlying beliefs supporting them, and in fact they may deepen their beliefs in the face of adverse evidence (Heath 1995; Staw 1976). In short, it is unlikely that policymakers will recognize any failures of their favored policies once they have themselves promoted them, built political relationships and reputations around them, and framed their understanding of the economy around them.[10] So even in the face of clear diminishing returns, committed policymakers create a strong force for stability and policy continuity.

Whereas committed policymakers do not recognize these costs, newer policymakers without such commitments are nonetheless introduced to policy circles through the day-to-day staff *turnover* of promotions, retirements, reorganizations, and hiring. In contrast to policymakers who have tied their reputations, good word, political identity, or career into specific policy goals, the newer policymakers introduced or promoted through turnover

[10] This is on top of a range of other barriers to learning. Confirmed both in psychological experiments (Lord, Ross, and Lepper 1979; Nisbett and Ross 1980) and social science research (Tetlock 1999; Goldgeier and Tetlock 2001), most individuals do not learn based on new experiences, information, or new ideas. People process new information in terms of the beliefs they already have, interpreting evidence as confirming preexisting beliefs or simply discounting its importance. However, these barriers to learning are presumably universal and not subject only to commitment.

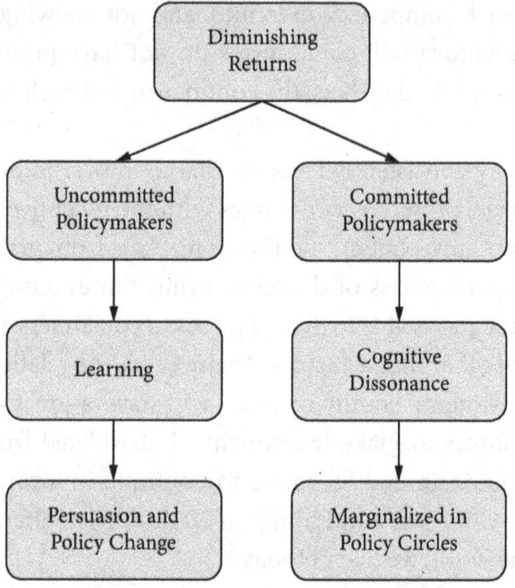

Figure 1.3 Learning and Policy Change

are willing to consider alternatives and learn about the costs of the policy regime, even if they agreed with it at the outset. These actors eventually *learn*, connecting the problems of diminishing returns to the existing policy regime. They eventually persuade, or displace, others to change policy trajectory. This set of mechanisms is represented in Figure 1.2.

This argument is empirically supported by the fact that most of the dramatic shifts in policy occur primarily under the leadership of the same party and the same executive leadership, particularly when policy changes correspond with turnover among core advisors who learn and persuade others of their views. For example, the Roosevelt administration underwent significant change in the late 1930s to favor antitrust enforcement after the turnover of key advisors and the addition of individuals who had shifted their stance on previous policies.

In contrast, this book argues that although different ideational and material factors matter as individual variables, they are mediated by a series of mechanisms: diminishing returns, commitment, staff turnover, and learning. The diminishing returns to competition do not destabilize a policy regime to leave an open field of institutional and policy options; rather, it is learning and material circumstances that push policymakers to anticompetition policy responses over time.

Case Selection

This theory will be developed and tested in the national contexts of the United States and France during the 20th century, drawing on extensive archival evidence from key moments of policy change over time. Within each national case, I focus analysis on two cases of policy change. The American cases cover a change in policy regime in the 1930s and 1940s from market power, under the aegis of "industrial self-government," to competition, under the SCP paradigm, and then a shift back to market power under the consumer welfare standard in the 1970s and 1980s. The French cases examine shifts in policy regime from competition to the market power of "national champions" in the 1960s, and then back to competition during the 1980s.

The cases are selected as "parallel demonstrations" (Skocpol and Somers 1980), showing how a series of policy regimes collapsed and were replaced via a common set of mechanisms across otherwise different institutional and political contexts. Cases are selected in this way for two reasons. First, the book seeks to explain change over time *within* national cases rather than to explain differences between each country. The main alternative approach, comparative case selection, is primarily helpful to highlight differences between cases, whereas here the goal is to understand the causes of a common pattern over time, for which parallel demonstrations are more appropriate. Second, the argument presented here is a theory of internal change—meaning that the policy regime intrinsically undermines itself over time—which precludes valid counterfactual comparisons between cases that would be required for other approaches to case selection. This line of reasoning is more fully developed in Chapter 2.

The two cases are also maximally different within these parallel demonstrations, meant to show that the theory proposed is independent of the specific institutional context of either a single national case or the details of a specific regulatory approach, such as common law antitrust or administrative state regulation. The United States and France represent dramatically different models. As a generality, the United States' economic policies with respect to competition and market power are implemented primarily through courts, via judicial rules proscribing permitted and prohibited behavior (antitrust) or the forms of private contracts that the state will enforce (IP, joint ventures, and common contracts). During the postwar period, France used entirely different regulatory tools for many of the same ends. Price controls were used to push industries into more or less competition, the position of nationalized industries as the sole purchasers in many markets was used to force or eliminate competition among private suppliers, the proximity of European neighbors increased the effects of import competition, and the state-controlled financial system could direct investment to ensure or prohibit the market power of established firms.

These regulatory differences, however, are not distinctions as to which state is "more" or "less" interventionist. Despite notions of the United States as a liberal state or a "liberal market economy" and France as "statist" or a "coordinated market economy" (Dobbin 1994; Hall and Soskice 2001; Schmidt 2002), the policy tools described for both governments are incredibly interventionist. Far from serving as the "night watchman" with regard to competition policy, courts in the United States proscribe, in detail, the agreements private parties are allowed to make, how much they are allowed to own, what they are allowed to do with their own property, the prices they are allowed to set, and in many cases what procedures are legal to determine all of the forgoing business decisions. The French policy tools of direct price controls, nationalized industries, and directed industrial policies are self-evidently interventionist, but legal rules and norms deeply shape American markets in a way that renders meaningless any assessment of which was more or less interventionist by comparison. The qualitative distinctions are important, but an over-emphasis on these differences, as well as the perceived nature of judicial intervention as "hands-off," often hides the extremely intrusive nature of many "liberal" governments like the United States.

The use of these two cases also provides some empirical leverage over competing explanations. Whereas some national cases follow similar timing in their shifts between market power and competition policy regimes (for example, the United States and United Kingdom), France and the United States exhibit very different timings for these shifts. In the 1960s, when the United States showed little to no hesitation in deepening its pro-competition regime in trade, antitrust, and regulatory policies, France was transitioning to its policy regime of national champions based around corporate consolidation. France's shift back to competition in the 1980s came on the heels of an American shift toward the market power-friendly consumer welfare standard. This variation in timing makes technological explanations, in particular, less plausible: among advanced industrial states, technology varies predominantly by time and not across countries.

Empirical Strategy and Research Design

The cases studies present rich and detailed evidence based on original archival research, tracking how governments monitored markets, what information was disseminated throughout the government, how that information was interpreted, how policymakers did or did not change their mind in light of new information, and how they used what they learned to persuade others.

In contrast to many works of comparative historical analysis, this book bridges a broader of understanding large-scale policy change with the day-to-day, mundane organizational politics of staffing, personal disputes, learning, and changing minds. Examining the individual policy elites who interpreted economic analysis and shaped policy decisions, it provides a micro-level analysis and framework for a macro-historical problem. By starting with specific policy actors, this book provides empirically concrete micro-foundations for these patterns by directly examining the beliefs and political preferences that policymakers had, the economic analysis they viewed, and the process by which they made policy choices.

The argument is not about individuals per se (i.e., whether one person as opposed to another was in a position of influence), but rather it uses evidence that can be gleaned from the fine-grained and rich level of detail of individual actors to test broader theories. Individuals can still be analytically categorized as committed or uncommitted, and their policy preferences categorized in terms of policy frameworks that are pro-competition or market power. This is true even though their views are more specific and their commitments may be from having sponsored certain legislation, having publicly campaigned on an issue, or having aligned one's career ambitions with a certain camp.

Archival evidence also helps overcome several methodological difficulties. First and above all, the archival record is among the best ways to get an accurate understanding of the economic information and analysis to which policymakers actually had access. Existing accounts of learning, policy change, or ideational evolution tend to rely on the effects of policy ideas that are publicly "in the air" at a particular historical moment. However, popular public arguments were often ignored or of little concern to policymakers in government at the time. By contrast, archival evidence provides access to both the government analyses, data, and reports that were never made public, as well as an accurate measurement of the subset of publicly available ideas and analyses that *were* influential in bureaucratic and policymaking circles.

Other analyses often rely on ex-post assessments of economic conditions that actors at the time may not have been aware of, such as the composition of unemployment or logistical problems in specific industries. Instead, this book focuses on the ideas and information that were "in the room" when policy debates were won or lost. Information, insights, or ideologies that are nowhere to be found in the archival record are unlikely to have been core drivers of policy change, particularly in comparison to facts, analyses, and assumptions that permeated the internal government discourse. For this reason, when assessing the economic evidence for diminishing returns, for example, the book focuses on the information that policymakers knew, even if better evidence was available elsewhere or is now available retrospectively.

Second, archival evidence often overcomes the problem of "revealed" preferences, in that policymakers are often not publicly honest about their beliefs, preferences, knowledge, or resolve. Succinctly, publicly stated beliefs about competition may simply be used to politically sell policies that were chosen for unrelated reasons. However, the archival record provides rich evidence of private correspondence among policymakers or with their non-political acquaintances, private or public statements of beliefs prior to public office, or their private actions to persuade others of their beliefs, any of which provide far more credible evidence of their genuine beliefs and motivations.

Third, the archival record provides a rich quantity of original qualitative data with which to test the argument against alternative theories based on the observable implications of each.[11] To summarize the theories against which this book's argument will be tested, *interest-group* or *lobbying* theories suggest that the state is easily captured by the lobbying of and close contact with concentrated private interest groups, and therefore the sustained political power wielded by pro-competition or anti-competition private interests leads to policy regimes. *Materialist* or *technological* theories argue that interests, government or private, are uniquely determined by the material circumstances of one's resources, technologies, and organizational position. In this context, this would suggest that policy and institutional change tends

[11] In many contexts, this is the meaning of process tracing (Bennett 2008; Bennett and Checkel 2015; Fairfield and Charman 2017), but it has also been referred to as "systematic process analysis" (Hall 2003, 2006) and is more widely considered the foundation to testing or evaluating theories by any particular method (King, Keohane, and Verba 1994; Van Evera 1997, 19–20 and 35).

to occur as the result of new technologies or market shocks. Lastly, theories about *economic ideas* argue that material positions and interests are far more ambiguous and in need of interpretation. Therefore, it is the ideas, ideologies, or economic models through which actors see their interests that determine their political preferences. These alternatives tend to see institutional or policy change as exogenous in nature, caused by the introduction of new ideas, technology, market pressures, or coalitional realignments, whose origins are not fundamentally intrinsic to the policy regime itself. Each of these alternatives is discussed in greater detail in Chapter 2.

Archival methods, however, come with the drawback of only being able to indirectly observe some observable implications of the theory, such as diminishing returns. Archives reveal what information policymakers and other officials had access to and how they thought about it, but it does not speak to the accuracy of the information or the soundness of the economic analysis presented to them. Policymakers can change their minds and "learn" from incorrect or inaccurate information, and archival methods do not provide a complete picture.

The book provides support for this argument with interpretations and conclusions that often clash with existing historiography on the basis of new evidence, in some cases more than others. Disagreements with existing, historically specific work are addressed in each of the case studies, but the research design and more general comparisons are reserved for these broader alternative theoretical approaches.

Outline of the Book

The remainder of the book is structured as follows. Chapter 2 elaborates on the theory and empirical strategy of the book, detailing the main claims and assumptions, the observable implications of alternative theories, and the approach to collection, measurement, and analysis of archival evidence. Chapters 3 through 8 represent the empirical content, consisting of case studies of the transitions from a market power policy regime to a competition policy regime, or vice versa.

Chapter 3 contains the first American case from 1930 to 1950, examining the collapse of the market power policy regime from the interwar years—built around industry associations, cartels, and price controls—leading to the subsequent rise of the postwar reinvigoration of antitrust and free trade.

American policy beginning in the late 1910s had increasingly favored a system of "industrial self-government" through which industries would be permitted to organize themselves voluntarily to share prices, wages, quality standards, and the like in order to avoid and stabilize "destructive" or "cut-throat" competition. The chapter shows how research done in the National Recovery Administration and Agricultural Adjustment Administration in the early 1930s New Deal concluded that the "administered prices" of large, dominant corporations were keeping prices high and holding back reemployment, and that industrial self-government policies were responsible. These conclusions made their way to the Department of Justice a few years later via a cohort of new policymakers disillusioned with early New Deal policies. There, these arguments were taken up in 1937 by policymakers facing independent problems of collusive bids on government contracts and a growing investigation into international cartels and patent agreements. This culminated in a ten-year trust-busting campaign from 1938 to 1948, entrenching the legal and legislative norms of a pro-competition policy regime for the postwar era built around the SPC paradigm.

Chapter 4, covering France from 1945 to 1970, examines the French government's pro-competition stance and policies coming out of World War II as they gave way to price protections and industrial consolidation in the 1960s. It first dispels with the conventional wisdom—of France as a fundamentally statist political economy opposed to market mechanisms—by demonstrating through new archival evidence that French policy favored expanding competitive mechanisms from the end of World War II through the early 1960s in an effort to modernize France through expanded output and productivity growth. The chapter then shows how an acceleration of these policies—through further tariff reductions, price ceilings, and industry reforms—threatened the profitability of French private industry and its prospects for making future investments. Established government advisors opposed changes to policy even as other areas of the government recognized it as a full-blown "crisis of investment." Only after this information was spread across government bureaucracies and consultative bodies in the 1960s did France turn to the market power policy regime of "national champions," built around corporate consolidation and price protections, precisely in order to restore private profits and investment.

The second American case—the shift from competition to market power in the 1970s and 1980s—is split into two chapters, both because of its complexity and because of its central importance to today's political dilemmas.

This case examines the collapse of the postwar antitrust consensus and the turn to weakened antitrust policy and enforcement in the 1970s and 1980s, in tandem with a strengthening of IP protections for firms on the technological frontier.

Chapter 5 examines the Nixon administration and the intellectual context around antitrust policy in the 1970s, including the debate between the Harvard "structuralist" school and the Chicago school. The Nixon administration initially adhered to strict enforcement of postwar antitrust law and supported free trade as principles of Republican market conservatism, all in the face of declining private profits and a declining balance of trade with Europe and East Asia. The chapter then shows how fears about the United States' international competitiveness were introduced by new White House staff in 1970 and 1971. These fears motivated the beginnings of a rethinking of antitrust policies as the administration grew closer to figures in the Chicago School of antitrust law and began introducing moderately anti-competition provisions into trade bills. Despite these internal debates, the Nixon administration was constrained by its prior pro-competition commitments, primarily making policy changes through the appointment of many corporate-friendly judges.

Chapter 6 shows this process playing out in the subsequent Ford, Carter, and Reagan administrations, as varying patterns of commitment moved policy change in fits and starts. The Ford administration, replacing Nixon after the fallout from the Watergate scandal, came into office at a time of high inflation. Seeking to keep prices down, Ford sought to further deepen pro-competition policies, committing his administration to them, even as many of his own advisors warned of a growing crisis of investment. The Carter administration was conflicted between commitments to antitrust policy and internationally trade competitiveness, as uncommitted policymakers in technology policy pushed for change, all of which happened as Nixon-appointed judges and administrative changes increasingly tilted policy in favor of market power. The Reagan administration came into office in 1981 with a clear ideological and policy agenda of weakened antitrust enforcement and strengthened IP rules—adopted from the Nixon administration and many changed minds in the antitrust profession—using the "competitiveness" of American business to masquerade these policies as pro-competition, despite internally knowing otherwise. Setting the stage for today's monopoly problems, merger policies were done away with, IP rules reinforced domestically and globally, and courts stacked with

Chicago-minded judges who reinterpreted antitrust to favor the consolidation of most industries.

Chapter 7 is the second French case from 1970 to 1990, as France abandoned the national champions policy regime and adopted competition policies more in line with standard antitrust, abolished all price controls, enhanced enforcement powers, and introduced merger controls. The chapter traces the expansion of the national champions policy early in the presidency of François Mitterrand, as his government attempted to construct vertically integrated industrial networks—*filières*—that would be completely insulated from the pressures of competition. As French firms increasingly showed themselves unable to redeploy capital resources—and the French economy proved to be pervasively cartelized by the national champion firms—influence within the Mitterrand government shifted. Key ministers were removed, and newer bureaucrats with experience in the failures of industrial policies gained influence. In 1985 and 1986, France removed all price controls, instituted competition policies with merger control, and privatized almost all of its national champion firms.

Chapter 8, the conclusion, revisits the main theoretical claims of the book, discusses the current implications for the United States and Europe, and discusses the implications for policy and academic research.

2

Understanding and Explaining the Internal Evolution of Policy Regimes

What explains these repeated alternations between policy regimes of competition and market power? This book and theory provide a microfoundational analysis of change by focusing on the details of behavior at the level of specific policymakers. Based on archival evidence gathered at this level of analysis, I argue that the complexity and ambiguity of policy around competition and market power pushes policymakers to adopt simple mental models favoring of one or the other, institutionalizing them into policy and law. Either type of policy regime generates *diminishing returns* – economic limitations intrinsic to the very approach to policy – that accumulate as the policy regime deepens. As diminishing returns accumulate, the information and evidence of this is ignored or denied by policymakers committed to the policy regime, who refuse to examine or reconsider the mental models underpinning the policy regime. Non-committed policymakers, introduced gradually through staff turnover, learn about the diminishing returns and push policy in the other direction, leading to policy change.

Scope and Limits of Theory

The dependent variable is policy regimes, which are long-term accumulations of many policy choices that systematically favor competition or market power. This book views competition solely in terms of *price competition* from classic microeconomic models, which refers to a state of a market with many buyers and sellers where producers face profit-maximizing incentives to reduce prices toward the marginal costs of production. This necessarily excludes alternative meanings of competition, like competing on quality or competing in the market for corporate control. By contrast, *market power*—the technical term for monopoly—refers to *any* deviation from price

Monopoly Politics. Erik Peinert, Oxford University Press. © Oxford University Press (2025).
DOI: 10.1093/oso/9780197789506.003.0002

competition that gives producers the ability to set prices independently of price-cutting competitive incentives.[1]

While conceptually narrow, using these definitions has several merits. First, even though markets will vary qualitatively along dimensions far beyond just how competitive they are—and most markets are characterized by a mix of competition and market power—any market can be seen somewhere along a continuum from perfect competition to monopoly pricing. As such, competition or market power retains conceptually broad meanings such that policies can be classified in terms of specific economic mechanisms and outcomes. Second, this narrow meaning aligns with the economic mechanism that one hopes to attain when speaking of competition: prices go down, consumers benefit, and efficiency improves. Third, many of the alternative meanings of competition are inconsistent: competing on quality, for example, implies the acquisition of market power through product differentiation. Lastly and most importantly, price competition is the analytically relevant meaning that corresponds to the diminishing returns of sustained policy regimes theorized in this book.

Policies include any action, law, bureaucratic rule, enforcement standard, or spending pattern taken by a government to further some goal, here either competition or market power, regardless of whether policies target individual sectors and firms or the economy in general. Table 2.1 provides several examples of how widely varied pro-competition and anti-competition policies can be and provides some examples of how they would be classified.[2]

Policy regimes consist of many policy changes that systematically favor competition or market power, embedded within an institutionalized understanding of the benefits or cost of competition and market power. The existence of a policy regime can be established by showing a systematic trend of policy changes in one direction, both in terms of the content of individual policies and the broader ideological and theoretic framework within which it is embedded. Some individual variation of lone policies that buck the trends of their time do not disprove the premise that there is a policy regime, but significant short-term mixing of pro-competition and anti-competition policies would do so. Policy regimes do not necessarily correspond with whether

[1] In this sense, competition and market power are viewed as opposite ends of a spectrum, approximated by the Lerner index in economics (Elzinga and Mills 2011; Lerner 1934).

[2] *Pro-competition* and *anti-competition* are used instead of more common terms like *procompetitive*, as the latter can conflate meanings. Procompetitive can be taken to refer to improvements to a firm's competitive position in ways that are different from or in opposition to the market process of price competition.

Table 2.1 Examples of Pro-Competition and Anti-Competitive Policies

Policy	Content	Coding	Explanation or Other Considerations
Price-fixing enforcement	Prohibits competing firms from colluding to set prices	Pro-competition	Price-fixing directly undermines the price competitive process.
Tariffs	Raises prices on imports	Anti-competition	Putting taxes on imports directly reduces competition from foreign firms, and likely increases prices.
Merger control	Limits on size of firms relative to their industry	Pro-competition	Limiting the size of firms via merger control lessens the possibility of either collusion or single-firm pricing power.
Resale price maintenance	Allows the original manufacturer to set final sales prices for retail	Anti-competition	Precludes price competition between retailers. Also allows manufacturers to hold wholesale prices higher than otherwise possible.
Competitive procurement	Requires government contracts to be subject to competitive bidding	Pro-competition	Precludes the possibility of government contracts given to single bidders able to set their own prices.
Price-setting in patent license	Legal jurisprudence permitting patent licenses to set prices at which licensees may sell	Anti-competition	This is indirect price-fixing, and it guarantees that there is limited price competition among licensees or with the patent owner.
Vertical integration	Legal jurisprudence permitting firms to expand from beginning to end of supply chain (i.e., from raw materials to sales)	Likely anti-competition	Vertically integrated firms do not face competition for intermediate products, and if the firm controls the market for an essential input or intermediate product, it can forclose competition from other firms or use it as leverage to put them at a disadvantage.
Regulatory burdens	For example, expensive privacy or environmental regulations with which only large and profitable firms can afford to comply	Possibly anti-competition	Environmental regulations may be entirely motivated by environmental concerns. If, however, the policy is motivated by the fact that the regulatory costs would remove competition from foreign or smaller firms inexperienced with such regulations, then the policy is anti-competition.

markets are competitive or monopolistic—policy regimes refer to the continuous trend of *changes in policy*, which take years to fully take effect as more firms react to them and additional policies complement them.

Lastly, it should be made clear what this book does *not* aim to examine or explain. In seeking to explain the general pattern between policy regimes that favor competition or market power, the book does not endeavor to explain all variation in pro-competition or anti-competition policies. Individual policies deviate from this trend, and many come about for reasons independent of the theory proposed. The category of policies that affect competition and market power is vast, with more policy variation than can be captured within a single theoretical framework. Similarly, I do not attempt to explain the success or failure of *individual policies*, but only the decline and limits of overall policy regimes. While some individual policies were so great in scale that their influence must be discussed on an individual level, the goal of this theory is to relate the diminishing returns of pro-competition or anti-competition policy frameworks that define a policy regime in its entirety.

The Political Economy of Competition and Monopoly

With the rising salience of antitrust and competition in public and policy discourse, this work builds on or contrasts itself with a growing body of literature across the social sciences. Existing work focuses to varying degrees on special interest lobbying, the ideological content and effect of different views of antitrust, the effects of technology and globalization, or—as this book does—on the long-run interplay between capitalist markets and the state.

Lobbying and Special Interests

Many scholars see competition, antitrust, and corporate regulation as a site of business and special interest lobbying. As antitrust generally targets the largest and most profitable firms, intuitively those special interests might lobby extensively to avoid enforcement or regulation. Most recently, Lancieri, Posner, and Zingales (2024) argue that the decline in antitrust enforcement in the United States since the 1970s was the result of concerted business lobbying, highlighting evidence such as increased general lobbying spending and the revolving door between antitrust agencies and the industries they regulate. Historiographic and political science accounts confirm that there was an outpouring of business lobbying beginning in the late 1970s (Hacker and Pierson 2010; Vogel 1989; Waterhouse 2013). Across policy areas and issues, lobbying proves influential, whether lobbying for antitrust deregulation to permit the franchise business model (Callaci 2018) or lobbying by technology companies to avoid competition regulation through international "digital trade" provisions (Li 2023).

Accordingly, *interest-group theories* argue policy is determined by conflict between and among interest groups, often taking the form of lobbying (Bawn et al. 2012; Culpepper 2010; Olson 1965). In these views, the state primarily aggregates the interests of private groups with competing policy preferences. Following the logic of collective action (Olson 1965), concentrated political interests like larger firms, narrow industries, or lobbying groups receive concentrated benefits from the resources expended on lobbying. Individual consumers and workers, in contrast, face high costs of political mobilization relative to diffuse benefits. As general theories, Rogowski and Kayser (2002) and Weymouth (2016) both see competition policy as a conflict between the general interest groups of producers (on the side of market power) and consumers and smaller businesses (who favor competition).

However, while many individual policies live or die as a result of extensive lobbying campaigns from private interests, broad changes in policy regimes are difficult to understand in such terms. Likewise, the logic of collective action would imply, in this case, that monopoly should almost always win, as market power tends to concentrate benefits in dominant firms, with diffuse costs on other stakeholders. Yet this is demonstrably not the case—for example with the Biden administration having continued with its competition agenda despite fierce backlash from big business and no countervailing interest groups in support.

Ideas and Economics

Others view antitrust and monopoly as a conflict between alternative theoretical and ideological understandings of how markets work. Many argue that the ideas of the Chicago school of antitrust caused the shift in antitrust in the 1970s, moving away from structural presumptions against mergers and large firms and instead favoring the consumer welfare standard, with its sympathetic view of economic concentration (Khan 2017, 2018; Fox and Sullivan 1987; Lande 1982; Paul 2020). Eisner (1991) and Berman (2022) argue that the slow introduction of formally trained economists, with a different style of microeconomic reasoning and analysis, changed antitrust to focus more on questions of efficiency, limiting enforcement by displacing the prior focus on fairness and legality. The Neo-Brandeisians are ideational theorists in practice, but I am saying that they are ideologically opposed to the Chicago school, not that they are ideational theorists in a way that Chicago school is not (Khan 2017, 2018).

Such ideational theories contend that since material interests and preferences are ambiguous, political actors are strongly influenced by the economic theories or models through which they view and interpret the economy (Beckert 1996; Blyth 2002; Fligstein 1990; Hall 1993). Rather than material or technological changes pointing to an obvious set of interests and policy preferences, new ideas and beliefs about how the economy works can lead actors to see previous institutions and policies as useless or in need of reform. Whether about antitrust and competition or more generally, ideational accounts tend to focus on the effects of ideas in reshaping political conflict, interests, and policy, often under-theorizing why certain ideas become more prominent than others.

While distinct, this book builds on these accounts to emphasize the long-term interaction between the ideational effects of mental models, commitment, and learning on one hand, and material diminishing returns on the other. Ideas and beliefs about the economy are causally important, but they are nonetheless constrained directly by the material feedback that policymakers receive.

Technology and Globalization

Many others argue that exogenous technological changes have been the primary driver of the rise of market power. Information technologies arguably create network effects that give a snowballing first-mover advantage in digital markets, concentrating revenue in the most productive firms, and as a result high-tech industries naturally end up more concentrated and less competitive (Autor et al. 2020; Kurz 2023; De Loecker, Eeckhout, and Unger 2020). Globalization arguably further favors this, as the most productive multinational companies with the logistics networks and transnational economies of scale will capture an increasing share of sales across all markets globally, leading to concentration as a result of real competition (Autor et al. 2020; Baccini, Pinto, and Weymouth 2017; Melitz 2003). Alternatively, as technology progresses, the high costs of research and development in industries like pharmaceuticals, silicon chips, and software may necessitate greater profits to cover those expenses or may limit the number of firms that a given market can support.

As the most prominent of these accounts primarily explain economic outcomes via technology directly rather than via policy, as a theory of policy change, these *materialist theories* see policy as responding to changes in technology or market opportunities (Frieden and Rogowski 1996; Iversen 1996; Thelen 2014). With technologies changing the relative costs and benefits of different institutions, governments and interest groups might prefer new institutions. So, for example, as research and development costs increase with breakthroughs in electronics, information technologies, and biotechnology, governments might strengthen intellectual property (IP) rights so that firms can recoup these costs. Or, popular, consumer-facing information technologies arguably encourage large-scale enterprise and limit the public opposition to such a concentration of power (Culpepper and Thelen 2020).

Technological change in industry, and particularly changes in capital costs, can have significant effects on policy, but it should be emphasized that the timing of these technological changes do not follow many of the policy changes in question. The American policy shifts in antitrust and related areas in the 1970s and 1980s occurred a decade or more before the rise of the global "superstar firms" discussed by Autor (2020) or the rise of the digital economy and the internet age. The technology giants that now make up the modern digital economy were founded and incubated in a policy environment that had become outright friendly to the acquisition of market power, using business tactics that had been specifically prohibited during the previous pro-competition policy regime (Khan 2017). Likewise, technology's effects on market structure are not always direct and unambiguous. The previous technological paradigm of mass production, with its high fixed capital costs, was once arguably a driver of concentration and monopoly (Baran and Sweezy 1966; Chandler 1977; Djelic 1998), but it also arguably contributed to overcapacity in the production of non-differentiated products and fierce price competition (Brenner 2006; Fligstein 1990; Piore and Sabel 1984).

Competition and National Models of Capitalism

One of the core questions for scholars of antitrust has been to understand the "Atlantic divide" in antitrust (Gifford and Kudrle 2015), whereby up until the past few years, European competition enforcement has been stronger and European markets generally more competitive (Philippon 2019). Arguments supporting these distinctions are many. Foster (2022) argues that the United States and Europe's divergence in competition policy is driven by distinct conceptions of competition that have become increasingly institutionalized over time, with the more administrative European approach to enforcement more effective than the adversarial litigation in the United States (Foster 2024). Ergen and Kohl (2019) emphasize the ordoliberal origins and traditions of European competition policy, noting that the "economization" of antitrust diminished enforcement less in the European Union than it had in the United States. Büthe (2007) argues that the supranational structure of the European Union, and the pattern of supranational political conflict among member states and subnational constituencies, led to the competition authority operating more autonomously than antitrust enforcers do in the United States. Others highlight longer-standing differences in the political economies of Europe and the United States going back to the late 19th century, resulting in enduring differences in competition policy and enforcement today (Prasad 2012; Berk 2009).

These perspectives generally follow the "national models" approach to political economy, according to which based on past historical differences, different countries have distinct combinations of institutions that represent different models of capitalism (Esping-Andersen 1990; Hall and Soskice 2001; Schonfield 1965; Thelen 2014). Through some event in the past, whether different timing of industrialization (Gerschenkron 1962), different responses to common economic shocks (Gourevitch 1986), or a series of self-reinforcing institutional complementarities (Hall and Soskice 2001), some countries adopted a "liberal" form of capitalism (e.g., the United States and United Kingdom), whereas other adopted various forms of "coordinated" capitalism (e.g., continental Europe). These extended out of historical institutionalist scholarship using "punctuated equilibrium" models of change, in which institutions are seen as stable and path dependent until external shocks like economic crises would create "critical junctures" that change the relative payoffs of institutions such that some groups would oppose or change them (Capoccia and Kelemen 2007; Gourevitch 1986;

Krasner 1984; Pierson 2000). Within these models, institutional and policy change is unlikely without exogenous shocks and therefore why national distinctions endure.

Accordingly, these perspectives have limited leverage in explaining the changes that we are seeing today, with anti-monopoly policy in the United States suddenly rising in political and policy prominence since 2020, superseding institutions that had appeared to constrain it. While the Atlantic divide in antitrust is very real, and as these scholars have shown, distinct national orientations can explain much about the administrative, political, and bureaucratic variation across countries, this approach is structurally limited in its ability to explain large-scale policy change within individual countries.

Competition, Monopoly, and Long-Term Change

Two notable pieces of scholarship already make similar arguments about the long-term evolution of business-state relations, antitrust policy, and corporate strategy in the United States.

First, Neil Fligstein argues that there have been discrete periods in American business history during which corporate managers understand corporate efficiency and competitive strategy according to distinct "conceptions of control" (Fligstein 1990, 2002). During these periods, most major corporations would adopt and adhere to a shared understanding of corporate strategy under which efficiency was understood in terms of, for example, maximizing market share through diversification and advertising rather than stabilizing markets through vertical integration, or avoiding price wars through trusts and cartelization rather than maximizing shareholder value. An argument formulated broadly in contrast to the argument of Chandler (1977), who saw the rise of large corporations as a direct response to the efficiency needs of new technologies, Fligstein emphasized the qualitative differences in each of these conceptions of control, seeing conception, and its associated form of industrial organization, as driven by government policies, the social and economic context, and the culture among the corporate elite. To explain these changes, Fligstein points to economic shocks like the Depression, or changes in government policy—antitrust policy above all—as driving the community of elite firms to change their conception of control.

Fligstein shows that most corporations in a given era adopted similar choices about their corporate organization and goals, but he does not categorize policy and corporate strategy across time periods by, for example, classifying multiple conceptions of control as competitive, expansionary, restrictive, or some other general category. As a result, general issues of competition and monopoly can appear to fall away when cartels, vertical integration, or mergers are no longer the focus of corporate strategy in a given conception of corporate control. Fligstein nonetheless effectively shows how diffuse legal rules and enforcement norms around antitrust and corporate governance can permeate to reshape a national market over time.

Second, Brett Christophers charts a very similar narrative as this book, of alternations between monopoly and competition in the United States and Britain (Christophers 2016). He argues that markets require a balance of competition and monopoly and that the state steps in to "right the balance" when markets go too far off track in favor of one or the other. Christophers argues that this balance has been successfully and functionally maintained in the long run by the intervention of the law to rebalance markets when markets fall too far one way or the other. For Christophers, the state intervened to do this, such as during the New Deal to steer policy toward competition or the Chicago School revolution reviving monopoly power in the 1970s, because it needed to in order to maintain the effective balance between monopoly and competition overall.

Unlike Fligstein, Christophers applies the general categories of competition and monopoly across many different times periods, expanding the analytical comparability across time periods. This book follows Christophers's approach, at the cost of treating different forms of market power or monopoly—such as a very concentrated mid-20th-century manufacturing industry and the contemporary tech industry—as broadly analogous, flattening qualitative distinctions between different policy arrangements, economic perspectives, and market dynamics in different time periods.

Punctuated Equilibrium and Endogenous Change

Following Christophers and Fligstein to examine repeated alternations between competition and market power, the question of this book is also a question of *endogenous institutional change*, meaning a process of change in policies or institutions without an exogenous cause or shock. To explain, it is not new to see certain economic or social phenomena occurring in repeated, periodic waves, such as a business cycle. Various "long-wave" theories theories, popular in the early 20th century (Kondratieff and Stolper 1935; Joseph Alois Schumpeter 1939), have seen a resurgence in recent years (Arrighi 1994; Arrighi and Silver 1999; Dafermos, Gabor, and Michell 2023; Mason 2015; Milanovic 2016; Owen 2010). Yet the variables that are the most common suspects for external or exogenous causes—new technologies, wars, and policy changes—in most cases have no particular reason, in and of themselves, to occur in regular cycles. However, in the abstract one can conceptualize an *internal* or endogenous dynamic for a social system to alternate in a predictable way, similar to a pendulum swinging back and forth without being pushed by external forces. And accordingly, wave theories tend to rely on endogenous mechanisms.

Nonetheless, there has been limited success in building productive, testable theories of endogenous change, whether in the context of repeated waves or more generally. In most theoretical formulations of institutional stability and change, endogenous change is a contradiction in terms. Following from similar intellectual traditions as the "national models" views outlined above, early historical institutionalism relied explicitly on "punctuated equilibrium" models of change. Institutions were seen as stable or "path dependent" until sudden external shocks like economic crises would change the relative payoffs of institutions such that some groups would oppose or change them (Gourevitch 1986; Krasner 1984). Different scholars emphasized different mechanisms, such as socialization through shared ideas (Blyth 2002; Denzau and North 1994; DiMaggio and Powell 1983; Meyer and Rowan 1977), game-theoretic Nash equilibria, or the use of institutions by the powerful to retain or further cement their advantaged positions (Knight 1992; Thelen 1999). However, this literature focused on clear distinctions between periods of institutional stability defined by path dependence (Pierson 2000) and shorter periods of change brought about by sudden, external shocks, often referred to as "critical junctures" (Capoccia and Kelemen 2007). Yet, if we think of institutions as "sticky" via any number of mechanisms—network externalities, socialization, or as game-theoretic equilibria—then institutions themselves are self-reinforcing and resistant to change. Endogenous theories, by contrast, must see institutional systems as dynamic with *self-contained* systemic properties, as if they were social perpetual-motion machines.

Scholarship extending these theories to address endogenous change has particularly looked to conceptual categories of mechanisms that might be able to account for endogenous change. Rational-choice scholars have theorized that endogenous *"quasi-parameters"* change slowly in the background, even as institutions remain otherwise stable, to then lead to change in the long run (Greif and Laitin 2004). Historical institutionalists have developed a series of gradual mechanisms of institutional change to describe how agents can change institutions slowly, whether by allowing them to whither away ("drift"), adding new policies and institutions on top of old ones ("layering"), or repurposing institutions for different goals ("conversion") (Hacker 2004; Mahoney and Thelen 2010; Schickler 2001; Streeck and Thelen 2005). However, these views describe broad, conceptual categories of mechanisms that could lead to endogenous change rather than specific arguments, causes, or variables.

To advance the literature on endogenous change, this book draws thematically on a series of "regime" literatures—which themselves drew inspiration from several wave theories—like the social structures of accumulation (Gordon 1978; Gordon, Edwards, and Reich 1982; Kotz, McDonough, and Reich 1994), the French regulation school (Aglietta 2000; Boyer 1990), and more recently growth models (Baccaro and Pontusson 2016; Hope and Soskice 2016; Baccaro, Blyth, and Pontusson 2022). These perspectives see history punctuated by a succession of different modes of economic organization that sequentially expand, burn out, and eventually collapse to be replaced by a new regime that restarts the cycle under an alternative form of organization (Arrighi 1994; Aglietta 2000; Boyer 1990; Kotz, McDonough, and Reich 1994). These views highlight ways that different modes of economic organization all face intrinsic limits to their expansion and growth.

Inspired by but expanding from these theories, an endogenous theory needs to rely on one group of mechanisms, self-contained within the theory, which are both the driver of stability and the later driver of institutional change. In effect, these mechanisms must reinforce institutional stability at one time, and yet at another time the very same mechanisms undermine the institution. This fits with our intuitive understanding of endogenous institutional change as carrying "the seeds of its own destruction." An endogenous theory should not rely on certain causes or crises "just occurring" unless it can be shown or safely assumed that those factors always or inevitably will occur.

Competition, Diminishing Returns, and Learning

This book argues that (a) policy regimes are adopted as policymakers seek simple mental models to frame and make decisions about competition market power, (b) policies regimes generate diminishing returns over time, (c) committed policymakers do not revise their beliefs about existing policies, (d) staff turnover introduces uncommitted policymakers to policy circles, (e) uncommitted policymakers learn and revise their beliefs, and (f) they displace committed policymakers and persuade others to change policy.

Ambiguity and Mental Models of Markets

At a general level, policymakers seek to maintain strong economic performance—whether because they must satisfy the demands of various economic constituencies, because they think that it is their professional obligation to do so, or because doing so will allow them to reap certain political or professional rewards. However, there is no objective standard of what strong economic performance means, and the web of policy areas that govern competition and market power—antitrust/competition, intellectual property, trade policy, industrial policy, etc.—is complicated, full of ambiguous trade-offs that are not straightforward to evaluate in either normative or economic terms. Consider the following, for example:

- Suppose that a large retail company is expanding, underpricing most of its smaller, local competitors, and putting many of them out of business. Is this (a) an example of a monopolistic firm using predatory pricing (selling at a loss) to control a market by putting competitors out of business, or is it (b) an entrepreneurial company taking advantage of new efficiencies and as a byproduct eliminating inefficient firms?
- Suppose that a firm develops a technology for a new product and licenses the patent out to other firms for them to manufacture the product, but the patent license includes a clause dictating the price at which the product can be sold. Is this license (a) a vehicle to provide sufficient incentive for a firm to innovate (since it would earn less if it were underpriced by its own licensees) or is it (b) price-fixing to capture monopoly profits?

- Claiming large predicted operational efficiencies, suppose a company is attempting to acquire one of its main suppliers. Many of its competitors also rely on this supplier for an important input. Is this (a) an attempt to lower costs by integrating the two firms and bring cheaper products to the market or (b) an attempt to undermine competition by cutting off its competitors' access to the supplier?

In these examples, it is easy to support either conclusion with some sort [of] evidence to support it. Drawing a clear line between the two is rarely obvious. It is a matter of both analytical and normative interpretation, and any realistic process of balancing the possible costs and benefits is time-consuming, laden with a variety of assumptions, and still subject to a great deal of uncertainty. Framing this policy area in such terms may prompt a rejection of the premise that competition and market power are inherently ambiguous, leading to a search for structured solutions and more specific prescriptions.

While not to deny the existence, utility, or general accuracy of any such models, I argue that this impulse—known in cognitive psychology as the *need for cognitive closure*—has an important effect on how policymakers understand economic information and translate it into policy choices. This "need for closure" refers to the felt need to come up with a conclusion to an issue, saving cognitive resources but eliminating ambiguity such that, as an issue, it does not need to be continuously reconsidered (Kruglanski and Webster 1996; Webster and Kruglanski 1994).[3]

While much of the literature on the need for closure focuses on individual-level variation in the need for cognitive closure (Golec de Zavala and Van Bergh 2007; Golec de Zavala, Cislak, and Wesolowska 2010; Webster and Kruglanski 1994), evidence indicates that it can be induced environmentally, and this theory emphasizes its commonality rather than individual differences. Importantly, evidence indicates that the need for cognitive closure

[3] In the psychology literature, this is more specifically referred to as the *nonspecific* need for cognitive closure. A specific need for cognitive closure refers to the desire for one's mind to be made up in favor of a specific conclusion (e.g., a preference to come up with a pro-competition conclusion). A nonspecific need for cognitive closure, by contrast, refers to the need to reach any sort of specific conclusion at all. Whereas the specific need may be based on motivated reasoning, the nonspecific need is only based on the discomfort of unclear and opaque situations that are hard to assess. In the social sciences, this is similar to the general effect that Blyth (2002) describes as Knightian uncertainty, whereby the lack of correspondence between one's understanding of the economy and its reality encourages actors to search for and seize on new economic ideas that provide this sense of closure, even apart from the truth or specifics of the ideas.

increases as (a) trade-offs between options become greater, (b) costs and benefits are less clear, (c) demands for deductive categories for decision-making increase, (d) the cognitive effort required to arrive at a conclusion increase, (e) as accountability for incorrect decisions is low, and (f) urgency or time limitations increase (Kruglanski and Webster 1996).

These stimuli closely resemble the context of economic policymaking in legal and regulatory settings, and particularly those related to competition and market power. Regulatory agencies are generally tasked to develop rules, guidelines, and laws that are applicable across many different contexts in a codified manner (deductive categories), and they are expected to do so in a timely fashion (urgency). For example, if a court—the most common venue where decisions on competition and market power are made in many jurisdictions—is asked to determine whether a particular practice is monopolistic (and therefore illegal), it must both (a) come to a conclusion in a relatively short period of time and (b) explain its reasoning in a generalized fashion that can be applied to other markets or future practices. These are, as mentioned, frequently difficult, complex decisions, where the wisdom of the choice taken is unlikely to be clear for many years, reducing any individual accountability. All of these factors favor "seizing" on simple, deductive, and translatable frameworks that eliminate much of the nuance, complexity, and ambiguity. In effect, even though individual policymakers usually want to make thorough and rational assessments about costs and benefits in each new context, time and resource constraints will push them to seize on simplified, deductive conclusions.[4]

These predispositions lead to the adoption of simple, shorthand economic models that are used to analyze and promote competition or market power and make decision-making more straightforward. The model of perfect competition is the most basic model in economics: in circumstances where many producers are selling similar products, competition forces firms to underprice each other until meeting marginal cost. The benefits of competition are clear: producers will make as much of the product as they possibly can for as cheap as possible. Firms have no individual power to set prices, ensuring that firms are forced to produce efficiently and that all the benefits

[4] Berk (2009) makes a similar argument in decrying the loss of Louis Brandeis's more contextual ideas about "regulated competition," in that American courts, regulators, and economists in the early 20th century were quick to revert to simple classification schema between monopoly and competition when determining the permissibility of different practices, ignoring more detailed and inductive criteria involving process, performance, power, and deliberation.

are passed on to consumers. What such a model does do, however, is largely sidestep the ambiguities and trade-offs between the costs and benefits of market power. By describing a world where there are no profits, no investment, and no technological change, it provides clear prescriptions in favor of competition.

Mental models in favor of market power are also simple and intuitive, and they similarly ignore the trade-offs and benefits of competition. Patents and other IP rights are most easily understood as necessary legal incentives to innovate or develop new products, even though they are, by nature, state-enforced monopolies that can be made even more restrictive via a number of contracting arrangements. Or, the market power of economically central firms can easily be framed not as a result of self-reinforcing market power but rather as evidence of the firms' success and efficiency relative to others, with the outsized profits it receives being necessary for them to continue their successful expansion.

In the case of either competition or market power, these models each provide analytically clear, if opposite, policy implications that allow policymakers to avoid constantly addressing difficult trade-offs and ambiguities. Suffice to say, a mental model of competition or market power has, built into its very conception, a certain degree of blindness to the economic problems that its further extension could create.

Mental models of competition and market power are usually more specific and vary across countries and time periods. For example, the consumer welfare standard, long the guiding principle of American antitrust policy, represents a grouping of mental models that simplify antitrust to maximizing consumer welfare, equating a multifaceted area of law to lower prices and maximized output (Leslie 2014). However, by including presumptions about the efficiency-enhancing effects of scale, vertical integration, and vertical restraints, it has served to enhance the market power of the largest firms. Yet the consumer welfare standard replaced a similarly simple "structure-conduct-performance" (SCP) framework from the mid-20th century. The SCP framework presumed that competitive conditions were shaped primarily by the degree of concentration in an industry, such that mergers and concentration were presumptively harmful. These assumptions tended to push policy toward pro-competition choices.

Policymakers are not completely trapped by obviously oversimplified models, and such models are more than the residual of a psychological impulse. Economic models, rigorously applied, provide valuable insights for assessing claims about competition, one way or the other. Rather the argument is twofold:(a) the appeal of such models is aided by the regulatory context and these psychological predispositions, and (b) such models can be and are used to avoid examining more conflicted or unclear realities that either contradict or do not fit into the world implied by the model. Furthermore, the mere holding of a mental model on its own does not make an agent unable to question it. Individuals can hold multiple sets of contradictory mental models simultaneously, and policy elites frequently do recognize that perfect competition or perfectly stable markets are both impractical and rare in practice. However, when faced with time constraints, ambiguity, and little accountability, the very same agents often quickly revert back to thinking in terms of price competition or market power in terms of shorthand models.

While policymakers are aiming for "good" economic performance overall, different mental models have value judgments associated with them, favoring certain groups over others. Market power favors large firms, and competition favors consumers and buyers. Likewise, the ultimate goals of policy change are influenced by the beliefs, models, and theories through which policymakers perceive economic problems (Hall 1993). As such, a shift in policy regime will correspond to a shift in which economic indicators policymakers prioritize. For example, in adopting market power mental models, higher profits come to be seen as a measure of success, even though they ultimately have their own deleterious effects on economic performance more generally.

Diminishing Returns

The adoption of these simple mental models leads to policy trajectories where governments continue making policies systematically enhancing competition or market power through their insertion into institutional, legal, and bureaucratic rules. Continuously pushing for more of one or the other will intrinsically lead to *diminishing returns*: the sought-after benefits of competition or market power will no longer come to fruition, and the policy regime will itself create a series of other economic maladies.

This is based on a premise, following Christophers (2016), that markets functionally require a balance between competition and market power in order to thrive. Empirical and theoretical scholarship has emphasized the need for both competition and market power to spur technological growth, innovation, consumer welfare, and efficiency gains. The literature on innovation and growth in particular emphasizes the need for a balance between the two, and extensive literature highlights the need for one or the other in a variety of ways. Most explicitly, Aghion et al. (2005) argue that the relationship between competition and innovation follows an inverted-U curve, in that innovation is greatest in a balanced position between competitive and monopolistic extremes.[5] Drawing from Joseph A. Schumpeter (1942), P. M. Romer (1990) argues that market power is the primary mechanism through which firms can be equipped and incentivized to invest in research and development. Market power both provides the resources, in the form of profits, to make investments in future growth, and the *prospect* of being able to obtain a monopoly position incentives to make those investments. Lester and Piore (2004) similarly argue that competitive pressures, left unchecked, strangle the collaborative processes within and across firms that allow for innovation. Galbraith (1952b) argued qualitatively that oligopolies were more effective innovators than either literal monopolies or firms under fierce competition. From the other side, Arrow (1962) pointed out that monopoly firms have little incentive to invest in innovation because they are already capturing monopoly profits.

The diminishing returns to market power can be illustrated as follows. As policy pushes for more and more market power, powerful firms obtain stronger monopoly positions, and profits are increasingly concentrated in firms lacking strong incentives to invest. Despite having the resources to invest, their economic position over competitors is assured, and further growth or innovation will not provide them significantly greater profits or earnings than their current monopoly positions already do. Non-monopoly firms, despite having the incentive to invest, predominantly lack the resources to make significant investments. This, in the aggregate, reduces consumption, stifles new commercial opportunities, and suppresses employment. In short, increasing monopoly undermines the very benefits it is supposed to provide by negatively effecting innovation, investment, and consumption.

Policy regimes in favor of competition face distinct diminishing returns. In a reasonable balance, competition pressures firms to continuously invest

[5] Aghion, Howitt, and Prantl (2015) extend this argument that pro-competition market reforms, combined with the market power of stronger IP rights, successfully achieves this balance. However, they primarily view market competition and IP monopoly rents as pulling in opposite directions: the incentive to innovate comes from the IP rights, which provide a temporary escape from competition.

to keep up with or get ahead of their competition, such that even substantial profits will be reinvested into R&D and expansion. However, with more and more competition, particularly as price competition puts the profits of lead firms in jeopardy, these benefits begin to disappear. Without profits, firms have fewer resources to make those investments and are less able to attract external financing for those investments, simply because the prospective rate of return to investors would be lower. Centrally, corporate investment declines. Through a series of secondary effects not sought by pro-competition policies, price competition undermines some of the very benefits expected from it.

It should be emphasized that markets are substantially more complex than this. Single industries in an otherwise competitive national economy can be characterized by monopoly or market power. Some firms in a supply chain can have extraordinary bargaining power over others that are subject to fierce competition. Many companies may experience cutthroat competition in certain markets while facing monopoly pricing in others. Therefore, the argument is not that diminishing returns occur because a policy regime pushes the entire economy fully to one extreme. Rather, pushing for market power or competition for decades, even in rather specific but consistent ways, will intrinsically result in diminishing returns. For example, by consistently strengthening IP rights and allowing vertical mergers and vertical restraints—as the consumer welfare standard policy regime has done in recent decades—profits have been redistributed away from industries and firms most likely to make investments in physical capital and toward IP-heavy firms and industries facing little competition and with little incentive to invest (Peinert 2023; Schwartz 2016, 2020).

Policy Failure, Commitment, and Learning

This book argues, however, that eventually policymakers recognize these diminishing returns, leading to an eventual change in the policy regime. However, whether and how these overall costs are recognized depends significantly on the policymakers in influential positions of authority and their willingness to learn and reconsider their beliefs based on the psychological mechanism of *escalating commitment*. This refers to the tendency for individuals to continue to support actions or goals in which they have already invested resources, whether those are political resources, social standing, or simply time and effort (Arkes and Blumer 1985; Heath 1995; Jervis 1976; Staw 1976). Agents who are responsible for certain choices and have made commitments have a tendency to double down on these choices, even in the face of adverse evidence, refusing to reconsider their decisions or the beliefs that originally motivated them. A politician or bureaucrat who has staked his or her career on a policy position will likely never reconsider either the position itself or the underlying beliefs that motivate it. Having spent significant resources in favoring either competition or market power, individual policymakers can serve as veto points to change in policy direction should there be any pressure to do so. We should expect such actors to not only refuse to change their mind but also to display cognitive dissonance when faced with evidence contradicting their beliefs.

This commitment is reinforced by other barriers to learning. Actors interpret new information as confirming their existing beliefs through a process of "biased information processing," even when the evidence is ambiguous or contrary to their beliefs. Experimental evidence shows that not only do individuals retain beliefs after encountering new information that should disprove them but also that this belief perseverance can be strong enough to maintain beliefs even after learning that the information that led to those beliefs was outright false (Ross, Lepper, and Hubbard 1975). Individuals often take information that is ambiguous—or is just poor evidence either for or against their beliefs—as further reason to reconfirm their beliefs (Lord, Ross, and Lepper 1979). This plays out in a similar way in the politics of competition and monopoly. Whereas dangerously declining profits by leading firms might be evidence that those firms are facing excess competition, to an agent with pro-competition beliefs, this can be evidence of the *success* of pro-competition policies, since they are meant to eliminate profits and ensure that surplus is passed to the consumer. Similarly, the outsized market share of a large firm might be evidence of excess market power, but to advocates of market power, it is evidence of the efficiency of the firm over competitors and the success of the policies that nurtured the firm to be so successful.

However, government bureaucracies and policymaking bodies are not only repopulated with hand-picked ideologues committed to existing policy positions. Processes of hiring, promotion, retirements, transfers, and intermittent reorganizations of bureaucracies are endemic, constant, and inevitable in—and thus *endogenous to*—nearly all government bureaucracies and policymaking entities. Such processes entail the removal, replacement, or even just the reshuffling of the actors who are most committed to established policy positions. It puts actors who are *not* committed to the established policy regime into positions where they have the knowledge to learn of policy failures and the position to persuade and influence others if they do. This can happen as new government agencies are created or bureaucracies reorganized, bringing in new actors and mixing up the positional influence and lines of communication between existing ones.

In contrast to committed policymakers, with or without prior policy preferences, uncommitted policymakers are able to *learn* and shift their beliefs and preferences in light of new information or circumstances. As the diminishing returns of the policy regime increase, non-committed policymakers learn about the diminishing returns and argue that there is too much competition or market power, that the approach to policy itself is responsible, and that policy should move in the opposite direction to address these failings. As these policymakers gain influence, they push for policy change from competition to market power, or vice versa. Thus, learning is mediated by commitment, suggesting that we should expect learning to occur primarily among uncommitted policymakers. Figure 2.1 visually explains this process of policy change, based on the sequence and process that is hypothesized to play out at the key moments of change in a policy regime.

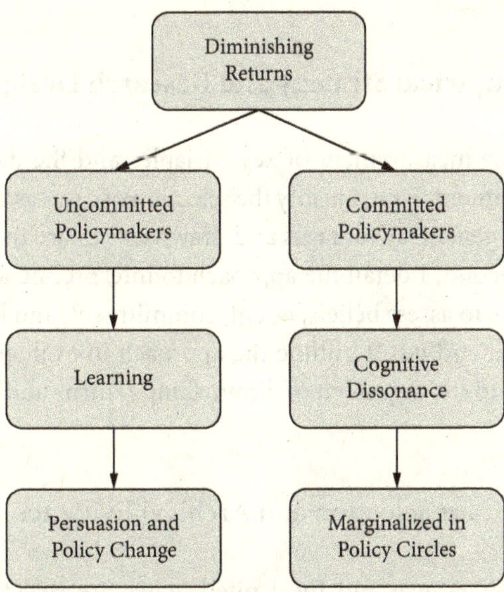

Figure 2.1 Mechanisms of Policy Change

To clarify, there is a key difference between (a) having a policy preference and (b) having a commitment (Arkes and Blumer 1985; Heath 1995; Staw 1976). Having stated or implicit preferences over policy simply means that an agent knows the policy outcome they prefer, but this may result from merely having learned certain analytical or ideational frameworks, having been educated a certain way, or having access to certain information. *Commitment*, in contrast, implies having expended actual resources in support of a position, whether those resources are personal, social, political, or material. Not just holding a policy preference, but having also expended resources, committed policymakers see their position and preferences as a sunk cost and will therefore escalate their commitment to it, even in the face of evidence contradicting it.

A policy regime in favor of competition or market power will over time produce diminishing returns. Committed policymakers, who spent significant resources implementing the policy regime, will not consider those costs. Only through the rise of uncommitted policymakers are opportunities for learning and recognizing policy failures made possible. After groups of policymakers have changed their minds about the regime and overall approach to policy, they are able to persuade others of these new beliefs and policy ideas, shifting policy from competition to market power, or vice versa, and establishing a new policy regime in the other direction.

Empirical Strategy and Research Design

I now turn to the measurement of key variables and the data collected to support this argument. First, I justify the selection of cases as parallel demonstration and the general advantages and drawbacks of archival evidence for this research. Second, I detail the approach to interpreting and structuring archival evidence to assess beliefs, intent, commitment, and learning of policymakers. Third and last, I outline the approach to evaluating alternative theories relative to the argument of diminishing returns and commitment.

Case Selection and Archival Evidence

The two cases of France and the United States are selected as "parallel demonstrations" (Skocpol and Somers 1980) in which "historical instances are juxtaposed to demonstrate that the theoretical arguments apply convincingly to multiple cases that ought to fit if the theory in question is indeed valid" (Skocpol, Theda, and Margaret Somers 1980, 176). This contrasts with comparative cases, which analyzes two instances that experienced different outcomes, leveraging key differences to isolate a purported cause, treating the two cases as sufficiently analogous counterfactuals to one another. Putting aside whether such cases can serve as meaningful counterfactuals more generally, in the context of endogenous change, counterfactual reasoning suggests imagining circumstances where the endogenous mechanisms do not occur, while all other internal dynamics of the institution remain "all else equal." For this approach to case selection to be valid theoretically, the causal mechanisms must be viewed as exogenously "just happening" for no reason dependent on the other features of the case that are all else equal, an independence that is prematurely rejected by the very premise of an endogenous theory. In short, comparative cases are predicated on the ability to separate mechanisms that an endogenous theory must see as unified.

By contrast, parallel demonstrations with rich empirical evidence that show multiple iterations of the theory across cases suffice for the more modest methodological aim of reducing the likelihood that the argument is a "just-so story" (i.e., that the theory appeared to "work" and fit the evidence in one setting alone merely by chance or as the result of theoretical overfitting). Furthermore, to the degree that the parallel demonstrations are in maximally diverse settings, it serves as strong evidence for generalizability. Nonetheless, the analytical burden of supporting the theory comes from the quality of evidence within each case rather than the structure of the case selection. Though not justified in such terms, many existing accounts of endogenous change are structured as parallel demonstrations.[6]

Within these parallel demonstrations, the theory and its alternatives are evaluated against original evidence by testing their observable implications against the observable implications of alternative theories.[7] This approach has variously been labeled process tracing (Bennett 2008; Bennett and Checkel 2015; Fairfield and Charman 2017) or "systematic process analysis" (Hall 2003).

[6] For example, see Blyth (2002), Chorev (2007), Greif and Laitin (2004), Owen (2010), Steinmo (2010), Van Bavel (2016), and Widmaier (2016).

[7] See King, Keohane, and Verba (1994, 19–20) and Van Evera (1997, 35).

The bulk of evidence consists of case studies constructed from original archival evidence from the United States and France, supplemented in a few instances with interview research and surviving audio recordings of key meetings. Archival research presents a series of important methodological advantages, as well as some important drawbacks. Archival evidence provides a more credible approach than alternative options for categorizing policies and policy regimes based on their intent, it provides direct evidence to assess the beliefs of key actors and how they learned in response to specific information. Moreover, it represents a wealth of original factual information about policy changes, detailing when and how they were made, by whom, and in relation to what alternative choices.

As a general matter, the archival approach of this book makes fewer assumptions about the beliefs of key actors, what information they had available, and how they viewed political and economic problems. By focusing on broad economic indicators, grand economic ideas, or structurally dominant political interest, many macro-historical analyses necessarily make, and rely upon, assumptions about the reasoning, decisions, and knowledge of individual actors. For example, a cross-national regression may be testing a theory about whether the power of business associations affects certain policy outcomes, or why political cleavages fall along class lines, regional lines, or by specific industries, but these analyses assume that political groups conceive of their interests, problems, and priorities in a particular way, skipping over the step of determining whether they actually do. By directly observing what agents chose to write, communicated to other policymakers and stakeholders, and how they framed problems, archival research makes fewer assumptions of this sort.

At the same time, the interpretive nature of historiographic, archival research comes with drawbacks, precisely because it sheds light *only* on what key actors chose to communicate, share, or otherwise put in writing, and it only provides information about those specific actors who appear in the archival record. Actors will often make calculated choices about what they are willing to put in writing—for example, if their genuine goals are not socially appropriate or legal (a problem that comes up, for example, with the Nixon administration). The archival record also does not tell us how actors weighed the importance of different factors or problems, nor does it tell us which actors' beliefs and choices were most decisive in coming to the policy outcome in question. Using archival evidence to support any such determinations requires interpretation, some assumptions about what is written versus not, and triangulation of the archival evidence with existing secondary sources.

While much of the archival evidence focuses on the beliefs and choices of individual key policymakers, and the theory refers to committed and uncommitted policymakers, this again should not be confused with the notion that the argument of the book is about the effects of individuals and their individual effects on outcomes. As such, individual counterfactuals that consider whether a different person had been promoted or selected for a key role, for example, are less relevant than *why* they were or were not selected for the role, specifically whether the events follow or conflict with the observable implications of the theory.

Assessing Intent, Beliefs, and Learning

With this archival material, the intent of policy, policymarkers' beliefs about how markets work, their commitments, and their learning are all gleaned from similar and overlapping evidence. The dependent variable, the policy regime, is measured by classifying policies as either pro-competition or pro-market power *in their intent* and then using those assessments to qualitatively categorize periods of policy continuity as a policy regime in favor of competition or market power. Deciphering policy intent, as well as the motivations and changing beliefs of policymakers, requires both determining the *genuine* beliefs of policymakers and mapping their stated understandings of competition or market power to those used by this book. Assessing commitment involves evaluating the resources policymakers have invested in a policy issue, as well as their own statements and those of others regarding whether and why they are committed. Lastly, as a mechanism, evaluating learning implies an assessment of prior beliefs, the information to which a policymaker was exposed, and their updated beliefs afterward.

There are similar difficulties in both evaluating policy based on intent and assessing policymaker beliefs. First, the intent and beliefs of policy may have been ambiguous, key supporters of certain policies may have had different reasons for supporting them, and in many cases some key policymakers may have been conceptualizing policies in terms unrelated to competition and market power. For example, policymakers might think about IP rights in terms of innovation policy, ignoring the rather obvious effects that they have on enhancing market power. Likewise, terms such as competition and monopoly have a range of both modern rhetorical meanings and historical meanings beyond strictly price competition as it is defined here. Consider how the neo-Brandeisian advocates of antitrust policy reject universally favoring competition, instead favoring more nuanced concepts of fair or regulated competition, which do not fit neatly within the categories described in this book.[8]

This problem is primarily obviated by relying on a single meaning of price competition, though coming at the cost of occasionally being at odds with the language used by the historical actors under analysis. Namely, with an understanding of how terms were used in the time period in question, combined with statements and arguments about the anticipated or intended economic effects policies, policies can broadly be categorized as pro-competition or anti-competition according the universal definitions used in this book. For instance, it is difficult to consider a policy designed to increase profits as pro-competition, regardless of how much language about competition is used to politically sell it, or policies marketed as protecting a favored category of economic actors from some form of economic threat or competition. While this approach does flatten substantive distinctions between policy beliefs, and does eliminate some richness of the archival record, this simplification corresponds to competition and market power in the forms they are theorized to lead to diminishing returns.

Similarly, both policy intent and motivation can be assessed at the individual level of specific policies as well as at the level of the policy ideas and mental models underpinning the overall policy regime. Policy regimes are not just built out of the accumulation of individual policies that happen to have anti-competition and pro-competition intent; they are built around coherent understandings of how markets work, such as the consumer welfare standard based on price theory, the structure-conduct-performance paradigm of industrial organization, or the beliefs around national champions and international competitiveness, which were the basis of French industrial policy for a time. As a result, where this book does show that

[8] For other examples, *competition* and *competitiveness* generally have distinct meanings that are, in fact, at odds. Competition refers to a state of a market where firms compete with one another by lowering prices or offering better products, whereas competitiveness generally refers to the ability of a firm or a country to beat its competitors. Similarly, the concept of monopoly can be conflated with the question of whether the firm is large or not, or it can be narrowed to refer only refer to illegal monopolies or to situations where there is truly only a single firm.

those economic theories favored competition or market power systematically, policies advanced within these frames can be considered as advancing the same goals.

Second, beyond the ambiguous meanings of these concepts, the archival approach to this theory means deciphering the honest, genuine beliefs of policymakers. Particularly for politicians, state actors, or interest groups lobbying for favored policies, there are a plethora of strategic incentives to misrepresent one's goals, intentions, strategies, and actual beliefs. Doing so can improve one's bargaining position, make one's position appear more legitimate, signal loyalty to one's party or political camp, or simply put one in agreement with a politically popular set of opinions. Furthermore, political agents strategically take advantage of the conflicted and overlapping meanings of words (competition, monopoly, etc.) to make their favored policies sound more palatable to existing rhetoric or interests. Bluntly, we would never expect advocates of market power to say "this is to promote monopoly" (though as the reader will see, this does happen), and advocates of competition are likely to hedge competition as more stable or safe than it is in order to make it sound more appealing to those who risk being put out of business by it.

Archival evidence can be particularly informative to address this, subject to the same qualifiers that the archival record is intrinsically incomplete. In private correspondence, policymakers often admit openly that a distinction exists between their true motivations and the positions they take in public, or why they took a position with one group of stakeholders and a different position elsewhere. First, opinions expressed in private correspondence with personal contacts who are politically disinterested are more likely to be genuine than politically strategic. Second, following Saunders (2011), opinions expressed prior to public office, and thus prior to strategic political incentives, also imply genuine beliefs. Third, circumstances where the actor knowingly pays a political price for expressing an unpopular view would also suggest that those views are genuine. For example, being the first to express the belief in a context where most disagree would indicate that the belief is genuine, as the political incentives would press one to express the opposite. Similarly, when an actor spends time and resources to persuade other actors in government of their beliefs i an indication that they are genuine. In weighing different statements of intent or belief, emphasis will be given to statements with the least motivation to misrepresent opinion.

Commitment itself is evaluated at multiple, albeit related, levels: the level of personal psychology and the level of public reputation. For that reason, there are two primary ways that a policymaker can take an action such that they will be considered committed for the purposes of this book. First, if they take action that expended effort—wrote a book supporting a certain position, got into heated arguments in policy circles, spent the time to convince others of their views, led enforcement actions with a certain policy goal in mind—that policymaker will be considered committed to that position. Second, more relevant for politicians than bureaucrats, if a policymaker makes very public statements in support of a certain vision of policy, they will be considered committed to that set of policies. The archival record also shows instances of staff discussing their prior commitments and the reputational costs of going back on those commitments if they change course.

To demonstrate learning, I aim to evaluate the state of a policymaker's beliefs both before and after they were exposed to information that plausibly could have changed their views. In many cases, this can only be provided by original archival evidence, which often consists of exactly what information was provided to various policymakers and stakeholders, as well as how they reasoned about or responded to it. While such a perfect comparison—seeing beliefs both before and after, as well as the information and reasoning that was put into it—is only possible in certain circumstances, this is also supplemented with evidence where policymakers will admit to having changed their mind or shifted their political and policy priorities in light of new information.

Evaluating Alternative Theories

The method of analysis for the empirical chapters is that of "process tracing" (Bennett 2008; Bennett and Checkel 2015; Fairfield and Charman 2017) or "systematic process analysis" (Hall 2003, 2006). Both are similar concepts, where process tracing "examines the observable implications of hypothesized causal mechanisms within a case to test whether a theory on these mechanisms explains the case" (Bennett and Checkel 2015, 7–8), and systematic process analysis refers to seeing "if the multiple actions and statements of the actors at each stage of the causal process are consistent with the image of the world implied by each theory" (Hall 2003, 394). In either case, both align with the most fundamental approach to research design: to test all of the observable implications of the theory relative to alternatives.[9] The idea is to examine the archival evidence to determine whether it is consistent or inconsistent with the competing theories in question. Here I highlight the most important distinctions between this argument and competing theories, not to highlight their substantial scholarly contributions, but rather to delineate their observable implications for the purposes of weighing the evidence for or against them in the empirical chapters.

Interest-group theories primarily focus on the efforts of private interests—business groups, organized labor, and consumers—to influence policy. While government archives focus more on state actors rather than private interests, the record used here is not a full account, but governments still keep extensive records of private interests attempting to sway them, how policymakers responded to them, and to what degree they were included in policy discussions. In short, these theories should expect government actors to be deferential to private interests when making large shifts in policy and for policy to shift in a direction that aligns with the preferences of the most politically powerful private interests. However, if interest groups were mostly ignored at the moments when new policy frameworks were being developed or where the direction of policy is shifting, this would be strong evidence against their importance for explaining broad policy regimes.

Technological and materialist theories emphasize the role of material economic shocks and technological change in shifting policy and market dynamics. While archives do not directly observe either of those, it does give a window into how policymakers understand technological change or exogenous shocks and how they react to them. Thus, archival evidence can show how policymakers saw their own constraints in material or technological terms. As such, these theories tend to predict that policymakers view technology or material conditions as a constraint on their policy choices or that material constraints create clear policy and political preferences. However, the archival record clearly shows that such questions were usually deeply contested in policy circles, that policymakers were ignorant about such questions, or that they simply changed policy in spite of them.

Ideational theories are addressed as alternatives in a particular respect, as this book relies on ideas as empirically important variables. Ideational approaches suggest that policy change results from the introduction of

[9] See King, Keohane, and Verba (1994, 19–20) and Van Evera (1997, 35).

new, comprehensive economic frameworks—Keynesianism, monetarism, the Chicago school, etc.— that reimagine the relationships between different economic variables on an entirely new set of premises (Blyth 2002; Hall 1989, 1993). However, they typically do not consider learning from material changes as the causal factor in that ideational change or in selection among competing economic ideas. As such, ideational theories see an "open field" of policy options in moments of crisis or policy change, whereas this theory would predict that uncommitted policymakers repeatedly turned toward anti- or pro-competition policy options in light of material feedback from diminishing returns.

That being said, many of the most decisive observable implications in favor of one theory or another are specific to individual cases. Some aspects of the theory are generally agreed upon in certain cases, and alternative theoretical frameworks would contest much more specific evidence than these general outlines. For example, most existing accounts agree that the French policy regime of national champions collapsed through endogenous internal limits, and the evidence brought to bear must focus on showing that it was the diminishing returns to market power specifically. Or, while most agree that the Chicago school of antitrust played a large role in transforming American antitrust in the 1970s, Chicago thinkers would never consider themselves to be, or at least admit to being, anti-competition in their outlook. Therefore, in that case, more empirical evidence is leveraged to indicate both that many Chicago thinkers were knowingly anti-competition and that politicians and other policymakers certainly took their views to be anti-competition regardless.

Conclusion

This book provides empirically realistic and concrete micro-foundations to explain long-term institutional and policy change regarding competition and market power. The theory focuses in detail on the specific actors responsible for both directly shaping policies and interpreting the meaning of broader economic and political forces. Combined with a research design well-suited to the question of endogenous institutional change, doing so allows this study to better capture many of the more fine-grained specifics of policymaking and learning in order to better understand how policy regimes can undermine themselves over time. I now turn to the empirical evidence in support of this proposition.

3

Monopoly, the New Deal, and the Postwar Policy Order

> Whenever in the pursuit of this objective the lone wolf, the *unethical competitor*, the *reckless promoter*, the Ishmael or Insull whose hand is against every man's, declines to join in achieving and end recognized as being for the public welfare, and *threatens to drag the industry back to a state of anarchy*, the *government may properly be asked to apply restraint.*
>
> —Franklin Delano Roosevelt, Commonwealth Club address, September 23, 1932

> Once it is realized that business monopoly in America paralyzes the system of free enterprise on which it is grafted, and is as fatal to those who manipulate it as to the people who suffer beneath its impositions, action by the government to eliminate these artificial restraints will be welcomed by industry throughout the nation. For idle factories and idle workers profit no man.
>
> —Franklin Delano Roosevelt, monopoly message to Congress, April 29, 1938

The Roosevelt administration dramatically changed its position relative to competition and monopoly over its first six years. Roosevelt came into office in alignment with a policy regime of "industrial self-government," which supported various forms of informal cartels, patent agreements, shared price lists, fixed wage scales, and a range of trade association policies to rein in "destructive competition." Despite reinforcing this through an experiment with anti-competition planning with the National Recovery Administration (NRA) from 1933 to 1935, the Roosevelt administration turned to an extensive campaign of trust-busting beginning in 1938, which extended through World War II. By the 1950s, this resulted in strong legal precedents against new forms of cartels and restrictive patent licensing arrangements,

Monopoly Politics. Erik Peinert, Oxford University Press. © Oxford University Press (2025).
DOI: 10.1093/oso/9780197789506.003.0003

along with reinvigorated government agencies enforcing antitrust laws and new anti-merger legislation, all built around a political consensus favoring competitive market mechanisms.

Existing literature on the New Deal suggests two principal alternative characterizations or explanations for these shifts. First, one view posits that the antitrust and antimonopoly movement of the New Deal largely failed and was replaced or forgotten as the focus turned to macroeconomic demand management and the subsequent mobilization for World War II (Brinkley 1995; Maier 1977). This view characterizes the postwar political economy as an accepted compromise of large corporations and oligopolistic competition, balanced by the countervailing power of labor unions (Galbraith 1952b, 1952a), with antitrust retaining at most a limited popular base or public following (Hofstadter 1965). Rather than denying that these shifts occurred, this argument broadly argues that antitrust and competition mattered very little in the course of the New Deal or postwar political economy.

A second view is that the New Deal politics of antitrust and monopoly were contingent or random, lacking a systematic pattern to them. Hawley (1966) sees New Deal anti-monopoly politics as a contingent back-and-forth of political and bureaucratic fights based on which advisors had influence at one moment or another, and does not see any systematic changes in the substance or direction of policy within the American political economy. This view does not, however, necessarily downplay antitrust's importance. Freyer (2006) and Wells (2002)—who both follow this general narrative—trace how postwar American antitrust policies were globally important, diffusing to the rest of the world through a mix of coercion, persuasion, and economic diplomacy.

This chapter examines how the gradually increasing costs of this anti-competition policy regime—the diminishing returns to market power—were noticed by new, uncommitted policymakers within various New Deal agencies. The pro-competition policies were driven largely by enthusiastic mid-level officials like Leon Henderson, Robert Jackson, and later Corwin Edwards,[1] around whom this analysis centers. However, just a few short years earlier, like most policymakers at the time, all such officials had

[1] See Wells (2002, 37–42) and Freyer (2006, 17–24) for other accounts that highlight these same actors.

supported the industrial self-government policies of the NRA, and they expressed genuine opinions in support of them. Through NRA research about the failures of the restrictive policies of industrial self-government, and other experiences with the anticompetitive trends of the time, they changed their views over the 1930s, reframing anti-competition policies as illegitimate. This formed the foundation of a new political and policy consensus around the strong antitrust and free trade policies of the postwar era, many of which eventually cohered loosely around the "structure-conduct-performance" paradigm.

Following a brief historical background of American competition policy and the market power policy regime that had been established by the interwar period, the analysis begins by showing that the NRA was an attempt to institutionalize the monopoly capitalism ideas of "industrial self-government," but that internal research in the NRA regarding price policy and competition revealed many of the policy's intrinsic failures. Second, the chapter traces the rise of pro-competition beliefs and enforcement actions within the Department of Justice (DOJ) in the late 1930s, as Robert Jackson took over and changed his opinion based on his own experience and policy ideas passed from the NRA through Henderson. Third, and stemming from this, the chapter shows how the DOJ campaign diffused across federal agencies, spread internationally as extraterritorial antitrust enforcement, and cemented a pro-competition policy regime in the few years following World War II. These uncommitted policymakers are contrasted with a group of policymakers, including General Hugh Johnson and Donald Richberg, who, despite seeing the same evidence, remained committed to industrial self-government.

Antitrust and Industrial Self-Government

Antitrust policy came to the United States following the rise of corporate, managerial capitalism in the late 19th century. Despite the size and concentration of the new industrial titans, and the prevalence of market power in many local markets, American markets in this era were fiercely competitive, characterized by regular price wars and bankruptcies (Chandler 1977; Dobbin and Dowd 2000; Fligstein 1990). Nonetheless, in response to populist and agrarian interests with little bargaining power relative to these new industrial giants, early anti-monopoly laws were passed at the state level in the 1880s, followed shortly by the 1890 Sherman Act, which banned agreements to restrain trade and attempts to monopolize. Although enforcement was initially unsure, the 1897 *Trans-Missouri* Supreme Court decision upheld the basic provisions of the Sherman Act, prohibiting inter-firm coordination and cartels.[2] These rules served to further reinforce competitive trends, removing some of the few remaining mechanisms available for business to limit price wars.[3]

The second wave of anti-monopoly laws deepened these trends. The 1914 Federal Trade Commission Act created the Federal Trade Commission (FTC), an independent regulatory commission that both shared responsibility for enforcing the antitrust laws with the DOJ and was bestowed with additional authorities. The 1914 Clayton Act included provisions to limit anticompetitive mergers to prevent firms on the scale of Standard Oil. It also included prohibitions on anticompetitive tying and exclusive dealing arrangements, as well prohibitions on directors serving on the boards of competing companies.

This pro-competition and anti-monopoly fervor was soon tempered by a different interpretation of economic problems: the notion of "destructive" or "cutthroat" competition. In good times, so the argument went, firms would over-expand capacity and build up inventories, only to enter prolonged and devastating price wars when demand collapsed by dumping all of this inventory and capacity on the market at a loss. In some versions of this view, price wars occurred because firms did not separate costs by product lines and therefore did not necessarily know when they were selling at a loss or making a profit (Berk 2009; Eddy 1912). The set of economic arguments and the policy ideas around this became more sophisticated over time, coming to include the argument that this competitive, downward pressure on profits suppressed wages as well, thereby lowering consumption and worsening competition for the remaining purchasing power. The proposed solutions were a variety of fixes in cost accounting, cooperation among industry associations, and various price policies, under the general banner

[2] *United States v. Trans-Missouri Freight Assn.*, 166 U.S. 290 (1897).

[3] They also, admittedly, led to a massive merger wave as firms sought to avoid price wars by merging, since doing so by inter-firm agreement was not prohibited. See Dobbin and Dowd (2000) and Fligstein (1990, Ch. 2); both emphasize the quandary into which the new antitrust laws put business, though it did lead to a merger wave in search of some way to legally coordinate and avoid price wars.

of "industrial self-government." While detailed in their analysis, these ideas and prescriptions opposed direct price competition, aiming at least to limit "excess" competition and, at most, to outright eliminate it through cartel-like arrangements.

This set of policy ideas formed the core of a market power policy regime that developed in the early decades of the 20th century. As the United States entered World War I, the American government managed the economic mobilization for the war under the aegis of the War Industries Board (WIB), a committee of government bureaucrats and industrialists who would determine production targets and prices noncompetitively and based on private cost accounting.[4] Emboldened by this experience and particularly driven by Herbert Hoover's Department of Commerce, the trade association movement took off in the 1920s. The Department of Commerce advocated expansion of industry associations' sharing of cost and price information to allow businesses to cooperate and "stabilize" overly competitive markets (Himmelberg 1976). By the late 1920s, the FTC held a series of trade practice conferences, giving government sanction to these policies, while the DOJ almost entirely stopped enforcing antitrust rules prohibiting many of these practices.[5]

Court decisions from this era similarly favored anticompetitive arrangements even when not based on ideas of industrial self-government. The 1920 *US Steel* Supreme Court decision ruled that "price leadership"—an arrangement where all firms follow the pricing choices of one central firm—is legal, despite the fact that the practice was not consequentially different from price-fixing in its economic effects.[6] Patent law followed similar trends. The 1926 *General Electric* decision ruled that patent holders had a complete and total right to restrict the prices at which licensees were permitted to sell the patented product,[7] which prevents competition between licensees and maximizes profits and market power for the patent holder.

[4] See Cuff (1973), Himmelberg (1965), and Himmelberg (1968) for background on the WIB as it pertains to competition and antitrust.

[5] See Himmelberg (1976, 54–65). See Berk (2009, 115–215) for an alternative interpretation of FTC policy at this time.

[6] *United States v. United States Steel Corp.*, 251 U.S. 417 (1920). See also Fligstein (1990) for an account of the importance of price leadership and the *US Steel* decision at this time.

[7] *United States v. General Elec. Co.*, 272 U.S. 476 (1926).

The Depression and the Price Problem

Rather than diminishing faith in such policies, the onset of the Depression in 1929 further intensified beliefs that reforming or removing the antitrust laws was the most important step to take on the road to recovery.[8] This consensus spanned both parties and many interest groups, with a plethora of bills to weaken or eliminate the antitrust laws being proposed by both parties during Hoover's presidency. After Roosevelt's election in 1932, a group of close advisers—including many from the original brain trust: Adolf Berle, Hugh Johnson, Raymond Moley, Rex Tugwell, and Donald Richberg—put together the National Industrial Recovery Act (NIRA) of 1933, which established the NRA.

The NRA was the hallmark early New Deal program, meant to stabilize the economy by placing each industry under a code that dictated fair practices for minimum wages, maximum working hours, restrictions on output, common cost accounting practices, and minimum prices (Barber 1996, 5–40). Each industry code was to be submitted by the industry itself, and the antitrust laws were suspended for the NRA, with the antitrust enforcement agencies like the DOJ formally re-tasked with to enforcing the new anti-competition rules of the NRA.[9] These trends were mimicked in trade policy, with the protectionist Smoot-Hawley Act of 1930 only being the most prominent example. The understood goals of the NRA and related policies were to increase prices so that businesses would earn more, be able to pay more in wages, and thereby increase purchasing power, further bolstering sales, prices, and profits. This intuition, that higher prices would lead to more employment, followed the practical experience that industries under conditions of "destructive competition" were rife with sweatshop labor, whereas those that were "stabilized" paid higher wages and generally treated employees better.

The Research and Planning Division

The Research and Planning Division was set up within the NRA on similar grounds, staffed by economists and statisticians from a mix of academia and

[8] See Himmelberg (1976, 110–180) and Schlesinger (1957, 181–183).

[9] The Agricultural Adjustment Act (AAA) of 1933 was a similarly anti-competition policy for agriculture, guaranteeing profitable prices for farmers by restricting output.

the financial industry. The primary task put to the division was to determine "the wage level which will maximize mass purchasing power,"[10] again figuring on being able to increase wages by increasing prices via anticompetitive cooperation. Ensuring that businesses had enough money to pay workers and make profits through high prices was seen as the primary path to recovery. For example, a May 1934 memo summarizes the NRA view that the primary determinants shaping employment decisions were "1. excess working capital or cash," "2. Ability to hold down unit costs," and "3. Possibility to increase prices without losing sales,"[11] the last of these being the modern definition of market power.

Leon Henderson was appointed as head of the Research and Planning Division in 1934 following a verbal confrontation with NRA Administrator Hugh Johnson.[12] Before this, he was a researcher with the private Russell Sage Foundation. Despite several years becoming one of the key advocates for pro-competition policies in the administration, Henderson's opinions at this time would indicate the opposite, if anything. Even before entering government, a private policy memo of his largely endorses the NRA view in support of open-price associations, which were are among the cartel-like arrangements of the time—price lists through which producers would be required to publish any price changes a certain period ahead of the price change.[13] These were ubiquitous in NRA codes and facilitated collusion. Henderson himself would later openly refer to such systems as equivalent to price-fixing.[14] Even several months into his time in the NRA, when he had become the head of the Research and Planning Division, he affirmed that price controls can "prevent the worst species of cut-throat competition,"[15]

[10] Alexander Sachs to Henry Allen Moe, June 24, 1933, Alexander Sachs Papers, Box 63, FDR.

[11] Vose to Henderson, May 19, 1934, John Hamm Office Files, Box 1, RG9, NARA.

[12] Henderson obtained the position at the NRA, temporarily as an assistant to the Administrator General Hugh Johnson, more or less on a dare following a screaming match with General Johnson in November 1933. Henderson was among a group of consumer advocates who were brought in to see Johnson, who proceeded to shout at them and slam on his desk before any of them even spoke. Henderson started screaming back, after which Johnson offered him a position as a "critical assistant" on consumer issues. Hawley (1966, 76–78) and Schlesinger (1958, 130–131).

[13] "Policy Memorandum (Confidential)", October 25, 1933, Leon Henderson Papers, Box 36, FDR. The handwritten draft of this memo shows it to be Henderson who wrote this. Compare to his handwritten diaries also found in Leon Henderson Papers, Box 36, FDR.

[14] Speech by Leon Henderson to the District of Columbia League of Women Voters, February 16, 1934, Leon Henderson Papers, Box 5, FDR. Similarly, in private correspondence with friends in academia, he expresses his primary concerns with the NRA in terms of the particulars of individual policy devices and the administrative burdens they make necessary. Henderson Letter to Frederick Mills, January 20, 1934, Leon Henderson Papers, Box 36, FDR.

[15] Henderson to Johnson, May 14, 1934, Leon Henderson Subject File, Box 4, RG9, NARA.

and it was his assessment that in 1931 "individualistic competition" was dangerously breaking out even in "stabilized" industries.[16]

That being said, since the Research and Planning Division was thrown together at the last minute with an unclear mandate, it was staffed by researchers with a variety of perspectives. Notably, chief statistician Victor von Szeliski, who had been in the Division for almost a year, wrote to Henderson a few months after his arrival:

> Some have said that the industries best able to take on workers and help with the reemployment problem are those which have the strongest price provisions, either direct or by way of limitation of production. *What evidence has come to my attention shows the contrary, if anything.*[17]

As in, he found that the firms least able to maintain prices and profits, and presumably in the most competitive markets, had the best employment records. Though only based on offhand figures at this point, he already identified the policies associated with industrial self-government as responsible: NRA policies like machine-hour limitations[18] and open-price agreements[19] may have "stabilized" prices, but in so doing also suppressed employment gains through high prices and lost consumption. Von Szeliski theorized that maintaining high prices, even if it improved employment for that firm, undid those benefits by draining consumer demand from elsewhere.[20]

This research continued, and in May von Szeliski backed it up with more industry-level data and figures, and with a far blunter conclusions (Figure 3.1). In a memo titled "Are High Prices Necessary for Recovery?", he wrote, "The industries with the 'worst' price records maintained employment much better that the industries that were able to hold their prices."[21]

[16] Hawley, 39.

[17] Von Szeliski to Henderson, April 26, 1934, von Szeliski Office Files, Box 7, RG9, NARA. Emphasis added.

[18] Machine-hour limitations were common in NRA codes, which required firms in the industry to only run industrial equipment for a maximum number of hours, in order to restrict output.

[19] Open-price agreements were price lists that firms in an industry would share with each other through the code authority. It was a common tool for collusion, as the public frequently did not see the price lists, and there were common waiting periods during which prices could not be revised.

[20] Von Szeliski to Henderson, "Relation between Prices and Employment," April 26, 1934, Victor von Szeliski Office Files, Box 7, RG9, NARA.

[21] Von Szeliski to Henderson, "Are High Prices Necessary for Recovery?" May 21, 1934, Leon Henderson Papers, Box 9, FDR.

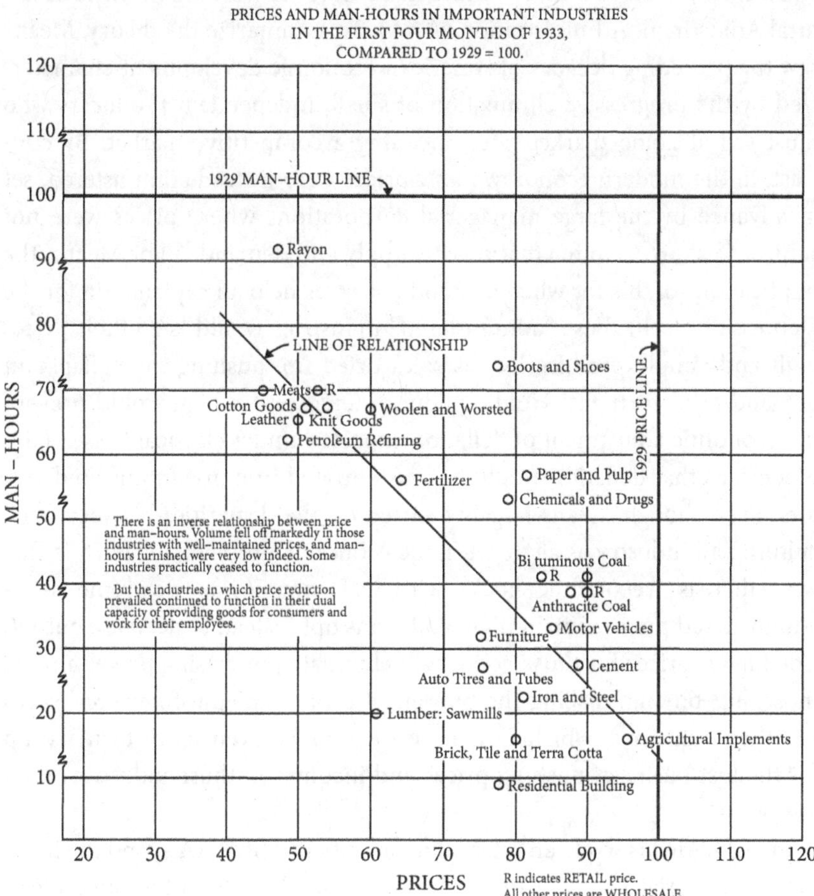

Figure 3.1 von Szeliski's Inverse Relation between Price Stability and Employment[22]

The Administered Prices Hypothesis

At the same time, elsewhere in the federal government, a similar theory with different conclusions was gaining traction: Gardiner Means's "administered prices" hypothesis.[23] Means began as a special economic adviser

[22] Chart V from Von Szeliski to Henderson, "Are High Prices Necessary for Recovery?" May 21, 1934, Leon Henderson Papers, Box 9, FDR.

[23] Means had originally developed this theory as part of his dissertation. See Gardiner Means, "The Corporate Revolution," January 1, 1933, Gardiner Means Papers, Box 2, FDR. Aspects of this

to Secretary of Agriculture Wallace in early 1933, working in the Agricultural Adjustment Administration (AAA). To summarize the theory, Means saw the preceding decades of American economic development characterized by the progressive elimination of small, independent producers who must sell at going market rates, meaning a competitive market. By contrast, in the modern economy, many prices were instead administered, set in advance by the large managerial corporations whose prices were not subject to short-term fluctuations of supply and demand.[24] For Means, the implications of this for when demand collapses held an explanation for the Depression itself: these "administered" industries would keep their prices high and simply produce less as sales dried up, pushing the collapse in demand even further.[25] Holding administered prices high would prevent the economic adjustment of deflation expected under classical laissez-faire models, as that deflation would be concentrated in non-administered sectors. Even though Means largely focused on the disparities between agriculture and industry as aggregates, the economic problem, in short, is that when there is an economic shock—with the Depression as an extreme case—administered prices remain high, and firms opt instead to decrease output. The higher prices for those goods will eliminate purchasing power among those still buying, placing the burden of economic adjustment on prices in other industries, which now have to produce even more to make up for the lost business, pushing prices and incomes in those industries even lower.

In 1934, Means wrote an internal memo titled "NRA, AAA, and the Making of Industrial Policy."[26] In it, Means rehashed many of the same ideas, but now with government statistics to support them, showing in particular that agriculture, despite a massive collapse in demand, continued to produce at the same levels with collapsed prices, whereas the prices for industrial sectors did not fall much, or at all, despite dramatically depressed sales (Figure 3.2). By the fall of 1934, based on widespread interest and

theory were included in his well-known work with Adolf Berle in 1932 (Berle and Means 1932). However, Means's work with Berle had little influence in policy circles, whereas a great number of reports, analyses, and memos in the 1930s follow Means's work on administered prices, particularly an internal policy memo eventually published as Senate Document 13, "Industrial Prices and their Relative Inflexibility" (Means 1935).

[24] Gardiner Means, "The Corporate Revolution," January 1, 1933, Gardiner Means Papers, Box 2, FDR, page 134.

[25] Ibid., page 144.

[26] "NRA, AAA, and the Making of Industrial Policy," January 15, 1934, Means Papers, Box 4, FDR.

connections that Means had made throughout the government, this memo was widely distributed, with recipients including the Federal Reserve,[27] the NRA,[28] and the Department of Labor.[29]

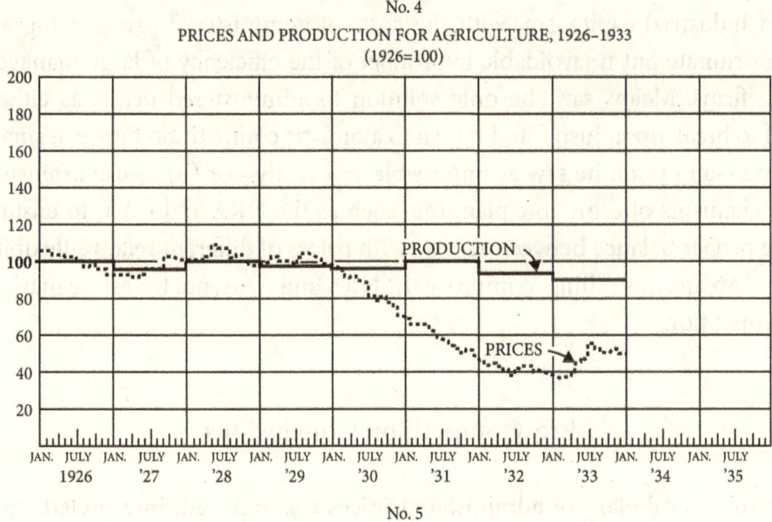

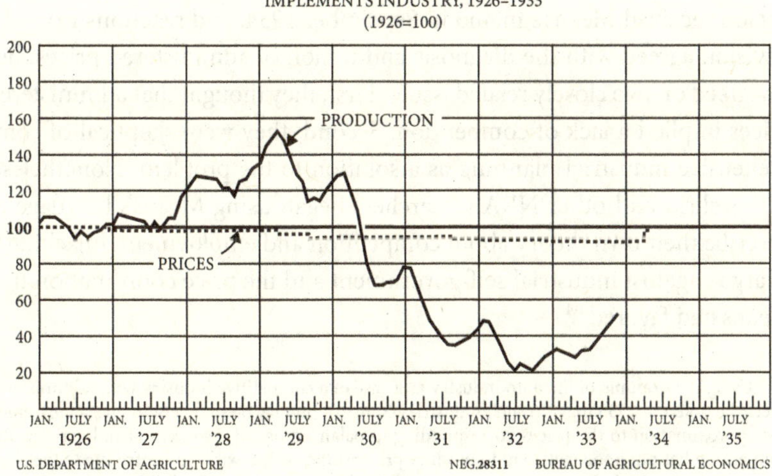

Figure 3.2 Charts 4 and 5 from Means's Internal AAA Memo[30]

[27] Currie to Means, March 4, 1935, Means Papers, Box 2, FDR.

[28] Galloway to Means, October 11, 1934; von Szeliski to Means, September 15, 1934, both in Means Papers, Box 2, FDR; Means to von Szeliski, September 14, 1934, von Szeliski Office Files, Box 3, RG9, NARA.

[29] Means to Clague, October 3, 1934, Means Papers, Box 2, FDR.

[30] "NRA, AAA, and the Making of Industrial Policy," January 15, 1934, Means Papers, Box 4, FDR. This same figure did also end up in Means (1935).

Means, however, saw administered prices and competition as somewhat unrelated issues. In fact, he wrote elsewhere, at the time in an unpublished work, that administered prices and monopoly were not the same thing.[31] For Means, administered prices were a fact and necessity of modern industrial capitalism, with the costs of administered prices being an unfortunate but unavoidable byproduct of the efficiency of large managerial firms. Means saw the only solution to administered prices as either (a) to break up industry and return to atomistic competition between small firms—an option he saw as impossible and costly—or (b) to use extensive mechanisms of economic planning, such as the NRA and AAA, to ensure the proper balance between sectors with prices of different relative flexibility.[32] Means was calling to improve the NRA and AAA, not to restore market competition.

Pro-Competition Conclusions

Means's vocabulary of administered prices was received, interpreted, and used very differently by the NRA's Research and Planning Division.[33] Henderson received Means's memo in September 1934, and reactions from the Division agreed with the diagnosis and notion of administered prices, but disagreed on two closely related issues. First, they thought that administered prices implied a lack of competition. Second, they were skeptical of comprehensive industrial planning as a solution to the problem. Nonetheless, von Szeliski and other NRA researchers began using Means's language to describe their own theory about competition and employment, hijacking it to argue against industrial self-government and the price coordination that Means had favored.[34]

[31] Using the example of the auto industry as a case of a competitive industry with administered prices, he noted in 1935 that "In such industries competition may be sufficient to give a fairly good first approximation to the prices corresponding to balanced use of resources at full activity. But competition has not boon sufficient to produce prices sufficiently flexible to contribute to the elimination of depression." Gardiner Means, undated confidential memo, "Possibilities and Limitations of Antitrust Policy," Means Papers, Box 12, FDR.

[32] "NRA, AAA, and the Making of Industrial Policy," January 15, 1934, Means Papers, Box 4, FDR, page 13.

[33] Franklin Ryan to Henderson, October 21, 1934; C.F. Roos Memo to Henderson, September 6, 1934; Von Szeliski Memo to Henderson, September 17, 1934; Simon Whitney to Henderson, September 26, 1934, all found in Leon Henderson Papers, Box 7, FDR. See also Barber (1996, 64) and Lee (1998, 39–41).

[34] Simon Whitney to Henderson, September 26, 1934, Leon Henderson Papers, Box 7, FDR.

After internal debates over the Means memo, the exact same conclusions the NRA had already reached came to be framed in terms of "flexible," "administered," or "rigid" prices. By March 1935, von Szeliski argued that investment, monetary, and banking, among other problems, were the primary causes of the Depression, but that "the price rigidities determined where and how it would hit: in rigid-price industries, employment down and prices fairly well-maintained; in the flexible price industries, prices down, wages down, but employment fairly well maintained."[35] Administered prices theory became a vocabulary for a set of anti-monopoly policy preferences that had been established prior and independently based on the limitations and failures of the NRA and similar policies.

Bear in mind that researchers at the NRA had already arrived at these same conclusions before Means.[36] Given the relationship between employment and output, von Szeliski's inverse relation between price stability and employment is, in practice, the same as Means relation between price stability and output. However, NRA researchers were far more likely to see this relationship as the result of the policy devices put in place by the NRA and similar policies before it, whereas Means did not look beyond the supposition that it was an unchangeable fact of modern industry. And while Means presents this as a novel theory of the economy, the empirical relationship he points to is very close to modern textbook understandings of market power: firms with market power do not need to change their prices in the face of competition. It was this latter interpretation of administered prices that increasingly came to be used in policy debates in later years, particularly by Henderson and other transplants out of the NRA.

[35] Von Szeliski, "Relation of Price Flexibility to Employment and the General Problem of Recovery," March 19, 1935, Victor von Szeliski Office Files, Box 9, RG9, NARA, page 2.

[36] Nonetheless, given the similarities in the nature of each argument, it should be addressed that these were entirely independent inferences—meaning that von Szeliski and the NRA Research and Planning Division reached their own conclusions *prior* to ever being exposed to the language or theory of administered prices. There is little indication of this possibility. Early interaction between the Research and Planning Division and the AAA occurred because of the creation of a price committee created at Roosevelt's request after reading a Brookings Institute report critical of the NRA. On May 11, 1934, in forming the price committee, Henderson reports that Secretary of Agriculture Wallace was to select one of his "underlings" for the committee, an impersonal reference for Means, implying Henderson did not know him at that time. See Henderson to Robinson, May 11, 1934, Leon Henderson Papers, Box 9, FDR. Likewise, on May 25, 1934, Isador Lubin forwarded an early memo about prices from Means on prices to Henderson, but the closest the memo comes to stating the administered prices hypothesis is in the assertion that "the hypothesis that there has been a radical change in the character of the pricing process should be tested." "See Minutes of Meeting of Cabinet Committee on Prices," May 23, 1934, Leon Henderson Papers, Box 9, FDR. And this memo is still *after* von Szeliski had his initial epiphany a month earlier.

The NRA had also collected far more robust evidence than Means had. Their reports had more specific numbers broken out by industrial subgroups, confirming that the least competitive industries, like steel or agricultural equipment, which according to the thinking of the time should have had the most resources to be able to absorb the costs of higher wages and more workers, had a consistently worse employment record.[37] Reports through the spring of 1935 detailed the inverse relationship between prices and employment, using simple regressions to estimate that around 30 to 35 percent of the variation in the employment performance of different industries since 1929 could be predicted based on the relative flexibility of their prices, again with the relationship being *opposite* to that of the policy consensus at the time. The industries subject to the most competition consistently seemed to employ and produce more.[38]

The pro-competition policy conclusions became clear over the course of 1934. As early as December 1934, internal reports were urging "fundamental reform in anti-trust laws."[39] Later, in 1935, rather than claiming that markets failed and that planning or non-market coordination was necessary, many NRA reports argued that the laissez-faire policy of letting private industry govern itself was a failure and that government intervention would be needed to restore market flexibility.[40] In April 1935, another statistician in the section writes to Henderson on the most important policies to stimulate recovery, and high on the list is "a revision of the NRA and Anti-Trust Laws."[41] Around the time that the NRA was shutting down, J. M. Clark, a consultant with the NRA and an early pioneer of the theory imperfect competition, put the conclusion bluntly: "Non-existence of ideal 'free competition['] doesn't necessarily mean the anti-trust policy is unjustifiable as an attempt to keep alive a working approximation which may produce better results than either more nearly complete monopoly or public control of a positive sort, e.g. prices."[42]

[37] Von Szeliski, "Effect of Price Levels on Employment," January 24, 1935, Von Szeliski Office Files, Box 7, RG9, NARA.

[38] Ibid., page 2.

[39] Von Szeliski to Henderson, "Boot and Shoe Codes," December 5, 1934, Leon Henderson Papers, Box 1, FDR.

[40] Von Szeliski, "Relation of Price Flexibility to Employment and the General Problem of Recovery," March 19, 1935, Victor von Szeliski Office Files, Box 9, RG9, NARA, page 8.

[41] T.J. Kreps to Henderson, "Positive Stimulants to Recovery," April 15, 1935, Theodore Kreps Office Files, Box 7, RG9, NARA.

[42] Clark to Henderson, "Notes on Seidler memorandum of March 15, 1935," Leon Henderson Papers, Box 2, FDR, page 1.

Leon Henderson's opinions about the monopoly problem were formed in this situation, with researchers poring over the NRA's track record.[43] Henderson increasingly questioned how the NRA framed problems and the solutions to them. In February 1935, he wrote to J. M. Clark, asking far broader questions about competition: "Has the essential nature of competition changed in recent years, or . . . Has the change been merely in the concept of unfair or destructive competition[?]"[44] By the time the NRA was closing down, Henderson suggested the work of the Division continue with research on "rigid pricesin which positive action to effect freer competition is needed."[45] Henderson began pushing for more pro-competition policies within the NRA by the end of 1934,[46] and he used the language and theory of "administered prices" for much of the rest of the 1930s to motivate and justify pro-competition antitrust actions.

Emphasizing the role of simple mental models and cognitive closure in this process, the NRA researchers oversimplified and overgeneralized their conclusions. Once they had decided competition was needed, other dynamics were shoehorned into this interpretation and framework. Having decided against the NRA regime, one memo asks other economists to develop deductive proofs that the NRA price protections undermine recovery.[47] Another memo circulating in the NRA, made in preparing a statement for Congress, noted that "a number of American industries do not conform to the orthodox concepts of competition and monopoly."[48] It expanded on the point by arguing that although a few industries fit the textbook models of monopoly and competition, "the preponderance of American industry is conducted" between the two.[49] But as a clear example of cognitive closure, on the following pages all this discussion of complexity, unclear categories, and fluidity is replaced by a fear of "an economy in which monopoly is far more prevalent tha[n] competition—where the quest for monopolistic profits has placed so

[43] Henderson was, in fact, the primary recipient of a majority of the reports and memos cited in this section.

[44] Henderson Memo to Clark, "Competition," February 1, 1935, Leon Henderson Papers, Box 2, FDR.

[45] Leon Henderson, "Preliminary Observations on President's Statement," June 6, 1935, NIRA Periodic Reports, Box 2, RG9, NARA.

[46] Barber (1996, 54–56) and Hawley (1966, 97–101).

[47] Von Szeliski to Roos, "The Effect of Price Protection Provisions," March 24, 1934, Victor von Szeliski Office Files, Box 2, RG9, NARA.

[48] Draft Memo, May 9, 1935, John Hamm Office Files, Box 1, RG9, NARA, page 6.

[49] Ibid., page 5.

many restrictions on the flow of goods and service that the standard of living is progressively declining."[50]

Nonetheless, this learning was not simply motivated by political party or electoral incentives in either direction. These researchers would openly refer to plans from other New Deal policymakers as "typical of some of the asinine logic of some of our Government agencies," in that case in reference to a relief plan for the federal government to directly finance textile mills to return unemployed to work.[51] Nor were these analysts simply conservative, pro-market hacks who managed to find themselves in the NRA. Von Szeliski himself disseminated reports contradicting opponents of the NRA,[52] and the debate about the Means memo was relatively open and heated within different groups in the Division.[53]

The Old Guard of Industrial Self-Government

In the short run, this was all for naught, as this rethinking occurred in certain circles contrasted sharply with the established policy leaders and political climate of industrial self-government. Furthermore, the National Industrial Recovery Act—the statute that created the NRA—was ruled unconstitutional in May 1935, for reasons largely unrelated to its anti-competition or pro-competition content.[54] The *Schechter* case gave two reasons to rule the NIRA unconstitutional. The first was not on the economics, ruling that it was an unconstitutional delegation of authority to the executive branch, since the law delegated authority to approve industrial codes to the president. The second was arguably more economic: *Schechter* gave a very narrow reading of the Commerce Clause of the constitution, fundamentally limiting the degree of permitted interstate commercial regulation. However, the case constrained much more whether the government had a right to regulate the national economy than whether it was going about it the right way, and

[50] Ibid., page 7.

[51] Roos to Henderson, "Relief Plan Aims to Return Millions to Work in Mills," June 13, 1934, Leon Henderson Subject File, Box 4, RG9, NARA.

[52] Von Szeliski to Lawson, "Criticism of National Recovery Administration by Senator Borah," February 17, 1934, Victor von Szeliski Office Files, Box 1, RG9, NARA.

[53] For examples of these arguments, see von Szeliski to Henderson, "Gardiner Means' Memorandum on NRA and AAA and the Reorganization of Industrial Policy Making," September 17, 1934; Roos to Henderson, "NRA and AAA and the Reorganization of Industrial Policy Making by Gardiner C. Means," September 6, 1934, both found in Leon Henderson Papers, Box 7, FDR.

[54] *ALA Schechter Poultry Corp. v. United States*, 295 U.S. 495 (1935).

little indicates that the decision was based at all on the economic failures or unpopularity of the policy.

The few years following the end of the NRA, from 1935 to 1937, were characterized by a dissonance between different officials and political leaders, going well past just the question of monopoly and competition. The overall direction of policy for the Roosevelt administration was put somewhat in question by the Supreme Court's willingness to strike down New Deal legislation, as well as waning political enthusiasm.[55] Nonetheless, administration officials, including Roosevelt himself, remained committed to the anti-competition approach to policy heralded by the NRA. After the NRA ended, and to get around the *Schechter* decision, legislation continued to spout out a series of "little NRAs"—regulatory commissions designed to perform the same functions but for individual industries.[56] These "little NRAs" included the Motor Carrier Act of 1935 (buses and trucking), the Bituminous Coal Conservation Act of 1935 and the Guffey-Vinson Coal Act of 1937 after it (coal industry), the Merchant Marine Act of 1936 (maritime transportation and construction), the 1937 Miller-Tydings Amendment to the Clayton Act (retail industry), and the Civil Aeronautics Act of 1938 (air transportation). These were an intentional choice by Roosevelt announced shortly after the NRA was ruled unconstitutional (Schlesinger 1960, 290).

Political support for the NRA remained strong among many industry and labor groups.[57] Even though some in industry viewed the NRA as giant conspiracy to help monopolistic corporations, restrictions such as maximum operating hours, as administratively difficult as they were, increased the prices received by smaller, less-efficient concerns such that they could stay in business. More efficient plants similarly received guaranteed large profits, contrary to the notion that monopolists were keeping prices "unfairly" low.[58] And even for those who saw the NRA as a tool of monopolies, the favored solution was not to enforce competition, but to expand price and market protections to cover themselves.[59] Organized labor was largely silent on the question of competition and monopoly, but rather fixated on internal

[55] See Brinkley (1995).

[56] See Hawley (1966, 149–280) for the best account of the "little NRAs".

[57] See, for example, Gibson to Senator Shipstead, May 18, 1935, Donald Richberg Alphabetical File, Box 1, RG9, NARA.

[58] Von Szeliski to Kreps, "War on Small Industries," February 11, 1935, Victor von Szeliski Office Files, RG9, NARA.

[59] Florsheim to Richberg, April 23, 1935, Donald Richberg Alphabetical File, Box 1, RG9, NARA.

disputes over whether to keep the NRA because of its labor protections or to decry those protections as insufficient.[60]

This was likewise all in the context among policymakers, bureaucrats, and politicians who consistently fell into the trap of seeing competition as risky or dangerous by default. External criticisms of the NRA largely agreed with its economic premises. The Darrow Commission, which investigated the NRA in 1934, accepted as given the anti-competition arguments that "unregulated competition forces down prices, wages, and salaries." It complained that small businesses are "driven into bankruptcy by low prices" brought on by larger producers" and saw the only choices as those between the NRA's "monopoly sustained by government" and a "planned economy, which demands socialized ownership and control."[61] Across the political spectrum, competition was dangerously ruinous as an economic mechanism.

Nonetheless, support for the NRA and its overall approach was most unwavering among those committed policymakers most responsible for it. The case of General Johnson, the appointed administrator of the NRA, is particularly illuminating. During World War I, Johnson had been one of the top aids for Bernard Baruch, head of the War Industries Board from World War I. He had spent much of the time since then advocating for a peacetime implementation of the same cooperative industrial activities that the WIB had temporarily but legally endorsed. He was called up by Roosevelt when the NRA was being designed and was central in writing and working out many of its main provisions. As such, Roosevelt thought him to be the obvious candidate for the position of administrator for the NRA. Once the NRA ran into difficulties, however, Johnson began to blame the problems on almost anything other than the NRA policy itself, even as evidence mounted that it was not performing what its advocates had said that it would. In a statement to the Senate about the NRA even after the end of his tenure there, he spoke about how genuine competition is impossible given modern industrial scale and concentration, that the WIB is a model policy to work from, and that "efficiency is attainable only by cooperation."[62]

[60] American Federation of Labor to President Roosevelt, May 3, 1935, OF466, Box 10, FDR; Wharton to President Roosevelt, May 3, 1935, OF466, Box 10, FDR.

[61] Clarence Darrow and William Thompson, "Special and Supplementary Report to the President," May 3, 1934, Material Sent to Finance Committee Hearing on Senate Resolution 79, Box 65, RG9, NARA, page 4.

[62] Johnson Statement to Senate Finance Committee, April 18, 1935, Material Sent to Finance Committee Hearing on Senate Resolution 79, Box 65, RG 9, NARA, page 9.

Donald Richberg, a member of Roosevelt's original brain trust and another of the primary architects of the NRA, had also been central to the antitrust revision movement in the late 1920s and early 1930s. Speaking in the Senate Finance Committee in February 1933, he said:

> We have reached the state in the development of human affairs where it has become intolerable to have our primitive capitalistic system operated by selfish individualists engaged in ruthless competition. . . . A planned control of the great essential industries in essential.[63]

He went on to be general counsel for the NRA, and later its administrator after Johnson stepped down. As the NRA was increasingly embattled, he continued to blame the NRA's failure on administrative problems of management and coordination, insisting that its limitations unrelated to its approach to addressing the Depression. Such interpretations were common within the NRA, and among its advocates after it ended.[64]

Especially noteworthy to the interpretation of the NRA's failure as an administrative failure is that the NRA succeeded in almost all of its policy goals unrelated to reaching economic recovery by restraining competition. Child labor, long endemic in American industry, was largely brought to an end. Section 7(a) of the NRA succeeded in ensuring collective bargaining rights and led to the unionization of most of the American labor force in a few short years. The NRA's price protections, furthermore, did succeed to protecting firms from competition: the rate of business failures fell to almost nothing relative to the time of the NRA's enactment, despite having steadily risen even prior to the Depression during the 1920s (Figure 3.3).

Retrospective economic research has also reached several of these same conclusions, namely that the early 1930s were paradoxically a period of both rising prices and recession, and that the NRA and similar anti-competition policies were responsible. More contemporary economic researchers have identified the price-fixing permissions of the NRA as a central explanation for rising prices during the 1930s even after the NRA experiment ended in June 1935, and as a key reason why the Depression dragged on for so many years. C. D. Romer (1999) concluded that the wage increases and

[63] Quoted in Brinkley (1995, 43).

[64] See Schlesinger (1958, 152–176) and Schlesinger (1960, 263–290).

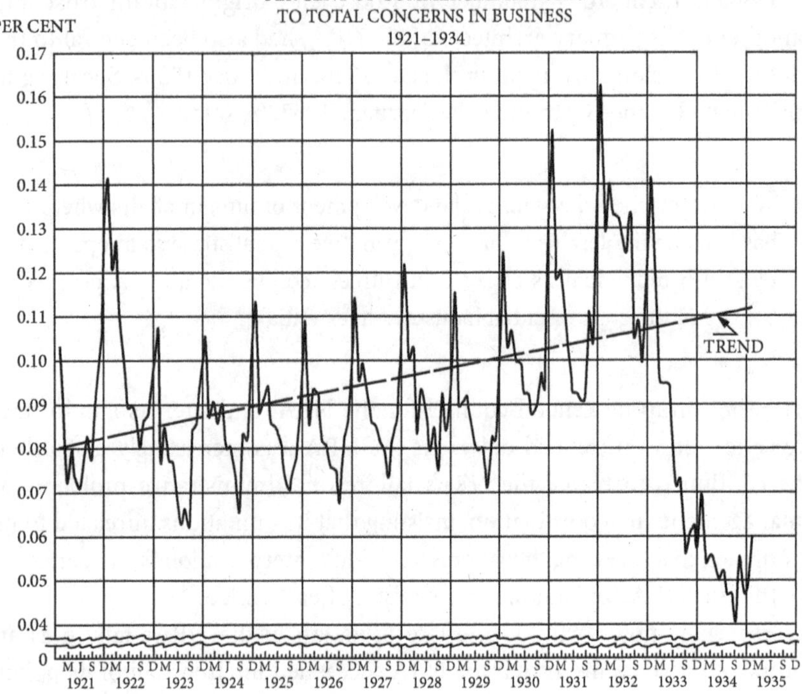

Figure 3.3 Percent of Business Failures to Total Business Concerns, 1921–1934[65]

collusive pricing arrangements of the NRA created the paradoxical recession with inflation, and Cole and Ohanian (2004) show how, by restricting output, the early anti-competition arrangements of the NRA likely led the Depression to persist longer than it otherwise would have.

Seeds of Trust-Busting in the Department of Justice

In 1938, however, policy began to change. Following a double-dip recession in 1937–1938, which was nearly as severe as 1929 and far more rapid, the Roosevelt administration began publicly blaming monopoly for the recession, contending that artificially high "administered prices" of large corporations were the primary drag on recovery. Attorney General Homer

[65] "Per Cent of Commercial Failures to Total Business Concerns in Business 1921-1934," Material Sent to Finance Committee Hearing on Senate Resolution 79, Box 64, RG9, NARA; Research and Planning Division, "Report on the Operation of the National Industrial Recovery Act," February 1935, Material Sent to Finance Committee Hearing on Senate Resolution 79, Box 64, RG9, NARA, page 24.

Cummings and Robert Jackson, the recently installed assistant attorney general of antitrust,[66] began a series of speeches railing against big business, blaming it for the double-dip recession and turning its back on the New Deal, and urging the reform and strengthening of antitrust policies. They followed this by filing a series of high-profile antitrust cases. The administration initially faced harsh criticism even among its supporters for these speeches, and even *within* the administration they were initially not popular. The origins of this change in policy are found earlier in 1937, and they directly connect to the lessons learned in the NRA.

Robert Jackson became the assistant attorney general of the Antitrust Division in early 1937. He was among the most influential advisers in pushing for the turn toward vigorous antitrust enforcement in April 1938 (Freyer 2006, 22), and he later became a Supreme Court justice and ruled on many of the pro-competition judicial decisions after World War II. However, his beliefs about competition and market power were rather different only a few years earlier. In remarks in rural Bemus Point, New York, in 1932, Jackson argued:

> Competition is essentially waste, it demands excess facilities and requires overproduction. Competition in labor is when two men are wanting a job that only one can have. Competition for labor is two jobs and only one man to fill them. Competition requires several concerns to bid on a construction contract that only one can get. Competition leads to overbuilding production facilities in good times, it sends out high pressure salesmen to sell you what you don't need, and invents an artificial obsolescence to make you discard it before its life is up. Competition forces installment sales, seduces people into extravagances and debt, accepts bad credit risks, builds up a surplus and then crashes."[67]

This was *before* Roosevelt was elected and *before* the NIRA was passed. Bemus Point had a total population of 280 as of the 1930 census. The political pressure to voice anticompetition views would presumably be weak at most. See also another speech the following year one town over, where Jackson refers to competition as "the god of the old economic order."[68]

[66] For readers not familiar with the American federal bureaucracy, the attorney general is the top law-enforcement official in government and head of the Department of Justice, and assistant attorneys general are the top officials for more specific enforcement areas, such as antitrust.

[67] Robert Jackson, "An Economic Plan for America", 1932, Jackson Papers, Box 32.

[68] Robert Jackson, Speech Delivered under the Auspices of the N.R.A. Committee of Jamestown, NY, 1933, Robert Jackson Papers, Box 32, LC, page 1.

This is followed by statements that "competition is dying by its own ruthless hand."[69] His beliefs on this matter appear to have persisted through the early 1930s.

Government Contracts and Identical Bids

Jackson's beliefs assuredly changed for a combination of reasons, but one of them was likely his experience with "identical bids," one of the most blatant and common examples of anticompetitive collusion in the 1930s. When the federal government solicited bids for materials or services from private contractors, at the time it was common to receive multiple bids that were identical—by cost, quality, quantity, delivery schedule, etc.—down to the cent. To give some particularly striking examples: fifty-nine independent government bids for steel pipe all came back at exactly $16,001.83; forty bids for cement all came back at $17,148.60.[70] Similarly, a series of Public Works Administration (PWA) contracts for steam power plant equipment received identical bids across six projects spanning multiple states, with identical performance and efficiency standards.[71] Regardless of the business arrangement used to reach such identical prices or its legality at the time, price competition was absent.

Determining whether such bids were legal fell to the Antitrust Division, which for several years had not been enforcing antitrust so much as enforcing NRA codes and defending the administrative planning of the early New Deal. The previous assistant attorney general for antitrust prior to Jackson, John Dickinson, had previously publicly defended such arrangements in December 1936, contending that there was nothing about "price uniformities" or "rigid prices" that implied illegal behavior, because "usually these practices may equally well result from natural and spontaneous growth in the course of the adaptation of the industry to its competitive conditions."[72] Nonpublic documents went to even greater lengths to justify

[69] Robert Jackson, "An Economic Plan for America", 1932, Jackson Papers, Box 32, page 14. The remarks were almost entirely a tirade against competition along with praise for Soviet-inspired economic planning.

[70] Homer Cummings, "The Unsolved Problem of Monopoly," November 29, 1937, Box 4, OF 10, FDR Library, page 3.

[71] Ickes to Roosevelt, February 14, 1936, OF 100, Box 1, FDR.

[72] John Dickinson Speech to Council for Industrial Progress, December 10, 1936, reproduced in Congressional Record, February 5, 1937, Robert Jackson Papers, Box 78, LC.

the practices, despite access to far stronger contrary evidence. One DOJ report from November 1936 discussed identical government bids for steel, even with knowledge of explicit private agreements between steel producers to maintain NRA price controls "whereby stability of price structure could be reestablished" and with knowledge that industry representatives were specifically looking for a loophole "which would not be violative of the antitrust laws."[73] However, the DOJ concluded that the wording of the agreement "taken alone, does not support the theory that it amounted to an agreement to adhere to *all* of the provisions of the [NRA steel] Code, including the price provisions."[74] The report concluded that since the only complaining party was "government officers to whom identical bids have been submitted," the practice was acceptable.[75]

Donald Richberg, another one of the NRA's committed architects, was also actively consulting the DOJ regarding identical bids. He agreed that there was nothing anticompetitive about them, as "it is unlikely that identical bids for standard products will be the result of a private agreement upon the prices quoted . . . and particularly because the price quoted will not be a special price but the quotation of a previously established price."[76] In essence, the identical bids in question were not price-fixing because they had already fixed the price according to shared price lists and shared cost accounting.

When Jackson arrived in the DOJ Antitrust Division at the beginning of 1937, the Division had more or less abandoned enforcement against identical bids, believing them to be technically legal absent proof of explicit collusion, and pushing it off as a problem for future legislation.[77] That, however, did not stop requests for advice from the Division. In a notable example, the Treasury asked whether the director of procurement was obligated to reject identical bids on government contracts for tires. Identical bids were so ubiquitous that Jackson and the Treasury faced the problem of repeat identical bids, where the Treasury rejected identical bids and solicited the contract again, only to get "a new set of identical bids . . . by the same

[73] Yost Memo to Dickinson, "Steel Investigation and Collusive Bidding on Steel Sheet Piling," November 23, 1936, Robert Jackson Papers, Box 78, LC, page 3.

[74] Ibid., Emphasis added.

[75] Ibid., pages 4–5.

[76] Donald Richberg, Confidential Memorandum for the Attorney General, "Steel Prices and Identical Bids," December 23, 1936, Robert Jackson Papers, Box 78, LC, page 2.

[77] Cummings to Roosevelt, April 26, 1937, Robert Jackson Papers, Box 78, LC.

bidders."[78] Jackson, rather than worrying about legal enforcement—because litigation would "probably be ended in two administrations from now"[79]—found a far simpler solution. The Treasury individually reached out to one of the companies, Sears Roebuck, and offered them the contract if they submitted a lower bid, which they did.[80] Bids for tires were increasingly competitive from that point on.[81]

At the same time, Jackson inherited a nascent investigation into a potential—but now famous—antitrust case against Alcoa, which had become an aluminum monopoly by the 1930s. Attorney General Cummings suggested Jackson look into the patent side of the case, as to whether Alcoa was holding onto patents for new technologies but not using them, both blocking technological advances but also preventing any potential competitors from using them.[82] While this suggestion was narrow, the DOJ asked the State Department to investigate the world aluminum cartel, opening an investigation spanning ten countries.[83] The resulting discoveries, however, revealed not just Alcoa's participation in the international aluminum cartel, but that Alcoa and other firms like it were able to maintain their domestic monopolies through a web of international, exclusive patent licensing agreements (patent pools) (Freyer 2006, 15–16).

As this was happening, the conclusions of the earlier research from the NRA came to Jackson through close contact with Leon Henderson, who had moved on to the PWA after the NRA shut down. Henderson had made a name for himself higher up in the Roosevelt administration, in particular because he wrote a memo to Roosevelt titled "Boom and Bust" in March 1937, which predicted that a second recession would come that year as a result of monopolistic pricing practices if stronger anti-monopoly policies were not implemented.[84] By summer his prediction appeared to be confirmed with the 1937 double-dip recession.[85] On July 20, 1937, Jackson

[78] Jackson to Assistant Solicitor General, June 1, 1937, Robert Jackson Papers, Box 78, LC, page 2.

[79] Jackson Memorandum for Assistant Solicitor General Bell, August 4, 1937, Robert Jackson Papers, Box 78, LC, page 2.

[80] Treasury Department Press Release, October 1, 1937, Jackson Papers, Box 78, LC.

[81] Cox to Oliphant, "Special Study of Automobile Tire Tie Bids in Government Purchasing," September 3, 1938, Cox Papers, Box 42, FDR.

[82] Cummings to Jackson, June 15, 1937, Robert Jackson Papers, Box 77, LC.

[83] Freyer (2006, 16); Cummings to Hull, August 17, 1937, Jackson Papers, Box 77, LC.

[84] Henderson to Roosevelt, "Boom and Bust," March 29, 1937, PSF, Subject File Series 5, Box 140, FDR.

[85] The direct cause of this retrospectively was almost assuredly the budget-cutting undertaken that year, but that was less well-understood at the time, and Henderson garnered attention nonetheless.

wrote for advice to Henderson with "a very rough sketch of a memo designed to encourage action against monopoly." This was meant as an outline of a broader program, but was very vague on details beyond a list of general topics.[86] In response, throughout the fall of 1937, Henderson continuously directed Jackson to NRA reports and data[87] and put him in direct contact with former researchers from the NRA's Research and Planning Division who had since moved to other government agencies.[88]

Railing on Big Business

At this point, only after seeing the common anticompetitive practices of the time, the sprawling international monopoly of Alcoa, and the research from the NRA tying it all together, Jackson started his famous round of speeches against big business in the fall of 1937. Jackson's rhetoric in these speeches focused almost exclusively on monopoly power. Rather than simply appealing to anti-business or anti-bigness sentiment, his arguments followed Henderson's and the NRA's version of administered prices theory,[89] based on facts and statistics from the Research and Planning Division. He detailed the same relationship between employment and price rigidity: "generally the more rigid and inflexible the price of a product during the depression the more calamitous was the decline in its labor's pay roll."[90] The overall conclusion was that reached by NRA researchers:

> The correspondence between rigid prices and low pay rolls is so general as to surpass the probabilities of coincidence. The kind of "industrial stability" which means the ability to avoid price concessions, does not promote, even if it does not injure, stability of employment or wage levels.[91]

[86] Jackson to Henderson, July 20, 1937, Jackson Papers, Box 77, LC.

[87] Henderson to Jackson, September 28, 1937, Jackson Papers, Box 77, LC.

[88] Henderson to Jackson, August 26, 1937, Jackson Papers, Box 34, LC.

[89] Robert Jackson, "Should the Antitrust Laws Be Revised?" September 17, 1937, Jackson Papers, Box 34, LC, page 4.

[90] Ibid., page 8. Jackson also cites an obscure report from the Canadian Royal Commission on Price Spreads that Henderson had sent around the NRA several years earlier. Ibid., page 11. For the original report, see "Report of Royal Commission on Price Spreads, Chapter II: The Economic Background," 1935, James Hughes Office Files, Box 2, RG9, NARA.

[91] Robert Jackson, "Should the Antitrust Laws Be Revised?" September 17, 1937, Jackson Papers, Box 34, LC, page 9.

He argued on the economic results of competition, noting that he has "no interest in 'trust-busting' for the sheer joy of 'trust-busting,'" and he emphasized that past "spectacular legal battles" over monopoly usually did not "produce any discernible economic effect."[92] He argued that "there is a silent conflict in this country between two kinds of industry. On the one hand we have high price, low volume industries, largely in the monopoly or semi-monopoly class. On the other hand we have competitive industry, large and small."[93]

When viewed in comparison with Jackson's previous views, some of his statements appear contradictory or hypocritical. Yet Jackson openly admitted that experience had changed his mind:

> I don't mind saying that I have amended my opinions on the functions and relations of business and government several times in the 25 years since I was admitted to the bar. . . . We have had the biggest war, the biggest boom, the biggest bust, the biggest recovery from a bust, and the biggest changes in constitutional law in our history. In the course of that procession we have had the biggest program of government financial help to business, and the most idealistic and devoted effort of government to help business stabilize itself through business self-government, that a democratic nation has ever known.[94]

He repeated similar sentiments again to a closed-door meeting of Democratic legislators, intended by its organizers to ensure that Jackson would "not be reluctant to present his views."[95]

As a point of adverse evidence, however, some private correspondence of Jackson shows political motivations to retaliate against the perceived or actual enemies of the New Deal and the administration. For example, the most well-known and controversial statement from these speeches was that there had been a "capital strike" against the New Deal.[96] Jackson, writing to his later replacement in the Antitrust Division:

[92] Ibid., page 2.

[93] Robert Jackson, "Cooperation between Government and Business," January 6, 1936, Jackson Papers, Box 35, LC, page 5.

[94] Robert Jackson, "Little Americanism," January 28, 1938, Jackson Papers, Box 35, LC, page 4.

[95] Patman to Estes, October 29, 1937, Jackson Papers, LC, Box 34.

[96] Jackson address to American Political Sciences Association, "The Menace to Free Enterprise," December 29, 1937, Robert Jackson Papers, Box 79, LC.

> The fact is that whatever may have been the cause of some decline in employment the "big business" crowd and the conservative Democrats and Republicans formed a loose sort of coalition to destroy the work or this administration. They showed their hand pretty well. All or us in the administration held our fire during the special session and let them give a demonstration of just what they had in mind. It got, however, to where we had to defend and you know I believe the only respectable defense is an assault. I think the last week has changed the whole atmosphere in Washington. Instead of asking what they can do to the New Deal, "big business" is now asking what the New Deal is going to do to them.[97]

However, this is unlikely to be in reference to the antitrust push discussed above. The "special session" referenced above was in October 1937, after Jackson had begun the more policy oriented speeches about antitrust reform, and this correspondence was two days after the one speech in which he did make the "capital strike" accusation.[98] It seems more likely to be in reference to those comments. Moreover, to the degree that antitrust policy was wielded as a cudgel, it was wielded indiscriminately across a surprising range of areas and potential political opposition, in a way that would be difficult to understand if the primary intent were political weaponization.

Price Studies and the Federal Trade Commission

In parallel, other investigations and conversations in the FTC came to make similar arguments through the fall of 1937 and early 1938. Just as Jackson was introduced to the problem of identical bids in 1937, a steady price increase for many products and commodities, paradoxically at the same time as the Depression worsened again, resulted in a chain of requests for investigation into many industries, pushing more public and government attention to the potential monopoly problem. Even as early as 1935, the FTC had been receiving around 500 complaints a month regarding high prices or price-fixing and had been progressively handling a several-fold increase in the number of cases during the NRA's existence.[99] Former FTC commissioner

[97] Jackson to Arnold, December 31, 1937, Box 77, Robert Jackson Papers, LC.

[98] Jackson address to American Political Sciences Association, "The Menace to Free Enterprise," December 29, 1937

[99] Ewin Davis to Roosevelt, December 31, 1935, OF100, Box 1, FDR.

Huston Thompson made multiple requests for broad, overarching investigations into the problem, seconded by the Treasury and the Department of Agriculture.[100] Thompson was suggesting such investigation to Roosevelt for years, but had been ignored until 1937, when other evidence and newer advisors began to align with his proposals.[101]

These complaints latched on to the passage of the Miller-Tydings Amendment to the Clayton Act as an impetus for action. Miller-Tydings was passed in August 1937 over the loud objections of the Roosevelt administration. The law permitted state fair trade laws to legalize "resale price maintenance," wherein a manufacturer could set the final price at which retailers were allowed to sell their products, eliminating price competition at the retail level. The bill itself passed that year in a contentious lobbying battle. Although Roosevelt made clear that he did not want the bill to pass, interest-group pressure made a decisive difference. With the exception of an early DOJ legal opinion that considered the bill "commendable" and stated "there is certainly much that can be said for permitting producers of trademarked and branded goods to protect their good will," almost all the relevant federal agencies opposed the bill.[102]

Despite this, the president received a flurry of lobbying demands in April 1937—several hundred a day—mostly from smaller businesses and retailers.[103] These were small businesses that one would think fall into the "little fellow" of the New Deal, and that definitely were viewed favorably during the NRA a few years prior, as most NRA retail codes had resale price maintenance provisions. Most tellingly, despite the substantial lobby, and Representative Miller requesting meetings on their behalf through back channels, Roosevelt refused to even meet with them.[104] The White House instead asked the FTC to deal with them.[105] When Roosevelt caved and signed the bill when it was tacked onto a tax rider, he did so with vocal and public objections.

Despite the legislative loss, the administration continued investigations on related price increases, which were all merged into one centralized FTC

[100] Thompson to Roosevelt, September 7, 1937; Taylor to Roosevelt, November 3, 1937; Wallace to Roosevelt, November 20, 1937; all in Box 1, OF 100, FDR Library.
[101] Thompson to Roosevelt, November 27, 1933, OF 466, Box 6, FDR; McIntyre to Hamilton regarding letter from Huston Thompson, December 19, 1935, OF 238, Box 1, FDR.
[102] Weston Memorandum to Jackson, February 8, 1937, Jackson Papers, Box 79, LC.
[103] McIntyre to Roosevelt, April 18, 1937, OF277, Box 2, FDR.
[104] Dargavel to McIntyre, June 16, 1937, OF277, Box 2, FDR.
[105] Roosevelt to Ayres, June 22, 1937, OF277, Box 2, FDR.

investigation by the end of the year.[106] Several months later, the FTC published a 700-page report that found fault in most industries examined and parroted the pro-competition theory of administered prices.[107]

The New Competition

With newer advisors in Roosevelt's inner circle—including Henderson and Jackson, but also Felix Frankfurter, Thomas Corcoran, Benjamin Cohen, and Homer Cummings—Roosevelt delivered his monopoly message to Congress in April 1938. He made the case that many of the troubles of the American economy were to be found in issues of excess corporate concentration, the "administrative" control of prices, and the restrictions that this system creates on free enterprise. Defending his new anti-monopoly position, he argued, "It is a program whose basic thesis is not that the system of free private enterprise for profit has failed in this generation, but that it has not yet been tried."[108]

The intellectual climate had shifted, but the committed adherents of the NRA stood their ground. Right before Roosevelt was to give his monopoly message to Congress, Donald Richberg wrote to Roosevelt, essentially in a panic, worried that Roosevelt had come to agree with the new trust-busting advisers, still openly advocating for a return to the NRA:

> The philosophy of the N.R.A. was wholly consistent with the New Deal. The philosophy of the fanatic trust busters, their hostility to all large enterprise, their assumption that cooperation is always a cloak for monopolistic conspiracy—this philosophy is wholly inconsistent with the New Deal.[109]

Richberg's objections fell on deaf ears.

Robert Jackson was promoted to solicitor general, and he and Attorney General Homer Cummings chose Thurman Arnold as a replacement. Arnold became a zealot for antitrust, dramatically expanding enforcement and completely overhauling and professionalizing the antitrust division. Funding for antitrust enforcement was dramatically and continuously increased for years through continuous requests for additional funding

[106] Roosevelt to Ayres, November 16, 1937, OF100, Box 1, FDR.
[107] Ferguson to Roosevelt, April 29, 1938, OF100, Box 4, FDR.
[108] Franklin Delano Roosevelt, Monopoly Message to Congress, April 29, 1938.
[109] Richberg to Roosevelt, April 23, 1938, Jackson Papers, Box 79, LC.

from Arnold. Arnold led the most expansive and aggressive trust-busting campaign in history, lasting a full decade from 1938 to 1948. Dozens of cases were filed against entire industries at once, including scores of foreign firms, and Arnold frequently urged all firms to accept quick consent decrees in order to achieve immediate economic results, rather than pursue drawn-out litigation. During his five years in the position, Arnold brought almost half of the cases under the Sherman Act is its first fifty-three years, increasing the staff of the Antitrust Division by a factor of five.[110] Under Arnold's leadership, the professional staff of the Antitrust Division increased from eighteen in 1933 to around five-hundred in 1942, and the rate of new cases filed went from eleven in 1938 when he began to ninety-two in 1940 (Waller 2006, 87).

Existing accounts often frame Arnold's fervor for antitrust as a happy coincidence—something that was not known even to antitrust advocates ahead of time (Brinkley 1995; Hawley 1966)—but correspondence between Jackson, Arnold, and Attorney General Cummings shows this to be unlikely. Arnold had been consulting with the DOJ Antitrust Division for much of 1937.[111] Behind the scenes, Arnold also helped several of Homer Cummings's anti-monopoly speeches that fall.[112]

Beginning in 1938 and extending to 1941, the Temporary National Economic Committee (TNEC) was launched as a congressional inquiry into the monopoly problem. The idea for such a committee had been passed around administration circles for a couple of years, largely based on early suggestions from Leon Henderson in 1935 and 1936. Deemed to be uneventful and largely unsuccessful by some, the TNEC served to greatly further the sharing of information across the federal government. Similarly, the behavior of administration policymakers during these events provides evidence about their intentions and strategies in their larger anti-monopoly campaign.

Despite the long, drawn-out process, the TNEC did serve as an effective conduit for information related to antitrust enforcement and economic policy. The above-referenced 700-page monopoly report from the FTC was originally not to be shared with Congress, as it contained a significant amount of confidential business and trade information. However, the nature of the inquiry got the FTC report released to the committee, passing information on potential antitrust violations in dozens of industries to the DOJ,

[110] Edwards (1943) and Barber (1996, 121).

[111] See Jackson to Arnold, September 28, 1938, and Jackson to Arnold, December 31, 1937, both in Robert Jackson Papers, Box 77, LC. See also Waller (2006, 64).

[112] Cummings to Jackson (handwritten), October 20, 1937, Box 78, Robert Jackson Papers, LC.

as Attorney General Cummings was seated on the committee.[113] Likewise, the TNEC was seen by its architects—most especially Leon Henderson, the secretary organizing the committee—as a platform with which to persuade and prove the scale of the monopoly problem to the public. In a private memo to FDR regarding the committee's position, Henderson wrote, "I hope you stress . . . that anything short of a complete delineation of the extent and abuse of concentration will not be convincing. We need complete and recorded evidence for next year's final report." He pressed the issue both as evidence and persuasion on one hand, and on the other as an apolitical aim of legitimate economic policy: "I hope you can emphasize that this Committee[,] by factual surveys, can prevent business cooperation principle from being diverted to restoration of former banking and business controls."[114]

These same policymakers took steps to undermine the counter-lobby expected in response to the TNEC and its conclusions. Oscar Cox, a central advisor to Roosevelt, wrote to Jackson in mid-1938, asking him to research the history and tactics of the relevant policy lobbies, since the TNEC proposals "will be infected and probably ultimately killed by the food, drug, cosmetic, liquor and proprietary association lobby," which "will probably be the nucleus for a larger lobby which can make the whole study futile."[115] Note that these industries, for the most part, were not typical "big business" that the administration would presumably oppose or rally against for political gain. The goal was policies against monopoly and to promote competition, and these simply happened to be the interest groups in the way.

This pattern played out inside and outside of the TNEC, with little to no evidence that the anti-monopoly push was initiated or promoted by private interest groups (Hawley 1966). It almost goes without saying that most organized business groups were extremely opposed to these new policy steps. And to the degree that private interests were involved in *promoting* the new policy, they were recruited after policy actions had already been taken, with support for Arnold's campaign coming primarily from disorganized small business (Freyer 1992, 212–223). For example, as soon as DOJ policymakers began making trust-busting speeches in 1937, Robert Wood, the president of Sears Roebuck—the company that was lured to break the identical bid

[113] R.F. to President, May 11, 1938, OF277, Box 2, FDR; and Freer to Roosevelt, July 19, 1938, OF100, Box 4, FDR.

[114] Henderson Memo to Roosevelt, "Suggestions re conference with Senator O'Mahoney and Congressman Sumners on Temporary National Economic Committee," March 7, 1939, OF3322, Box 2, FDR.

[115] Cox to Jackson, July 28, 1938, Oscar Cox Papers, Box 41, FDR.

collusion—wrote in support.[116] Agricultural interests, in the form of the American Farm Bureau Federation, unsurprisingly and quickly got on board with Arnold's campaign and lobbied Congress in support, but again *after* the campaign started.[117] Even organized labor, a central New Deal coalition member, had little involvement. Arnold even controversially pursued cases against organized labor.[118]

The Foreign Cartel Threat

The new antitrust and anti-monopoly policies took on new dimensions in the lead up to World War II. The TNEC had stoked fears of a foreign threat in the form of cartels, and based around this issue, the committee's early attention turned to the otherwise uninspiring topic of patents (Wells 2002, 39–40). By late December 1939, right as World War II broke out in Europe, the patents investigation of the TNEC had found that a great deal of "control exerci[z]ed by foreign governments and business enterprises upon American Industries."[119] This was particularly true of German firms, who had entered in a range of patent licensing cartels with American companies. For example, to do this and hide the nature of the agreement, Siemens had an American firm take out patents on beryllium, refuse to license them to anyone else, and also not produce any itself. This essentially prevented the existence of a beryllium industry in the United States.[120] These problems appeared common in defense-related industries, and the TNEC found that multiple European countries had used the American patent system for similar legal devices.[121]

With this framing of foreign cartels, World War II did not stop Arnold's antitrust campaign. Cases were filed throughout the war despite loud opposition from defense contractors. Within weeks of the opening of World War II in Europe in September 1939, Arnold requested a large appropriation of over $900,000 for the Antitrust Division with the goal of cracking down on war profiteering.[122] With the war, a section of the Antitrust Division

[116] Wood to Roosevelt, June 1, 1937, OF327, Box 2, FDR.
[117] O'Neal to House Appropriations Committee, February 2, 1940, OF277, Box 3, FDR.
[118] Arnold Memorandum to the Attorney General, June 25, 1940, "Activity of Teamsters' Unions in Pittsburgh, Pa.," Jackson Papers, Box 85, LC.
[119] Borkin to Henderson, December 2, 1939, Henderson Papers, Box 24, FDR, page 1.
[120] Ibid., pages 1–2.
[121] Ibid., page 7.
[122] Arnold Memo to Attorney General, September 25, 1939, Jackson Papers, Box 83, LC.

refashioned itself as the "Department of Economic Warfare," using litigation to arguably remove German economic influence in other regions of the world. While this new target of international cartels helped justify their campaign as part of the war effort, it also gave them access to a plethora of information about the corporate relationships between major multinational firms in chemicals, oil, optical instruments, explosives, aluminum, and many other industries.

To summarize the general cartel problem, the interwar years had seen an unprecedented proliferation of international cartels in most industries, with agreements spanning almost every region of the world and commercial interests on both sides of the war. The permissive standards of patent law and the nonexistent reach of antitrust beyond borders[123] had allowed multinational firms, in the United States and abroad, to cooperatively partition product and regional markets entirely among themselves, and use the full force of national authorities to defend their rights to do so.[124] For example, if the best version of a product at the time were made using a mix of technologies covered by patents that only a few firms held, they could come to an agreement that they would license all their patents to each other (a patent pool) and agree on fixed prices for the product or to each only operate in mutually exclusive geographic regions (a territorial allocation agreement). Not only would they all have effective monopolies, but the state of patent law required the state to enforce that monopoly on potential competitors.[125] Revelation of these agreements sparked public outrage, as German and American military suppliers often had agreements that they restrict output—and which were obeyed right up to the start of hostilities—any of which could be seen as aiding the enemy.

As the DOJ made these sorts of discoveries, the public press, the administration, and DOJ officials published widely read exposés and books of the involvement of American firms in international cartels, and particularly

[123] For an example of each, the Webb-Pomerene Act of 1922 allowed American firms so set up cartels as long as the final market was abroad, and the 1926 *General Electric* case allowed patent holders to set the price of the final product for licensees (*United States v. General Elec. Co.*, 272 U.S. 476 1926).

[124] For the best accounts on the international campaign and the cartel practices involved, see Wells (2002, 43–136) and Freyer (2006, 24–59).

[125] For example, based on this exact arrangement, there was an interwar cartel agreement between Imperial Chemicals (UK), Alkasso (an American export association mostly controlled by DuPont), and Solvay et Cie (Belgium), to split the world market for alkali among themselves: Solvay got Europe, ICI got the British Empire and South America, and Alkasso got Central America, Canada, and East Asia. "Memorandum re: Alkali—Cartel Control of Markets," November 8, 1943, page 1, Box 1, Records of Roy A. Prewitt, RG 122, NARA.

their anticompetitive agreements with German firms in defense-related industries. Berkeley economist Robert Brady wrote *The Spirit and Structure of German Fascism*, arguing that the Third Reich was a "dictatorship of monopoly capitalism" (Brady 1937). Franz Neuman likewise argued in his book *Behemoth: The Structure and Practice of National Socialism* that Nazi aggression and imperialism was driven by concentrated capitalistic interests (Neumann 1942). In June 1941, *Click* magazine published an exposé of American defense orders for Plexiglas, which it argued were directly going to the coffers of German industry, and by extension the Third Reich.[126] Arnold's successor at the DOJ, Wendell Berge, published *Cartels: Challenge to a Free World* (Berge 1944), and Borkin and Welsh published *Germany's Master Plan: The Story of Industrial Offensive* (Borkin and Welsh 1943). Public speeches would detail the interdependence between American and German companies in magnesium, optical instruments, beryllium, and tungsten carbide, focusing on the patent agreements, territorial divisions, and price controls in the cartel agreements.[127]

Following the war, antitrust experts from the DOJ and FTC were instrumental in the occupation authorities of Germany and Japan. As the war was coming to a close and as the Antitrust Division was preparing for its postwar litigation spree, James Martin, the former head of the Antitrust Division's "Economic Warfare Unit" followed Allied armies into Europe with a team of cartel specialists, seizing records and assets of German firms (Haley 2001, 27). The Decartelization and Deconcentration Branch in the German occupation after the war was likewise staffed by transplants from the DOJ's Antitrust Division, ardent believers that a democratic and non-aggressive Germany required radical deconcentration of industry. Corwin Edwards had been moved with a similar group of antitrust experts to the occupation authority in Japan (Freyer 2006, 168–198), where he pushed to break up the complex structure and web of relationships between the Japanese zaibatsu, based on a shallow understanding of that country but in light of his own understandings of business collusion elsewhere.

At the center of this nexus of antitrust, international affairs, and trade policy was another policymaker, Corwin Edwards, who had followed a similar path as Henderson and Jackson, bouncing around in the 1930s and 1940s

[126] Click, 1941. This was misleading, as the United States had obtained the technology from Germany but cut off relations in 1940 following the outbreak of war (Wells 2002, 49–50).

[127] Norman Littel, "The German Invasion of American Business," January 25, 1941, OF10, Box 6, FDR.

between the NRA, the FTC, the DOJ, the State Department, the postwar occupation authority in Japan, and congressional committees after World War II. An expert on antitrust and cartels, most accounts consider him to be a doctrinaire antitrust zealot against cartels (Freyer 2006; Haley 2001; Wells 2002).

Yet as with others, Corwin Edwards's opinions had been initially more muted. Edwards was brought into the Consumer Division of the NRA from academia in 1933 (Hawley 1966, 76), and worked closely with Henderson and the Research and Planning Division. Even as the NRA was shutting down, he wrote to Gardner Means regarding the Guffey Coal Bill—a pending "little NRA"—that "with a vivid memory of the chaotic conditions which unchecked competition formerly produced in this industry. . . . Public regulation of the industry has, we hope, come to stay," though he admittedly argued that the bill should not be given the complete exemption from the antitrust laws that it was eventually granted.[128]

The planning for the postwar world economic order was influenced by Edward's and other trust-busters' views, and the Department of State's postwar trade plans took these issues seriously, in consultation with the DOJ. With free trade as an increasing priority for the planning of postwar economic policy, tariff-free borders would mean little for free trade if markets were still mostly governed by restrictive cartel agreements. International trade negotiations increasingly centered on the issue. In the late summer of 1944, the State Department created a special advisory Committee on Private Monopolies and Cartels to guide these trade negotiations, including Edwards. These same policymakers advised the negotiations for the International Trade Organization (ITO) treaty, which included specific provisions against cartels and other anticompetitive practices. During his time on the Cartel Committee, Edwards also chaired the Policy Planning Board at the DOJ, which was simultaneously seeking to expand the reach of American antitrust law abroad to combat foreign cartels and the agreements among multinational firms.

Even though the Senate never approved the ITO treaty, and therefore its eventual replacement in the form of the General Agreement on Tariffs and Trade (GATT) did not include specific antitrust provisions, and there were attempts to resolve the patent and cartel issue legislatively and through these trade negotiations, the antitrust campaign created strong legal precedents

[128] Edwards to Means, June 12, 1935, Means Papers, Box 1, FDR.

once court decisions came in. The cases brought by the DOJ leading into and during the war led to a wave of federal court decisions in the late 1940s and early 1950s that struck down a range of patent pools, cartel agreements, and joint venture arrangements as illegal, enshrining the fruits of this campaign into law.[129] American antitrust law had already been expanded greatly to govern the behavior of American firms overseas. These were almost across the board pro-competition changes. IP rights, and particularly patent license provisions, were significantly limited based on antitrust and competition concerns, and the extraterritorial reach of American antitrust law abroad was dramatically increased to cover the behavior of American firms internationally.

This was not, however, a matter of judicial luck. The Supreme Court that decided some of these cases included the antitrust enforcers who initiated similar cases before being promoted to the court, such as Robert Jackson and Tom Clark.[130] Furthermore, there is an indication that the economic and national security concerns motivating these cases were directly communicated, with pressure, to the judges making these decisions. As part of a patent study committee in Congress, in late December 1941 Secretary of the Interior Ickes suggested to Roosevelt that he "consult both [the Department of] Justice and some of your friends on the Supreme Court" to grant the DOJ "the right to intervene in patent litigation between private parties," expanding the DOJ's enforcement powers. This argument was made specifically citing the "interrelationship between American patents and those of foreign countries" based on the fact that Germany had "penetrated very far and very successfully into our American economy" using such tool.[131] This is unlikely the only time that administration officials sought to directly influence the Court.

This was followed by legislative action with the 1950 Celler-Kefauver Act, which closed a loophole in Section 7 of the Clayton Act that had allowed firms to avoid merger controls by buying the assets of a competitor rather than the corporate entity. The law also expanded the law to cover "vertical" mergers, where the merging companies that do not directly compete with

[129] The most important of these cases were *United States v. Alcoa*, 148 F.2d 416 (2d Cir. 1945), *United States v. National Lead Co.*, 332 U.S. 319 (1947), *United States v. General Electric Co.*, 80 F. Supp. 989 (S.D.N.Y. 1948), *United States v. General Electric Co.*, 82 F. Supp. 753 (D.N.J. 1949), *United States v. Minnesota Mining & Mfg. Co.*, 92 F. Supp. 947 (D. Mass. 1950), and *Timken Roller Bearing Co. v. United States*, 341 U.S. 593 (1951).

[130] Clark was the head of the Antitrust Division for a short period after Arnold resigned in 1942.

[131] Ickes to Roosevelt, December 29, 1941, OF3k, Box 8, FDR.

one another. This law, like other policy changes before it, was based on the experiences of policy elites from the cartel campaign, the early New Deal, and in this case foreign occupations of Japan and Germany.

Outside of merger control, many were already pushing "to repeal some or all of the acts granting exceptions to the antitrust laws such as the Miller-Tydings price maintenance law and the Reed-Bulwinkle law exempting the railroads from the antitrust laws."[132] In January 1950, President Truman asked the secretary of commerce to head an interdepartmental committee tasked with developing "a program to promote the spirit and practice of business competition; to foster the growth of new and independent enterprise; to encourage voluntary compliance with the laws against monopoly, unfair competition, and restraints of trade; and to increase the effectiveness of these laws as bulwarks of free competitive enterprise." Experts who were consulted about the matter were asked questions solely aimed at increasing competition and suggested the removal of the antitrust exemptions enacted as the "little NRAs" in the 1930s.[133]

Conclusion

This chapter provided an account and analysis of how key groups of New Deal policymakers learned—via economic analysis, interaction with private economic and political interests, and daily experience—about the scale and nature of the monopoly problem. Early research about administered prices and the diminishing returns to market power stemming from industrial self-government policies led policymakers in the NRA to reject the existing policy regime. They diffused this information across federal bureaucracies and used contingencies such as World War II to entrench new pro-competition policies into place. This established the competition policy regime that pushed for stronger antitrust, freer trade, and fewer regulatory restrictions for the following thirty years.

Non-committed policymakers changed their minds, even as committed policymakers refused to do so, even with the same information. Henderson, the intellectual architect of the anti-monopoly push, was in favor of many

[132] Statement of Congressman Emanuel Celler, July 29, 1949, Box 105, Berle Papers, page 2.

[133] Sawyer to Berle, January 21, 1950, Box 105, Berle Papers, FDR. These antitrust exemptions were not all removed until the deregulation movement in the 1970s, but they were criticized by antitrust advocates for decades.

of the NRA's anti-competition policy devices before he dealt with them up close in the NRA, and within a year he was advocating for strong antitrust policies. Robert Jackson, considered one of the ultimate trust-busters in American history, had favored industrial self-government at the beginning of the 1930s. While Corwin Edwards never expressed views as opposed to competition as either of those two, his views clearly became stronger as the decade wore on. Likewise, established policymakers—who had implemented or staked their reputation on anti-competition policies—refused to reconsider their views, even with access to the same information.

Out of all of this, it is hard to view the outcome of this change as the antitrust movement having failed, as some have argued. After 1938, economic policy changes favored competition, and many of the laws and regulations around war mobilization included antitrust provisions. The price-and-output orientated antitrust policies favored by these newer policymakers may have been consistent with the new Keynesian demand management, but that does not mean that antitrust policies were unimportant and subsumed into this new macroeconomic paradigm, as Brinkley (1995) argues.

Nor were these changes contingent coalitional or bureaucratic conflicts. Even with consistent back-and-forth lobbying fights among interest groups, policy change showed a consistent and steady shift away from market power and toward competition. The most notable coalitional realignment in the 1930s—when organized business increasingly turned against the New Deal—did occur at around the same time in 1937 and 1938, but the personal and professional correspondence presented here shows that policy preferences changed prior to the most notable of those conflicts and that the Roosevelt administration pursued pro-competition policies even against many of its own core constituencies.

4
Ententes and National Champions in Postwar France

> Our vulnerability was all the greater because of a set of public and professional rules that limited internal and international competition.
>
> —Planning Commissioner Pierre Massé in 1960[1]

> This undoubtedly shows that it is necessary to rehabilitate cartels and monopolies.
>
> —Economist François Perroux in 1966[2]

Driven by fears of international cartels and a parallel commitment to free trade, the Allied triumph in World War II gave the American government leverage to push other countries to adopt antitrust policies: Japan in 1947, the United Kingdom in 1948 and 1956, France in 1953, and Germany in 1957. In the case of France, the 1953 anti-cartel policy was part of a wave of pro-competition policies that continued until being displaced in the 1960s by a market power–focused industrial policy of "national champions," under which the state would coordinate and suppress competition to create a small number of international-scale corporations.[3] The government implemented tax, regulatory, and financial incentives to encourage mergers and international expansion in order to create firms of sufficient size to command market power and capture market share in international markets.

[1] Pierre Massé, "Note sur les Obstacles à l'Expansion Économique," March 24, 1960, 81AJ/260, AN, page 5.

[2] Procès-Verbal, Conseil Économique et Social – Section de la Production Industrielle et de l'Énergie, July 7, 1966, 19920430/104, AN, page 5.

[3] Many European countries in this period had firms referred to as national champions, as well as policies to support them. In many cases, these were in nationalized industries. For the purpose of this chapter, I refer to the national champions policy as specifically anti-competition policies of concentration and protection, in reference to private sector firms only.

Monopoly Politics. Erik Peinert, Oxford University Press. © Oxford University Press (2025).
DOI: 10.1093/oso/9780197789506.003.0004

This chapter shows that this policy shift was motivated by a central problem: the perceived costs of competitive pressures following decades of procompetition policies, above all France's entry into the European Economic Community (EEC). Though ignored by many French economic managers committed to the results of procompetition policies, the ensuing foreign and internal competition led to a collapse in French corporate profits and investment. National champion industrial policies were not the only attempted solution to this problem, but internal debates revealed the nature of the problem and the lack of other realistic options. As they were adopted, these policies were explicitly discussed in terms of creating monopolies, permitting cartelization, and preventing competitive mechanisms from interfering with the financial ability to maintain profits.

This partly contrasts with the frequent characterization of France to as the "statist" or "dirigiste" model of national political economy (Dobbin 1994; Hall and Soskice 2001; Loriaux 1991; Schmidt 2002; Schonfield 1965; Vail 2017; Zysman 1983). While this typology emphasizes the central role of the state in managing the economy, highlighting a state-run financial sector directing investment based on state economic plans (Hall 1986; Loriaux 1991; Zysman 1983), this has occasionally be extended to characterize postwar French economic policy as broadly anti-competition, with distrust of markets and market mechanisms. Several scholars recognize the increasingly market-based economy over the latter half of the 20th century, but often attribute this to external factors such as the EEC or the General Agreement on Tariffs and Trade (GATT) (Adams 1989; Schmidt 1996).

A second set of accounts implies or argues that the industrial and competition policies of this era were a single, coherent policy. France, along with other European countries at the time, came to adopt the American industrial model of mass production, with large firms with large economies of scale engaging in oligopolistic competition (Djelic 1998; Piore and Sabel 1984). Popular books such as Jean-Jacques Servan-Schreiber's 1967 *Le défi américain* (The American Challenge) highlighted that American companies out-classed their European competitors in technological sophistication, management, scale, etc. (Servan-Schreiber 1967). In adopting this model, France imported assumptions about economies of scale and mass production technologies being more efficient (Djelic 1998, 150). In recreating this model, so the argument goes, both competition policies and corporate consolidation were functionally necessary. In this vein, Didry and Marty (2016) contend that the anti-cartel policies from the immediate postwar years were a tool in a more comprehensive plan for industrial policy, in that breaking up cartels among the suppliers for nationalized firms would lower the input prices for nationalized firms and other national champions, allowing their market power to be developed a decade later.

This chapter shows how heavy-handed state intervention can enhance competition as well as restrain it. The new archival evidence collected for this book shows that policy consistently favored competition from 1945 through the 1960s. However, a decline in profits and private corporate investment was the primary driver of the anti-competition aspects of the national champions policy. Industrial policies shifted from favoring maximal output and lower prices in the 1940s and 1950s to prioritizing corporate high profits and investment in the face of foreign multinationals. The policy aim was motivated more by a desire to restore profits and investment than it was by any technological requirements, interest-group conflict, or functionalist institutional design of a directed economy. The technical needs of newer technologies were openly discussed but were not the motivation for corporate consolidation or integration. Interest-group conflict occurred broadly within the bounds of the policy framework defined by the national champions policy, rather than supporting or opposing the policy change itself.

The chapter begins by detailing the institutional background of the postwar French state, showing that pro-competition policies were aggressively pursued through the early 1960s. It then analyzes an acceleration of procompetition policies in the early 1960s, showing that warning signs about the downsides to these policies for private profits and investment were ignored by committed policymakers. Policy opinions changed through learning in the early 1960s, centered around "*autofinancement*" and the reinvestment of lagging corporate profits. New understandings about market power and international competitiveness were adopted and transposed into existing policies and institutions, with the Fifth Plan (1966–1970) advancing a new wave of industrial policies to consolidate most industries. Throughout the case, specific committed and uncommitted policymakers are highlighted to show that patterns of turnover and learning were still central to these changes.

Institutional and Policy Background

An Introduction to French Economic Institutions

Prior to the 20th century, economic thought in France was almost universally liberal in the *laissez-faire* sense. The state was to stay out of private business, taxation was for revenue and not for regulatory purposes, and deficits were considered unsound public finance (Kuisel 1981, 1–30). However, with respect to competition, this liberalism belied a *de facto* preference in favor of protectionism, combined with accommodations for anticompetitive practices like cartels and trade associations (Kuisel 1981, 15–26). During the interwar years, as in most of Europe at the time and inspired by the German example, cartels were favorable seen as an effective way to stabilize industries in the face of fluctuating exchange rates and unpredictable business cycles (Barjot 2013, 2014), despite some unsuccessful pushes for anti-cartel laws by the Popular Front in the 1930s (Chatriot 2008). The wartime occupation Vichy regime further entrenched anti-competition policies, creating a series of *Comités d'organisation* (Organization Committees) with broad powers to set production schedules, decide quotas, and regulate prices and competition. While the occupation was primarily concerned with extracting resources, these organizations were nonetheless often headed by French business leaders with experience in interwar industry associations and cartels (Nord 2010, 92).

France's quick defeat in World War II upset political and economic understandings of France's place in the world. French elites came to recognize that they were now outscaled in a world of industrial giants, and resistance leaders latched onto various understandings about France's backwardness premised around business conservatism and the lack of dynamic competition.[4] By the time of liberation, leaders came to blame the decline and backwardness of the country on protectionism and "Malthusianism" (Duchêne 1994, 126–131). In the rhetoric of the time, Malthusianism was understood as rigid, defensive, and extremely risk-averse business behavior (Adams 1989, 2) or as

[4] For example, the March 1944 action program of the *Conseil National de la Résistance*, a federation of wartime resistance groups, explained future outlines of economic planning, but highlighting primarily that the trusts, financial combinations, rents, and *situations acquises* (broadly meaning vested interests) of the interwar years would no longer be the dominant force in the economy and would not be the primary beneficiaries of its expansion (Nord 2010, 101).

> a conviction that the market was fixed and one trader's gain meant another's loss, a preference for high profit and low turnover, and a willingness to mitigate competition sufficiently to keep weaker firms afloat. (Williams 1964, 3)

Socialists like André Philip, Pierre Mendès France, George Boris, and Robert Marjolin pushed ideas about freeing the economy from restrictive trusts, monopolies, and moneyed control over industry.[5]

For these and related reasons, right after the war France created a spate of new institutions, akin in scale to the explosion of bureaucracies in the American New Deal (Nord 2010). A number of industries—finance, insurance, coal, electricity, and railroads—were nationalized.[6] Beginning with the First Plan in 1948, the Planning Commission (*Commissariat Général du Plan*), directed investment funds, economic priorities, and industrial and social policies through non-coercive policy tools, based on five-year plans for the social and economic development of France. In 1946, the bureaucracy responsible for reporting economic statistics, INSEE (*Institut national de la statistique et des études économique*), was created. State control of finance, combined with an underdeveloped equity market, meant that credit was available mostly to the types of firms, or even specific firms, that the state favored, and macroeconomic policy at the *Bank of France* was largely operated in order to allocate credit to specific industries according to the dictates of the plan (Monnet 2018). Price controls from the Ministry of Finance covered a wide range of industrial and consumer products (Dumez and Jeunemaitre 1989; Franck 1958). It is this grouping of institutions that often lead to France being exoticized as a fundamentally different model of "statist" political economy (Dobbin 1994; Hall and Soskice 2001; Loriaux 1991; Schmidt 1996; Schonfield 1965; Verdier 2002; Zysman 1983), a view that can give the impression that policy and economic outcomes were functionally intended (Hayward 1986, 2), overlooking more mundane ways in which these institutions operated less-than-smoothly or similarly to those in other countries.[7]

[5] See Kuisel (1981, 157–159 and 167–179) and Nord (2010, 101–102).

[6] This is along with the car manufacturer Renault, which as an exceptional case was managed and operated by the state but as if private.

[7] For example, in correspondence with Planning Commissioner Massé in 1962, American economist Kenneth Arrow wrote that he was "at our own equivalent of the Commissariat au Plan," at a time when he was serving on the American Council of Economic Advisors. Kenneth Arrow to Pierre Massé, April 2, 1962, 19930276/5, AN.

Pro-Competition Policy Background

However, these institutions did not themselves determine the policy priorities that these institutions would pursue.[8] Countering both anti-market representations of France and the argument that the national champions policy represented continuity as an extension of earlier policies, France pursued as pro-competition policy regime during the immediate postwar period through the 1960s, meant to modernize business practices, eliminate old vested interests, and increase productivity.

Even so, France did not have a well-defined "competition" or "antitrust" policy prior to 1986 (Gerber 1998, 193). Prohibitions on restrictive economic practices like price-fixing or quotas go back to the Napoleonic codes, but for most of the postwar decades, there was only a loosely related set of norms, regulatory rules, and policy priorities around price controls, trade, public procurement, and industrial policy, spread across different bureaucracies such as the Ministry of Finance, the Ministry of Industry, and the Planning Commission. Despite their distinct locations within the French administration, connections across and within these did amount to a coherent understanding of both policy priorities and the economic problems that motivated them.

These priorities were clear as early as the First Plan in 1948. A Productivity Commission set up by Jean Monnet to advise the plan conducted analyses of the United States' economic advantages as the result of a continent-wide, price-competitive market with little to no internal barriers to the movement of goods or economic factors.[9] By contrast, cartels, at this point referred to as *ententes*,[10] were considered dangerous supports for the "Malthusianism"

[8] Other accounts tend to see a more automatic link between these institutions and policy context. For example, Loriaux (1991) refers to the entire postwar period as that of an "overdraft economy," with French economic planners unable to restrain their intention to intervene, plan, and cartelize. Schmidt characterizes France's postwar policies as beginning from a strongly dirigiste position and moving progressively but largely continuously toward more market-oriented policy, most of all because of France's exogenous entry into the European common market (Schmidt 1996, 73–74).

[9] M. Allais, "Pouvons-nous atteindre les hauts niveaux de vie américains?" Undated document, 81AJ/176, AN; Commissariat Générale du Plan - Group de Travail de la Productivité, Programme français pour l'accroissement de la procuctivité, Chapitre II: "Les causes de la faible produtivité française," undated document, 81AJ/176, AN. Both of these documents are likely from 1948, as they reference events or data from 1947 and 1948 and are with other documents from those years.

[10] The term *entente* is used because it was understood to include a broader array of possible business agreements. Cartel has a relatively specific economic meaning of agreements to fix prices or restrict output.

of French industry.[11] The Productivity Commission's views highlighted the role of domestic competition in lowering prices, increasing productivity, and eliminating the domestic rents that had been responsible for business conservatism.[12]

Whereas the strict price controls from World War II remained in place from 1945 to 1948 to prevent an explosion of inflation when pent-up consumer demand was released from wartime restrictions, most of these controls were lifted in 1948 by the Price Directorate (*Direction des Prix*) within the Ministry of Finance. Minutes of the National Price Committee reveal these choices to be justified in terms of the benefits of competition on lowering price and benefiting consumers.[13]

The Price Committee was, however, also aware that prices might end up determined by ententes once liberalized.[14] To their understanding, agreements left over from the Vichy period and the interwar years reasserted themselves as soon as state quotas and narrow price controls were eliminated. From 1948 through 1953, the Price Committee frequently discussed the need to eliminate ententes and restore a competitive system to the French economy, but they struggled to do so within the constraints of remaining price controls and existing business organizations. To mitigate this, price ceilings were used to prevent price-gouging by concentrated interests or ententes (Franck 1958, 25–26), and certain price controls were maintained as a counter to the anticompetitive behavior of French firms and ententes.[15]

This was in conjunction with a more direct solution, whereby the nationalized industries (electricity, railroads, coal, etc.) would use their position as the sole purchaser in public procurement markets (referred to as *marchés publics* or public markets) to force firms in cartelized industries to compete, creating a central commission to oversee these policies, the *Commission Centrale des Marchés*.[16] Not only had a series of central industries been nationalized—railroads (*Société Nationale des Chemins de Fer* or SNCF), electricity (*Électricité de France* or EDF), coal (*Charbonnages de France* or

[11] Ministère des Finances et des Affaires Économique - Direction des Programmes Économiques, "Esquisse d'une politique de productivité," November 18, 1949, 81AJ/178, AN, page 2; "Esquisse d'une politique de productivité," undated document, 81AJ/179, AN, page 9.

[12] Comité National de la Productivité, "Memorandum sur la politique française de productivité et l'assistance technique," July 1951, 81AJ/179, AN, page 17.

[13] See, for example, Procès-Verbal - Comité National des Prix, June 22, 1948, B-0055902, CAEF, page 2.

[14] Procès-Verbal - Comité National des Prix, April 23, 1948, B-0055902, CAEF.

[15] Procès-Verbal - Comité National des Prix, February 17, 1950, B-0055904, CAEF.

[16] See Didry and Marty (2016), Franck (1958, 34, 99–102), and Marty (1999).

CDF)—but the state accounted for most investment in the immediate postwar years and directed most investment to just these sectors (Quennoüelle-Corre 2000, 4–12). This put the newly nationalized firms in an even greater position of extreme power over private industry.

A formal anti-cartel policy, the *Commission Technique des Ententes* (hereafter CTE) was created in 1954 according to a decree from 1953, following several years of political pressure from politicians and the public. There was a strong public sentiment against restrictive ententes, and reporting to political leadership from the bureaucracy frequently pointed to noncompetitive and outdated market organization, as well as anticompetitive practices, as a core driver of higher French prices.[17] Even though many earlier attempts to pass an antitrust or entente policy were thwarted by an intransigent business lobby, in 1953 the legislature endowed Finance Minister Edgar Faure with total control to submit a decree on *ententes*, giving little space for lobbying opposition to thwart the decree.[18]

Along with restrictions on horizontal cartels, starting in the 1950s France was particularly harsh in prohibiting vertical restraints—restrictions by firms against others up or down the supply chain (Adams 1989, 216–226). Many rules from the 1953 decree were reimposed with more enforcement in the 1960 Fontanet Circular (*Circulaire Fontanet*), which banned vertical restraints of trade like refusal to sell or resale price maintenance. The circular has a well-known background story.[19] Édouard Leclerc, a wholesaler, began to sell products to general consumers at wholesale prices in 1949, against the exclusive contracts and resale price maintenance (*prix imposés*) imposed by his suppliers. After a decade of disputes, with suppliers often refusing to sell to him, Leclerc met with the Finance Ministry and the Planning Commission, who were both anxious to reduce inflation.[20] They saw distribution and wholesale reform, and the competitive practices it implied, as an effective means to reduce consumer prices and therefore pushed for the ban on those vertical restrictions.

These domestic policies were paired with the pro-competition content of most European treaties, which removed tariff barriers and imposed

[17] See, for example, the Nathan Commission Report: "Rapport Général de la Commission créée par arrête du 6 janvier 1954," March 20, 1954, 1A-0000390, CAEF and R. Nathan to Ministère des Finances, March 20, 1954, 1A-0000390, CAEF.

[18] See Chatriot (2008) and Gerber (1998, 186–190).

[19] For much greater context, see Billows (2016, 2017) and Jacques (2016).

[20] For example, see Commissariat Général du Plan d'Équipement et de la Productivité, Procès-Verbal: L'Expérience Leclerc, June 9, 1961, 19930275/34, AN.

competition rules. The entente problem was, in fact, among the primary economic motivations for the 1951 Treaty of Paris, which created the European Coal and Steel Community (ECSC).[21] The ECSC's final form was the most pro-competition of the options considered during negotiations for the Treaty of Paris (Kipping 2002, 92–119). Furthermore, the competition sections of the treaty were demanded primarily by the French negotiators, not the Germans or by American influence (Montalban, Ramirez-Perez, and Smith 2011; Kipping 2002), despite being based on American antitrust law and partially written by an American antitrust expert (Freyer 2006, 272–273). Despite its later failures, the French policymakers who initially designed and were put in charge of the ECSC, namely Jean Monnet and Pierre Uri, considered control of cartels and trust-busting as among the ECSC's highest goals (Duchêne 1994, 246–249), to the dismay and anger of European partners.

The 1957 Treaty of Rome, which created the EEC, also contained strong competition articles, many of which, again, were favored by the French delegation (Warlouzet 2011, 274–275). Many industry groups had opposed the treaty in its entirety, arguing that French prices were too high relative to those abroad to withstand foreign competition.[22] Research from the Ministry of Finance showed these claims to be greatly exaggerated, as, in fact, France was competitive in a range of industries.[23]

Nonetheless, these EEC competition rules only went into effect with Regulation 17/62 in 1962, which ended up being rather weak. It permitted some cartel agreements and required that all agreements be submitted to the competition authority, DGIV, for approval. The French, backed by the American observer to the negotiations, was alone in opposing the German-backed rule for mandatory declaration of all cartel agreements.[24] This was on the (largely correct) assumption that the most harmful cartels, or even any that were illegal, would never be declared, all while overwhelming DGIV with

[21] The ECSC was seen as major pro-competition victory even at the time (Franck 1963, 20). See Kipping (2002) and Montalban, Ramirez-Perez, and Smith (2011) regarding the pro-competition interests regarding the ECSC. For an example of characterizations of the ECSC as a *dirigiste*, anti-competition policy, see Loriaux (1991, 115–132) and Milward (1984, 137 and 467).

[22] For an example in steel, see Roland Labbe to Commissaire Général au Plan, August 27, 1956, 80AJ/137, AN.

[23] Warlouzet (2011, 39–40). More studies in later years continued to support this more mixed conclusion as the common market opened. Direction Générale des Prix et des Enquêtes Économiques, "Comparaison du niveau des prix dans les pays du marché commun," October 1958, 80AJ/137, AN.

[24] "Avant-Projet de Note," November 21, 1960, Premier Ministre – Comité Interministériel pour les Questions de Coopération Économique Européenne, 19790791/264, AN, page 7.

due diligence about the most innocuous business agreements.[25] The French delegation went so far as to say "the system of the Commission is useless, complicated, ineffective, and dangerous."[26]

Furthermore, the most effective aspects of early EEC competition policy came not from Regulation 17/62 but from outright bans on vertical restraints inherited from domestic French policy. In negotiations, the French administration successfully demanded that the rest of the EEC accept the strict bans on vertical restraints that it had imposed domestically in the Fontanet Circular in 1960 (Warlouzet, Laurent, 2011, 292–294).[27] And, the earliest EEC case to enforce competition rules, the Grundig-Consten case in 1966,[28] was based on these vertical prohibitions, not the horizontal cartels that the Germans otherwise emphasized (Adams 1989, 138–139).

The Rueff-Armand Committee of 1960, instigated by liberal economist Jacques Rueff, capped much of this off with a series of proposed interventions and policy changes. While many of them focused on macroeconomic policy and financial regulation, it also recommended the deregulation of protected sectors and a harsher enforcement against ententes.[29] It is often noted that the committee's recommendations on these topics were never implemented, but at that moment they explicitly held off on new rules for *ententes* because the European Regulation 17/62 was still being negotiated.[30]

Policies to promote economic concentration did exist in the 1940s and 1950s, but had different justifications than often assumed. In 1948, reports

[25] See Warlouzet (2011, 303, 314, 327) and "Note sur le fondement juridique de l'autorisation préalable des ententes et du régime transitoire prévus dans le projet de règlement proposé par la Commission de Bruxelles," Bureau de la réglementation du maintien de la concurrence et du contrôle des Ententes, December 14, 1960, 19790791/264, AN, pages 2–4. Internal memos from the Price Directorate to the French delegation would take the exact same position, for the very same reasons: that it was burdensome, not necessarily effective, and that most entente agreements were to be banned outright by the Treaty of Rome in the first place. "Projet d'intervention pour le chef de la délégation française," October 3, 1960, Direction Générale des Prix et des Enquêtes Économiques, 19790791/264, AN.

[26] "La déclaration obligatoire des ententes: Examen du projet de la comission – schema de contre-propositions," January 17, 1961, 19790791/264, AN.

[27] "Note: Réglement d'application des articles 85 et 86 du Traité de Rome," Primier Ministre – Comité Interministériel pour les Questions de Cooperation Économique Européenne, November 27, 1961, 19790791/265, AN. Joseph Fontanet himself intervened with the Director General of the Commission to ensure that vertical restraints were outright banned. Fontanet to Verloren van Themaat, October 1960, 19790791/264, AN.

[28] Consten SaRL and Grundig GmbH v Commission (1966).

[29] "Programme des travaux du comité avant le depot du Premier Ministre," Comité institué par le décret No. 59-1285, February 23, 1960, 81AJ/260, AN.

[30] Bertrand Balaresque, "Note pour le Ministre: Séance de travail du 18 novembre relative à l'examen des avis et recommandation du Comité Armand-Rueff," November 17, 1960, 540AP/1, AN.

would favor the creation of larger production units to make use of newer technology and economies of scale, but would also propose "anti-trust" policies to mitigate the potential abuse of concentrated industry.[31] When the Ministry of Finance conducted industry studies in the early 1950s, it focused on the relationship between plant size and the marginal cost of the final product, motivated to ensure that French firms were producing at low cost.[32] While the financial conditions of the industry would be mentioned, the primary concern was to ensure that competition would eliminate marginal producers and that those remaining would be efficient.

This all occurred at a time of limited industrial policy of the sort that statist perspectives emphasize. France did have a *regional* industrial policy (*Aménagement du territoire*) that distributed loans for the industrialization of underdeveloped regions (i.e., outside the Paris region). This policy was created in 1954 and included funds for general development, to increase plant size away from small workshops, and to retrain workers.[33] The loans were directed toward smaller firms, and the committee overseeing these loans often justified their actions in terms of suppressing "artificial protections that government authorities had either established or tolerated" in favor of certain vested interests.[34]

Growing Competitive Pressures

As this policy regime continued into the early 1960s, the overriding problem known to all was inflation, ranging from 3 percent to 6 percent per year. Industry would argue that wage and benefit demands from organized labor pushed up business costs that they were forced to pass to consumers. Labor blamed business for increasing prices. Some economists and bureaucrats

[31] Commissariat Générale du Plan - Group de Travail de la Productivité, "Facteurs de la productivité: Role de l'État," 1948, 81AJ/176, AN.

[32] Direction Générale des Prix et des Enquête Économique, "Concentration dans l'industrie cimentière," October 27, 1954, B-0057658/5, CAEF; Direction Générale aux Prix, "Concentration et Reconversion de l'industrie du superphosphate," September 1954, B-0057658/5, CAEF; Commissariat Générale aux Prix, "Modernisation et concentration de l'industrie de l'ammoniac," August 26, 1954, B-0057658/5, CAEF; Direction Générale des Prix et des Enquête Économique, "Spécialisation et concentration dans l'industrie cotonière,"August 8, 1954, B-0057658/5, CAEF. For a full list of the studies completed, see "Étude sur la structure économique au point de vue de la concurrence – (Liberté des Prix)," undated list, B-0057658/5, CAEF.

[33] "Note d'information sur l'aide en faveur de la conversion de l'industrie, du reclassement de la main d'oeuvre et de la decentralisation industrielle," Comité de Gestion du Fonds de Conversion, January 10, 1955, 19920430/86, AN.

[34] Ibid., page 3.

argued that the *Bank of France* was providing loans to the nationalized firms and the private sector through seigniorage, pushing the money supply past available resources. Jaques Rueff, in particular, was of this opinion, which was reflected heavily in the Rueff-Armand Report of 1960.[35] This began a slow move to reduce the reliance on *Bank of France* loans.[36] Nonetheless, coming into the early 1960s, the desire to control inflation added pressure for more pro-competition policies.

Entente Doubts

Yet concerns related to these policies preceded the 1960s. Before the Treaty of Rome was finalized, some in the Price Directorate in the Ministry of Finance argued that even the mild restrictions of the CTE—the cartel commission—could weaken French industry's position in the European market, with committed policymakers pushing back. Louis Franck, the director general of the Price Directorate since 1947, had spent the entirety of World War II in Washington, DC, and much of the 1930s in the United States observing the American New Deal. Therefore, he was well connected and well informed about the United States' aggressive antitrust movements at the time and was a committed advocate for more pro-competition policies through his carreer, writing two books on prices and free competition (Franck 1958, 1963). He was instrumental in the creation of the CTE but nonetheless was disappointed with its results, finding that competition was often a second priority relative to rationalization, productivity improvements, or market stabilization.

Even before the Treaty of Rome passed, other policymakers formed doubts. Yves Le Portz was a senior official under Franck who had coordinated with the Ministry of Industry to select the most important industries to scrutinize for anticompetitive practices.[37] But, as the Treaty of Rome was being negotiated, Le Portz argued that while the EEC would hopefully encourage competition, the need to maintain full employment in France, combined with the inefficiency and high costs in many French basic

[35] Jacques Rueff to Antoine Pinay, June 10, 1958, AG/5(1)/2366, AN, pages 2–3.

[36] See Monnet (2018).

[37] Franck to Le Portz, April 26, 1954, B-0057625, CAEF. The Ministry of Industry, otherwise a proponent of industry's interests before and after this time, does not appear to have opposed this. Rather, the list of industries chosen to investigate was based mostly on those about whom the most complaints had been received.

industries, meant that they should not ban French participation in European market-sharing cartels.[38] The instability of competition combined with the French competitive disadvantage would put employment at risk without controls of some kind on competition. He concluded that "French internal legislation must therefore be such that it can authorize intra-European market-sharing cartels in the cases where they are necessary to protect French industry."[39] He listed off a number of potential anti-competition reforms to CTE, namely expanding the exceptions for cartel practices that would promote cooperative research, rationalization, and improvements in productivity.[40]

These suggestions were ignored in the immediate term, and France continued to push competition policies in the EEC. Beyond ignoring these concerns, Louis Franck instead was noticeably irate in other instances when competitive public procurement rules were not followed to the letter.[41] In any case, after the plan was reinvigorated by Charles de Gaulle and Michel Debré in 1961, the Fourth Plan (1962–1965) put new emphasis on massively expanding public projects and investments rather than in promoting private industry (Warlouzet 2011, 342–344). Planning Commissioner Pierre Massé summarized his take on France's economic conditions to Prime Minister Michel Debré in 1960, with the *lack* of competition as the main concern: "Our vulnerability was all the greater in this domain because of a set of public and professional rules that limited internal and international competition."[42]

Tariff Acceleration and Internal Competition

Multiple times from 1959 to 1962, France accelerated the elimination of its tariff barriers beyond what was required the Treaty of Rome (Warlouzet, Laurent. 2011, 227–228). Whereas the treaty in 1957 was multilateral and

[38] "Note sur la révision de la politique en matière d'ententes professionnelles industrielles," Yves Le Portz, B-0057641, CAEF, page 3.

[39] Ibid., page 4. Market sharing cartels or agreements are where multiple producers agree to divide a market either by territory (such that each producer has an exclusive area with no competition) or quota (whereby price competition is impossible or limited because supply is fixed). These were particularly common in international cartels during the interwar period and were among the primary motivations for the anti-cartel provisions in both the CTE, the ECSC, and even the Treaty of Rome itself.

[40] Ibid, page 4.

[41] Franck to Marcille, September 22, 1960, B-0057632, CAEF.

[42] Pierre Massé, "Note sur les Obstacles à l'Expansion Économique," March 24, 1960, 81AJ/260, AN, page 5.

arguably not a policy decision by France alone, the accelerated tariff reductions were unilateral and surprised France's European partners. Internal Ministry of Finance reports likewise frequently justified tariff elimination as a way to control inflation by exposing French producers to external competition.[43]

This policy did not come without its detractors, however. Valéry Giscard d'Estaing was elected as a deputy in the National Assembly for the rural Puy-de-Dôme department in 1956, and in 1959 was tapped to be the secretary of state for finances, in 1962, mere months after being nominated as the minister of finance, d'Estaing suggested both that the tariff reductions for the common market not be accelerated and that fiscal measures to favor investment and mergers should be implemented.[44] However, the technical advisor communicating this plan to President Charles de Gaulle, J. M. Lévêque, voiced his disagreement and argued that import competition from tariff reductions is the best way to limit inflation.[45] Similarly, writing to Finance Minister Michel Debré in 1961, Jaques Rueff—who had just the previous year given public recommendations in support of further tariff liberalization—applauded the accelerated tariff reductions as the "most effective possible brake on internal price increases."[46]

Whatever the underlying causes of inflation, the downward pressure on prices from import competition was deemed important, and not without reason, as it had been shown to be effective, as seen by the falling prices of imports and exports over this time (Figure 4.1).

However, trade barriers at the border were not the only issue. In a May 1962 memo to the prime minister, Phillippe Huet, Louis Franck's successor as director general of prices, noted that many of the pro-competition policies meant to contain inflation—imports, exchange liberalization, and price ceilings—had only had a limited effect and encouraged deepening them.[47] He called for stronger enforcement against ententes as a necessary complement to tariff reductions, using the example of a recently formed

[43] See, for example, "Note sur un action douanière sur les prix," Ministère des Finances et des Affaires Économiques - Cabinet, March 6, 1961, 540AP/2, AN. The same report notes that the common external tariff of the common market limits the amount by which they can remove tariff barriers, indicating that they might have considered going even further.

[44] J.M. Lévêque to de Gaulle, "Programme économique et financier de M. Giscard d'Estaing," February 14, 1962, AG/5(1)/2366, AN.

[45] Ibid.

[46] Jaques Rueff, "Note pour le Premier Ministre," February 28, 1961, AG/5(1)/2366, AN, page 1.

[47] Philippe Huet, "Note sur l'état et l'évolution des prix etablie en vue de définir les éléments, conditions, et moyens d'une politiques des prix," May 18, 1962, 540AP/2, AN, page 8.

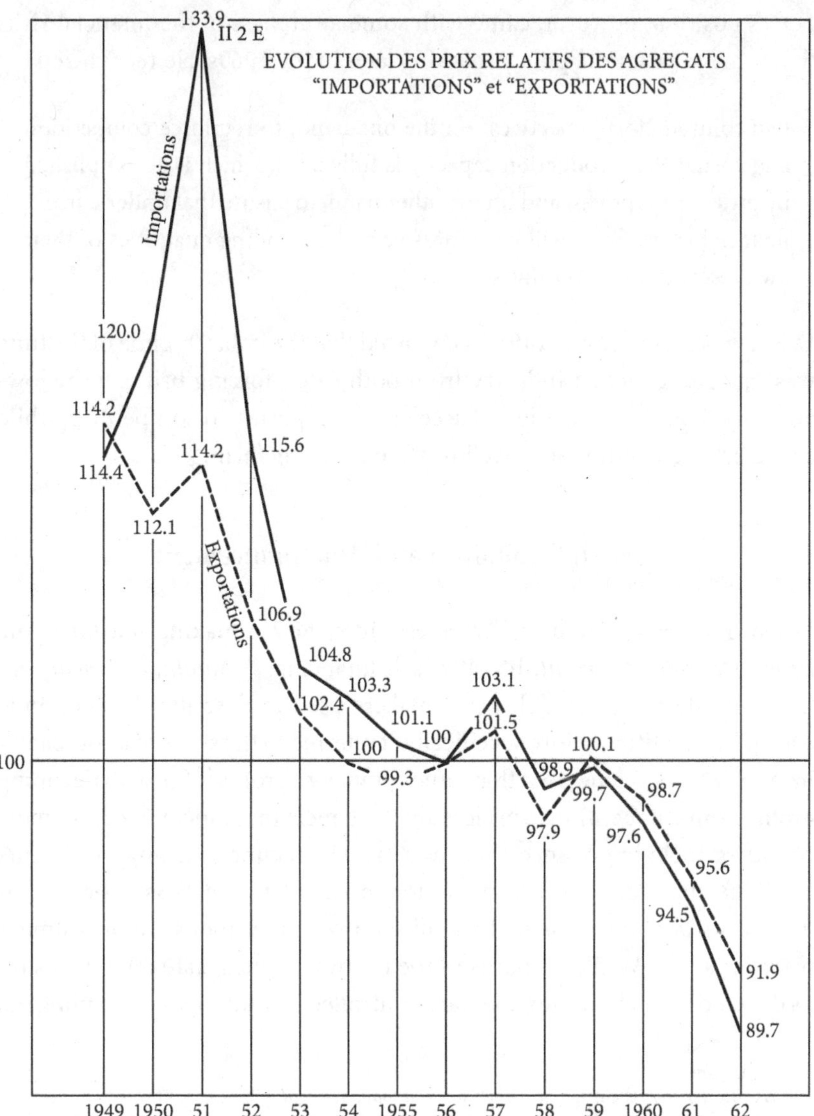

Figure 4.1 Decline in Prices of Imports and Exports through the 1950s[48]

Franco-Japanese cartel agreement in electrical equipment that was setting import quotas and thus undermining the intended benefits of open trade.[49]

[48] "Document No. 1: Les Prix," attached to Annexe Technique, Tableau économique d'ensemble de l'année 1970, April 1964, 19930277/2, AN.
[49] Ibid., pages 16–17.

Huet's position, however, came with some awareness of the financial risks that came to permeate policy thinking later in the 1960s. He recognized

> two contradictory objectives: on the one hand, to reinforce competition and ensure that production capacity is fully used, which is accomplished by pressure on prices, and on the other hand, to ensure that under current financial rules, firms will have massive and expanding quantities of their own resources to cover investments.[50]

Even advocates of competition recognized that the policy regime of the time was squeezing French industry from both sides, forcing prices to be lowered based on a combination of accelerating exposure to competition while conversely demanding massive investments for the plan.

French Capitalism and *Autofinancement*

When Huet referred to firms' "own resources," he was making allusion to the issue of *autofinancement*, literally "self-financing."[51] *Autofinancement* was the vocabulary that French policymakers used to describe the economic costs of competition. More specifically, it referred to the share of a company's investments that came from that same company's profits.[52] So, with declining profits from competition came less ability to meet investment needs. In most countries, including France, this investment by retained earnings represents the lion's share of total private sector investment, and thus a significant decline in *autofinancement* had substantive implications for investment more broadly.[53] While accounts of the postwar French state often focus on its directed financial sector, the state-controlled institutions surrounding the

[50] Ibid., page 15.

[51] As with entente, the original French word *autofinancement* will be used throughout because, although its meaning has some similarities to self-funded investment or investment from retained earnings, it has a particular meaning and measurement in this period in France that does not have a suitable translation.

[52] In most instances, *autofinancement* included amortization payments because replacing capital goods was a form of investment in times of rapid development. *Autofinancement* also occasionally included investment borne from temporary liquidity in amortization funds (sometimes called "sinking funds"). Simon Nora, "Autofinancement et le Plan: Problèmes de l'autofinancement dirigé," March 1947, 20030362/2, AN, pages 6–10.

[53] Note that *autofinancement* was not well understood even by French policymakers at the time. A March 1947 report by economist Simon Nora characterizes *autofinancement* as not widely known, without either solid numbers or theoretical devices to understand it. Ibid. In 1952, the Planning Commission noted the debate, highlighting that many thought of *autofinancement* as reinvested profits while others considered it in terms of a firm's available cash. Commissariat Général du Plan

Treasury, and the strong limitations on credit, a vast majority of investment in the French economy came from *autofinancement* (Quennoüelle-Corre 2000, 5–6), albeit less so than in most other countries.

However, *autofinancement* had a negative reputation in the government. Following understandings of "Malthusian" French business as backward, conservative, and rent-seeking, policymakers often understood *autofinancement* to exclusively be produced by raising prices on consumers. Given that France had been a relatively closed economy for generations prior, it was intuitive that businesses would be able to simply raise prices to meet their investment needs without any market constraints.[54] Even in 1953, the Planning Commission considered *autofinancement* as the independent variable in the relation between prices and investment, with reports titled "Impact of Autofinancement on Production Costs" ("*Incidence de l'autofinancement sur les prix de revient*"). That is to say, they considered that prices could be set according to the desired level of investment from *autofinancement*, rather than vice versa.[55] Policy memos from the era show this understanding of prices to have been common in both public and private thinking prior to the 1960s.[56]

Lastly, *autofinancement* was often measured in a way that obscured the reason for its economic importance. It would be reported in terms of the rate (*taux*) of *autofinancement*, which referred to the percentage of total investment that came from *autofinancement*.[57] So, for example, there would be times when investment from retained earnings would be falling, yet the rate of *autofinancement* would be increasing, because investment from

de Modernisation et d'Équipement, Réunion de Commission de l'Energie, December 15, 1952, 80AJ/39, AN, page 1. They then identified three different meanings of *autofinancement* used in France at the time: (1) the portion of net profits directed toward investment, (2) the balance of cash available for the firm to spend, and (3) gross profits before amortization. Far from a mere conceptual dispute, the first was the meaning understood by the public, though it was not used by any of the firms included in the Planning Commission study, and most nationalized firms appeared to be using the third meaning. Commissariat Général du Plan de Modernisation et d'Équipement - Commission de l'Energie, "Note sur l'auto-financement," January 8, 1953, 80AJ/39, AN.

[54] Nor did policymakers see investment from borrowed funds very differently; the Planning Commission frequently reached the conclusion that paying back loans would also require firms to increase prices in the future. Commissariat Général du Plan de Modernisation et d'Équipement, Réunion de Commission de l'Energie, December 15, 1952, 80AJ/39, AN, page 2.

[55] Commissariat Général du Plan, "Incidence de l'autofinancement sur les Prix de Revient," January 8, 1953, 80AJ/39, AN, page 1.

[56] A note to Minister of Finance Michel Debré from his chief of staff in 1966 complains of competitive pressures preventing price increases to fund investment—as if that were an intuitive solution. DuPont-Fauville Note to Debré, January 13, 1966, 98AJ/5/80, AN, page 2.

[57] Maurice Polti Report to Section des Finances, du Credit et de la Fiscalité of the Conseil Économique et Social, "Problème de l'autofinancement," April 26, 1967, 19920430/106, AN, page 48.

borrowing or equity financing was declining even faster.[58] Similarly, firms targeting a certain rate would react differently to maintain it if it were set as a policy target. Sheltered sectors (*secteurs abrités*) not exposed to competition might maintain or raise their prices to increase investment and hit the targeted rate, whereas firms exposed to competition (and thus cannot raise their prices) might *decrease their other investments* to meet the desired rate of *autofinancement*.[59]

From the CNPF to the Planning Commission

The earliest conversations making this connection were within the business community, who were the most proximate to the issue. However, these initial conversations, and the communication of this information to the government, was greeted with a mix of skepticism and hostility. As early as 1958, the *Conseil national du patronat français* (CNPF), the French peak employers' association, held meetings regarding investment and *autofinancement*.[60] It was in 1961 at the latest that this was communicated to the state, directly to Planning Commissioner Pierre Massé, when CNPF discussions contended that *autofinancement* had declined continuously since 1949, despite its increasing importance as a source of investment for French business.[61] Even at this early stage, the main interpretation was that competition was the main threat, as *autofinancement* depends "above all on the prices permitted by competition."[62]

In concert with representatives of the CNPF, Planning Commissioner Pierre Massé had requested that Rexeco, a private think tank created in 1957, complete a study on *autofinancement*, finished in late 1961.[63] The Rexeco report was primarily concerned with a growing disparity in the capital-labor income ratio in France, which was tilted increasingly toward labor, reducing the amount of profit available for *autofinancement*. The report noted that

[58] Procès-Verbal – Section des Finances, du Credit et de la Fiscalité of the Conseil Économique et Social, February 28, 1967, 19920430/106, AN, page 4.

[59] Raymond Courbis, "Prévision des prix et étude sectorielle des entreprises pendant la préparation du Ve Plan," 1968, 19930277/115, AN, pages 43 and 62–69.

[60] This conclusion is based on archives of the CNPF. Robert Pelletier of the CNPF, had been discussing the *autofinancement* issue as early as 1958, with regard to the reduced margins that French firms had for investment under the price blocages at the time and the ECSC rules. See Note de R Pelletier du 21 février 1958, Compte-Rendu de l'exposé de Perrin, vice-Président Usine à l'IEP, 72AS 1315, CNPF (based on notes from Laurent Warlouzet).

[61] CNPF compte-rendu, "Autofinancement," December 12, 1961, 19890471/19, AN.

[62] Ibid.

[63] Ibid.

the existing draft for the Fourth Plan (1962–1965) seemingly intended to use foreign competition to eliminate *autofinancement* entirely and thus end private control over investment:

> For the Planning Commission the doctrine seems to be the following. Autofinancement will be reduced in the course of the next few years by foreign competition. This evolution will allow the last investments that still escape the control of the Plan, financing by autofinancement, to fall under its authority.[64]

Nonetheless, the Rexoco report and the CNPF conversations both saw *autofinancement* as being chipped away primarily by wage gains. However, at this stage, the later policies of concentration, market power, mergers, and so on were not even mentioned.

Pierre Massé had warned business leaders in the CNPF that they would face resistance to demands for greater flexibility in *autofinancement* from supervisory organizations overseeing the plan, which were still focused on price and competition.[65] The CNPF began developing arguments to counter political objections that *autofinancement* was a way to price-gouge, or that it was merely diverting resources that could be wages.[66] For the CNPF, the greatest fear appeared to be that the government primarily opposed *autofinancement* because "use of the firm's own resources prevent all control over investments by organizations or individuals external to the firm."[67] Nonetheless, the CNPF had told the Planning Commission by 1961 that investment was going to be limited as a result of rising competitive pressures.

Market Feedback

Early News

Nonetheless, other news about the economy, competition, and even profits and investment remained quite positive through 1962. A Ministry of Finance report from July 1959 commented that private investment was still growing

[64] Rexeco, "Document de Travail: Note sur l'autofinancement des sociétés françaises," Copy of René Damien, December 1961, 19890471/19, AN, page 2.

[65] CNPF compte-rendu, "Autofinancement," December 12, 1961, 19890471/19, AN.

[66] This was a disingenuous position for the CNPF, since their policy preference was to supplement *autofinancement* by taking income from labor.

[67] Ibid.

as it had been,[68] and reports in 1960 from INSEE to the president's office and within the Ministry of Finance all showed investment had been expanding.[69] The Planning Commission indicated the same for 1961 and 1962.[70]

That said, some reporting to policy elites indicated a problem. A section of the *Conseil Économique et Social*—a comparatively powerless consultative body to the legislature—had noticed the *autofinancement* problem, in that with tariff liberalization and rising competition, profit margins dropped and the financial position of private firms worsened.[71] A report from November 1962, on the progress and difficulties in executing the Fourth Plan, remarked that there had been a tightening of the resources for *autofinancement* for the private sector,[72] though this is buried among the other mundane concerns about regional development, agricultural incomes, the balance of payments, and employment. Likewise, a 1962 report from the Planning Commission on the same subject lauded the growth in overall investment during the previous year,[73] even though it had separately noted a fall in private sector profits. While considering competition as "a stimulant to the effort of productivity in companies," reports argued that "it could then go beyond a certain threshold and instead limit our industrial dynamism, otherwise exposed to the hazards of the world and to the pressure of foreign competition."[74]

The Stabilization Plan of 1963

Competitive pressures were exacerbated by the Stabilization Plan of September 12, 1963, which was designed to stop the inflation of the prior few years. The plan came after bank reserve requirements from the Treasury had been

[68] Vaez-Olivera note to Secretaire d'État aux Finances, July 10, 1959, 540AP/1, AN, page 5.

[69] Meraud to Méo, INSEE "Note sur les perspectives d'investissements des industries privées pour 1960," AG/5(1)/2441, AN; Bertrand Balaresque to Ministre, "Point de la conjoncture et perspectives à court terme dans l'industrie," June 30, 1960, 540AP/1, AN, page 5.

[70] Conseil Economique et Social – Section du Plan et des Investissements, "Resumé des principales questions étudiées par le rapport sur l'éxécution du Plan pour les années 1961–1962," October 18, 1962, 19920430/72, AN, pages 7–8.

[71] Ibid., page 1.

[72] Maurice Halff, "Problèmes posés par l'exécution du IVème Plan," November 21, 1962, 19920430/72, AN, page 14.

[73] Comissariat Général du Plan, "Rapport sur l'exécution du plan en 1961 et 1962," 1962, 19930275/96, AN, page 55.

[74] Ibid., page 11.

increased a few times to control inflationary pressures, but to no avail.[75] The Stabilization Plan reduced tariff schedules by another 15 to 20 percent past previous accelerations, directly limited markups for importers, added new price ceilings, strengthened control over public procurement to fix prices against upward revisions, furthered reforms of distribution and wholesale to eliminate inefficient retail, and added new credit restrictions for consumers.[76] Each facet of the plan would further exacerbate the rising *autofinancement* problem, by either directly increasing competitive pressures or deepening their impact: price ceilings would limit private sector earnings, tariff reductions would increase competition and also reduce earnings, and the credit restrictions for consumers would lower demand further, on top of the prior credit restrictions for other sources of investment. But the pro-competition mental model held by most policymakers at this time prevented them from seeing this. If one believed that French industry was a collection of Malthusian firms with comfortable rents, then their profits *should* be made lower by competition, and these outcomes would be signs of success.

Nonetheless, other information was ignored in the formulation of this plan. By early 1963, almost every report on investment and the overall economic outlook coming into the Ministry of Finance or prime minister's office noted the decline in private investment in the prior years, and yet policy documents almost always simultaneously favored more competition, particularly in retail and distribution.[77] A mere two months before the plan was implemented, an INSEE survey—sent to the president's office—asked managers about their intent to invest in 1964. Across the board, almost all business leaders said they would invest less, after already two years of general declines in the rate of private sector investment.[78]

Then, after the plan was implemented, the costs mounted up rapidly. By February 1964, routine INSEE reports noted the deteriorating financial

[75] INSEE Direction des Synthèses Économique – Division de la Conjoncture, "La situation économique en fevrier 1964 et les perspectives pour les prochains mois," February 1964, 540AP/3, AN; Monier to Ministre des Finances, "Plan de stabilisation – Premiers résultats d'une enquête de l'Inspection Générale de l'Économie Nationale," October 3, 1963, 540AP/3, AN.

[76] Direction Générale des Études et du Crédit, "Mesures annoncées par le gouvernement pour lutter contre la hausse des prix," September 1963, 540AP/3, AN; INSEE Direction des Synthèses Économique – Division de la Conjoncture, "La situation économique en fevrier 1964 et les perspectives pour les prochains mois," February 1964, 540AP/3, AN, pages 2–4.

[77] Untitled Memo, "Politique Commerciales," 540AP/3, AN; Ministère des Finances, "Amélioration de la concurrence," undated memo, 540AP/3, AN; Ministère des Finances – Cabinet, "Note sur la situation économique," April 30, 1963, 540AP/3, AN.

[78] Blanc to Deniau, "Les projets d'investissement pour 1963 et 1964 dans les entreprises industrielles privées," July 26, 1963, AG/5(1)/2441, AN.

condition of private sector firms: with prices blocked, facing foreign competition, and bank credit limited, firms could not raise prices, so there was little way to make up losses other wage cutting, which was not an option with a militant, unionized workforce.[79] Other reports, to Finance Minister Michel Debré, noted complaints from key industries about their financial conditions, but even then advocated further competition by arguing that rising imports "constitute one factor of productivity growth and are nothing but the other side of a better division of labor in the common market."[80] Specific numbers from INSEE at this time put the private sector investment decline at 5 percent between 1962 and 1963, but indicated that most firms surveyed said that they their investments would decline an additional 4 percent on average in 1964.[81] In the grand scheme of economic growth, these numbers are not enormous, but the Planning Commission had specific investment targets for the private sector. With the risks of declining investment becoming increasingly clear, the government was contemplating adding coercive measures to ensure compliance with the plan—by adding a profit tax for non-complying firms—rather than address the reasons they did not have the financial resources to make the plan's investments.[82] It was in this flurry of reports that the government, but the Ministry of Finance, in particular, began to appreciate the scale of the problem, assembling data showing the decline in *autofinancement* through the early 1960s (Figure 4.2).

These concerns were initially ignored because political leadership was blinded by a set of pro-competition mental models that prioritized output and low prices, with limited profits seen as a good outcome. With that perspective, seeing overall investment grow while the share of private investment falls would not be negative news. Similarly, all of this did come in the context of otherwise very positive news about the state of the economy. It was not the case that productivity or growth was declining in any

[79] INSEE Direction des Synthèses Économique – Division de la Conjoncture, "La situation économique en fevrier 1964 et les perspectives pour les prochains mois," February 1964, 540AP/3, AN, pages 29 and 38–41.

[80] Note au Ministre, "Le Plan de stabilisation – Point de la situation," March 7, 1964, 540AP/3, AN.

[81] H. Cachin Note pour le Ministre, "Enquête de l'INSEE sue les investissements dans l'industrie en 1963 et 1964," July 10, 1964, 540AP/3, AN.

[82] "Projet de loi instituant un prélèvement de compensation sur les entreprises qui ne respectent pas les objectifs du Plan de développement économique et social." Undated document. This document was in folders of other documents from 1963 or 1964 that all focused on issues from the fallout after the stabilization plan.

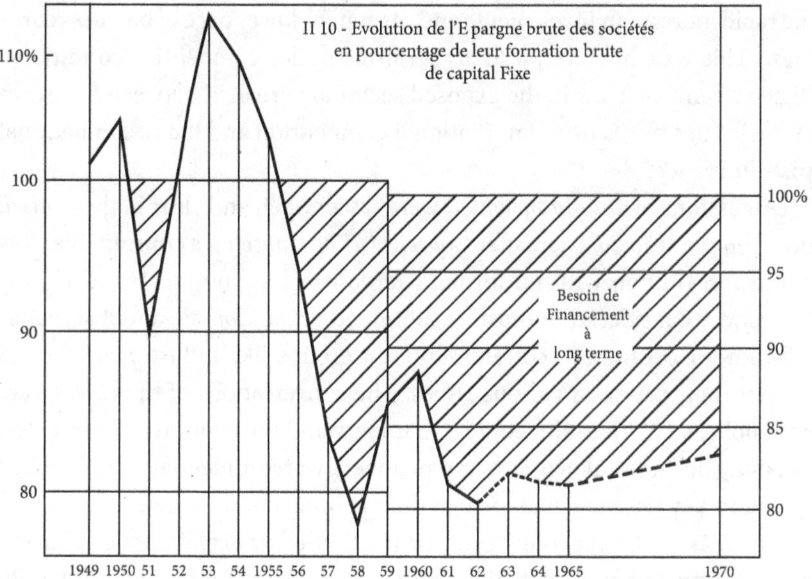

Figure 4.2 The Decline in Corporate Savings as a Percentage of Gross Fixed Capital Formation[83]

way. Instead, production, wages, and productivity were all increasing.[84] And while inflation control, not competition itself, was the primary goal of this plan and prior policies, it nonetheless remains that case that competition—from imports, internal reforms, or price restrictions—was among the first mechanisms that policymakers would reach for in order to attain this goal.

The Policy Debate

Referred to the *Conseil*

The CNPF moved publicly voicing concerns over *autofinancement.* Paul Huvelin of the CNPF, speaking to the *Assemblée Générale* in 1964, stated that "the main cause of the indebtedness of French firms is that disparity between

[83] Ministère des Finances, "Annexe Technnique, Tableau économique d'ensemble de l'année 1970," April 1964, 19930277/2, AN.

[84] There was, however, discussion on how the positive estimates were, if anything, underestimating productivity growth. Commissariat Général du Plan – Service Productivité, "Note sur les progrès recents de productivité," January 1967, AG/5(1)/878, AN.

the rapid increase in investments and the much slower pace of business earnings." This was, however, a focus on firms under competitive conditions: "The margins of firms in the exposed sector are crushed between pressures on their sales prices from international competition and the rise in national costs in France."[85]

Discussions of *autofinancement* were rather open and clear in the *Conseil Économique et Social* (hereafter *Conseil*).[86] The *Conseil* is a consultative, corporatist institution with no formal decision-making power. However, any laws under consideration must be submitted to the *Conseil*, and it serves as a forum for organized economic interest groups like industry or labor to express their views on various issues. The conversations of the *Conseil* are not public, so it is a useful context to understand the contours and interests in policy debates. Likewise, many members were influential in this policy area, and key decision-makers like the planning commissioner or director of the Treasury would come to advise the *Conseil* or explain policy choices. A 1964 report shared with the *Conseil* by Robert Pelletier of the CNPF warned of the costs of the common market's shock on previously protected industry,[87] and it suggested that *autofinancement* would largely disappear in around five years in private French industry if general private sector profitability were not restored.[88] None present in the *Conseil* openly contested this representation.[89] When attending one session, the director of the Treasury argued that "in the ever-increasing international competition, price competition is becoming more and more the dominant factor, so it is essential that our firms benefit from a sufficient profit margin which gives some flexibility to their commercial policy."[90]

Another concern raised in the *Conseil* was that the statistics previously used to assess and monitor the problem were distorted to hide the decline in profits and investment, and its scale in the private sector specifically. In this and other reports by Pelletier, the CNPF argued that French national

[85] Paul Huvelin Speech to Assemblée Générale, January 14, 1964, 19890471/19, AN.

[86] Procès-Verbal, Conseil Économique et Social – Section des Finances du Crédit et de la Fiscalité, October 20, 1964, 19920430/87, AN.

[87] Robert Pelletier to Conseil Économique et Social, "Le Financement des Investissements," December 17, 1964, 19920430/87, AN, page 30.

[88] Ibid., page 177.

[89] Procès-Verbal, Conseil Économique et Social – Section des Finances du Crédit et de la Fiscalité, December 1, 1964, 19920430/87, AN, page 6.

[90] Procès-Verbal, Conseil Économique et Social – Section des Finances du Crédit et de la Fiscalité, December 9, 1964, 19920430/87, AN, page 6.

accounts mixed the investment of private industry in with those of housing construction, public administration, and the nationalized firms, viewing investment in the aggregate from all of these sources.[91] The most recent INSEE study had broken these sectors apart and determined a 3 percent drop in investments from 1963 to 1964.[92] Nor was this the first recognition of this sort of problem. In April 1963, INSEE sent a downward revision of previous estimates of private sector investment to an advisor for de Gaulle, suggesting the problem was even worse than previously thought.[93] In hindsight, many of the positive reports about investment growth in the very early 1960s had been overly optimistic. This concern, about aggregate statistics hiding the extreme drop in profits and investment in the private sector, was later echoed in *L'impératif industriel* (The Industrial Imperative) by Lionel Stoleru, one of the architects of the national champions policy in the late 1960s and early 1970s (Stoleru 1969).

Clappier Reports on Exposed Industries

These discussions in the *Conseil* occurred at the same time as the release of a series of widely read reports on three industries exposed to international competition. In 1962, the minister of industry had commissioned a working group on "exposed" industries: singling out aluminum, organic chemicals, and heavy machinery for study. Headed by Bernard Clappier of the *Bank of France*,[94] all three reports were released in early 1965. Despite some variation based on industry-specific issues or strengths,[95] the reports all spoke to a common set of problems: the risks of the "colonization" of the

[91] R. Pelletier, "Rapport destiné à la Commission des Investissements et du Financement du CNPF. Étude sur le financement des investissements productifs," October 1965, 19890471/19, AN, page 1.

[92] Ibid., page 2.

[93] Gruson to Deniau, April 4, 1963, with attached report from INSEE "Les Investissements des entreprises industrielles privées (Pétrole exclu) en 1962 d'après les chefs d'entreprises," AG/5(1)/2441, AN.

[94] Groupe de Travail sur les industries exposées, "Rapport sur l'industrie du gros matériel d'équipement mecanique," May 1965, 98AJ/5/80, AN (hereafter "Heavy Machinery Report"), footnote 1 on page 2.

[95] For example, the aluminum industry had apparently kept up with technological advances, built state-of-the art plants, and was even successfully licensing its technologies abroad, as well as undertaking a series of mergers on their own. See Groupe de Travail sur les industries exposées, "Rapport sur l'industrie de l'aluminium," January 1965, 98AJ/5/80, AN (hereafter "Aluminum Report"), page 1. The report on heavy machinery likewise extensively discussed how public contracts were awarded based on the centrality of the government as a customer, something not true of the other industries studied. Heavy Machinery Report, pages 12–13.

French market by American firms, insufficient *autofinancement*, and, above all, insufficient corporate concentration.

What is most telling for this analysis, however, is *why* concentration was seen as necessary, contrary to the justifications based on price and efficiency previously given in the 1940s and 1950s. At no point was it suggested that newer technologies required larger production units or plants, or that smaller firms were economically inefficient for organizational reasons. In fact, the reports explicitly state that the problem of size is *not* in terms of economies of scale, cost efficiency, or quality. The heavy machinery report states the following:

> This disparity in total business does not necessarily mean that the sizes of the production units are always exceeded by those that may exist among our competitors, or that the production of a type of equipment by a French company is necessarily worse than that produced by one or another of its foreign competitors. It even happens that the opposite is true: where a French company has a larger plant than the largest German company, which is true, for example, for turbines or large boilers. But in this case, the French company is smaller because it is much less diversified than its German counterpart.[96]

The report instead focused on *financial* concentration along with manufacturing specialization.[97] The chemicals report highlights that most French firms are too small only in terms of financial limitations.[98] When noting the lack of research and development, the report stresses this only in terms of amount of funding (e.g., "Large French chemical firms devote a much lower percentage of their operating budget to research than that done by large American firms."), denoting that these costs are seen in financial terms, not in terms of an operational efficiency.[99]

The reports advocate for tax advantages for mergers and concentration and even in some cases the maintenance of tariff barriers within the common market for the industry.[100] These reports contended that other

[96] Heavy Machinery Report, page 9.

[97] Ibid., page 10.

[98] Groupe de Travail sur les industries exposées, "Rapport sur l'industrie des grands produits intermédiaires de la chimie organique," May 1965, 98AJ/5/80, AN (hereafter "Chemicals Report"), page 10.

[99] Ibid., page 14.

[100] Aluminum Report, page 16.

firm-level solutions to this financial problem were not available, as France's financial markets were not deep enough at the time to cover the needed investments.[101] Price ceilings prevented firms from raising prices, even though in the case of aluminum, these price ceilings kept French prices *lower* than those abroad.[102]

Fixing *Autofinancement*

By 1965, the drop in private investment was well known and discussed widely at high levels of government, with advisors to President de Gaulle referring to "the crisis of productive investments."[103] While it is argued here that the growing crisis of private sector investment and profitability was the primary motivation and driver of the national champions policy, it was by no means the only option considered. The debates in and around the *Conseil* are particularly useful for examining the alternatives to address *autofinancement*, even though conversations quickly, if indirectly, centered around market power.

As already mentioned, policymakers' understanding of where profits and investment came from was profoundly shaped by the legacy of a protected, closed economy prior to World War II, and as such one of the earliest considered solutions to the problem was the possibility of simply increasing the prices that firms would be allowed to charge in order to increase profits and investment. Even though price ceilings could be raised, as a solution this is not possible in a competitive economy.[104] But these discussions came after years of attempting to address inflation by suppressing prices, and some policymakers still favored continuing these policies. In one early discussion, when one representative in the *Conseil* mentioned that many economists felt that profits were improperly influencing final prices,

[101] Ibid., pages 9–10.

[102] Ibid., pages 10–11.

[103] J. Chabrun to de Gaulle, "Audience de MM. Chalandron et Bloch-Lainé," April 28, 1965, AG/5(1)/2441, AN.

[104] Jean Dromer, a technical advisor to de Gaulle, noted that higher labor costs, the price block in 1963, and international competition made it impossible for firms to make up the losses anywhere, especially not via prices. Dromer to de Gaulle, "Le financement des investissements des entreprises et la fiscalité," March 11, 1965, AG/5(1)/2441, AN, page 6.

Jaçques Rueff—author of the Rueff-Armand report and committed to liberal competition—seconded this, and another suggested even *more* import competition to limit inflation.[105]

Others proposed external sources of financing, like the stock market or banks. However, the resources simply were not there. Prior reports on the state financial system were clear that private demand for investment had already well exceeded what the Treasury would be able to provide, even in 1962 before the issue of *autofinancement* was considered critical.[106] This assessment, that the Treasury and *Bank of France* would not be able to help, had also been confirmed by a director of the Treasury to the *Conseil* in 1964. While acknowledging that the private sector's investments were in grave risk, Director General of the Treasury Maurice Pérouse emphasized all of the other financial obligations that the Treasury had to local governments, nationalized firms, and even foreign governments, suggesting that private firms would need to find ways to attract more capital and that increasing their rate of autofinancement would be desirable.[107]

On top of this, the cost of borrowing was generally at around 8 percent.[108] Given that inflation in this era was consistently between 4 percent to 6 percent, the inability to repay loans with a real interest rate of between 2 percent and 4 percent implies a remarkably poor outlook for profits. The final report of the *Conseil* on *autofinancement* accepted the conclusions that the decline in investment could neither be attributed to a lack of external financing—as that had actually increased—nor be solved by growth in external financing.[109] Restoring the profitability of French firms was seen as the only way to resolve the problem.[110]

Conversations turned to market power. One representative from labor (CGT), Jean Duret, commented that the only clear way known to increase *autofinancement* would be to expand cartelization internationally, even

[105] Conseil Économique et Social, Compte Rendu Sommaire, July 9, 1963, 20090342/2, AN, page 2.

[106] Commissariat Général du Plan, "Note pour le Ministre des Finances," February 22, 1962, 19930275/39, AN, page 3.

[107] Minutes of Section on Finance, Credit, and Taxation, Conseil Économique et Social, December 9, 1964, 19920430/87, AN.

[108] Robert Pelletier to Conseil Économique et Social, "Le Financement des Investissements," December 17, 1964, 19920430/87, AN, page 104.

[109] Ibid., page 111.

[110] Ibid., page 144.

though this would conflict with existing price policies to control inflation.[111] Jacques Rueff, again, objected to these policy moves, constantly arguing that the only ways to increase prices would be cartels or trade protections, and he argued that France still did not have a functioning competitive market anyways.[112] The *Conseil's* final report nonetheless focused on market power:

> Autofinancement by reinforcing acquired situations[113] would accentuate the natural tendencies of the economy to create monopolistic units.
>
> Autofinancement would, moreover, be a factor in price increases, tending to return the burden of paying for investment to consumers.[114]

These policy discussions show that policymakers themselves clearly saw the anti-competition policy options they were considering to be contrary to the pro-competition policies of the preceding decades, and that competition and investment were increasingly seen as trade-offs.

The Fifth Plan and the National Champions Policy

The national champions policy was directly outlined in the Fifth Plan (1966-1970):

> The Fifth Plan therefore proposes as an objective the creation, or reinforcement where they already exist, of a small number of companies or groups of international size capable of confronting foreign corporations in areas where competition is established: technical autonomy, dimensions of production and marketing units, versatility and balance between different customers and different geographic markets, reserves to be able to

[111] Procès-Verbal, Section des Finances, du Crédit et de la Fiscalité, Conseil Économique et Social, December 8, 1964, 19920430/87, AN, page 6.

[112] Procès-Verbal, Section des Finances, du Crédit et de la Fiscalité, Conseil Économique et Social, December 1, 1964, 19920430/87, AN, page 10. In other sessions of the Conseil, Rueff had the same argument over *autofinancement*, responding similarly as members of the *Conseil* would point out that the profit margins gained from cartelization or concentration in Germany or the Netherlands were an important source of investment there. Procès-Verbal, Section des Finances, du Crédit et de la Fiscalité, Conseil Économique et Social, October 10, 1964, 19920430/86, AN, page 10.

[113] *Situations acquises* refers to vested interests or rents, but does not have an exact translation.

[114] Robert Pelletier to Conseil Économique et Social, "Le Financement des Investissements," December 17, 1964, 19920430/87, AN, page 114.

> respond quickly to the release of a new product, etc. In most major sectors of industry (aluminum, steel, mechanics, electrical engineering, electronics, automotive, aeronautics, chemistry, pharmacy, etc.) the number of these groups should be very limited, often even reduced to one or two.[115]

To support this, the state introduced tax and financial incentives for mergers on the belief that positions of market power were necessary for French firms to compete with foreign, and particularly American, multinationals.[116] The law of July 12, 1965, granted significant tax advantages for mergers. When the restrictions from the 1963 Stabilization Plan were lifted, this was supplemented with exemptions to *encadrement du crédit*, credit ceilings normally imposed by the *Bank of France* (Hall 1986, 153). In making these changes, the Fifth Plan also aimed to increase the rate of *autofinancement*.[117]

To emphasize how much policy understandings had shifted, it is difficult to overstate how many reports in the 1960s—from the Planning Commission, from the Ministry of Finance, from the Ministry of Industry, from the prime minister's office—begin with two pages that elaborate on some form of this exact argument:

> (a) France has been exposed to competition with the Treaty of Rome, the liberalization of exchanges, and other procompetition policies;
> (b) This has decreased profits in French industry and limited firms' means to finance further investments via autofinancement, and
> (c) We need to create concentrated, larger firms of international scale that will have the financial and technological resources to compete, with the economic power to survive in international markets.[118]

It was well understood by this point that the increases in *autofinancement* were to be drawn from concentration and market power, and this was reflected across policy areas adjacent to the Fifth Plan.

[115] Commissariat Général du Plan, "Cinquième Plan de Développement Économique et Social (1966-1970)," pages 68–69. Retrieved from https://www.strategie.gouv.fr/sites/strategie.gouv.fr/files/atoms/files/cinquieme-plan-1966-1970.pdf on June 5, 2019.

[116] See Adams (1989, 54), Hall (1986, 148), and Piore and Sabel (1984, 140)

[117] Jean Chardonnet, "Projet de Rapport Général sur le Vème Plan," Conseil Économique et Social, September 24, 1965, 20090342/2, AN, page 3.

[118] For example, see Commissariat Général du Plan, "Pour des structures financières compétitives," 81AJ/259, AN, page 1; Commissariat Général du Plan, Groupe de Travail sur les Problèmes de l'Adaptation, "Pour l'étude des problèmes de l'adaptation," March 28, 1966, 19930277/226, AN; INSEE, Direction de la Prévision, "L'Évolution recente des fusions d'entreprises en France," March 15, 1967, 98AJ/5/81, AN.

Industrial Development Committee

The Industrial Development Committee of the Fifth Plan was proposed by an advisor to Prime Minister Pompidou to coordinate concentration policies.[119] François-Xavier Ortoli, the new planning commissioner, opened an early meeting of the committee seeking to address the problems of (a) low profit margins in France, (b) how to encourage corporate concentration, and (c) how pro-competition public procurement policies were interfering with industrial development.[120] Looking into the history of industrial development policy in France, the committee's understanding was that it saw *there was no such prior policy.*[121]

The Industrial Development Committee's final recommendations were, in order: 1) reform of competition policies, 2) research and development aid, 3) aid to specialized SMEs, particularly subcontractors for larger firms, 4) reform of public procurement as a tool of industrial strategy, 5) European-level mergers, 6) simplify regulations, 7) improved education, and 8) encouraging improved management methods.[122] Almost every area related to firm-level regulation or industrial policy was aimed at limiting the competitive forces that French firms would face, and the section on competition policy stated, "Adaptation of competition policy with regard to *ententes*, dominant positions, and price policy in France and in the Community, to take into account the need to prepare the necessary industrial specializations and groupings as well as outward FDI."[123] In deciding how to report these conclusions to the *Conseil des Ministres*, the committee framed their proposals in terms of generalized deficiencies of competitive market mechanisms.[124]

[119] Monjoie Note to Premier Ministre, "Préparation des travaux du Comité Interministériel 'Structures industriels,'" January 3, 1966, 81AJ/258, AN.

[120] Compte-rendu, Comité de Developpement Industriel, May 5, 1966, 19930277/226, AN, page 2.

[121] When discussing industrial policies, it discussed the need for a "critical study of past policies (or the absence of policies?)." Projet de compte-rendu, Comité de Developpement Industriel, June 30, 1966, 19930277/226, AN, page 4. This sentiment is likewise echoed throughout the Committee's final report and Stoleru (1969).

[122] Commissariat Général du Plan, "Projet de relevé de décisions du Comité de Developpement Industriel," May 6, 1968, AG/5(1)/878, AN, pages 2-3.

[123] Ibid., page 2.

[124] "Projet de Note de Présentation du Rapport du C.D.I. au Conseil des Ministres," May 2, 1968, 81AJ/259, AN, page 2.

"Public Markets" and Strategic Industrial Policy

This spread to government procurement policies (public markets or *marchés publics*).[125] The markets where nationalized firms bought from private suppliers were a central tool for the French state to enforce competition.

And even prior to the Fifth Plan, the public markets and their pro-competition bidding policies were a central target for proponents of industrial policies. In 1964, Planning Commissioner Massé had pressed anti-competition reforms to Minister of Finance Michel Debré as a solution to rising capital costs and international competition for the electrical equipment industry, in order to assist with the *autofinancement* of private suppliers by reducing the number of suppliers in any given market to just two or three.[126] The Clappier reports complained that procurement rules limited firm size by requiring multiple bids even for very large projects,[127] and they recommended that concentration should not be impeded by any anti-entente legislation or EU competition rules and that industry representatives be added to procurement committees (*Commission des marchés*) to ensure adequate profits.[128]

With the Fifth Plan, Finance Minister Debré asked the commission overseeing all public procurement to examine possible reforms to aid industrial restructuring.[129] The resultant report for implementation complained of past public buyers too concerned with maintaining low prices and not giving private suppliers sufficiently predictable contracts. It suggested that procurement as an excellent method to protect French industry from competition.[130] Other conversations noted that suppliers had often been accepting contracts at a loss because public buyers were overly zealous about maintaining competition.[131]

[125] This is also the exact policy context in which Didry and Marty (2016) argue that earlier pro-competition policies were part of a coherent policy for the later creation of national champions. However, the reforms in this exact area erased the earlier, anti-entente policies from the 1950s, and those reforming these policies in the 1960s as a form of "strategic industrial policy" clearly saw their choices as at odds with earlier decisions.

[126] Pierre Massé to Michel Debré, July 10, 1964, 19930276/2, AN, pages 1–2.

[127] Heavy Machinery Report, pages 12–13.

[128] Ibid., page 18–20.

[129] Ministère de l'Économie et des Finances – Commission Centrale des Marchés, "Rapport sur les problèmes posés par les marchés publics en tant qu'eléments d'une politique économique visant à renformer les structures industrielles," July 24, 1967, 19930277/233, AN, page 1.

[130] Ibid., page 12.

[131] Compte Rendu, Mission Centrale des Marchés, July 7, 1967, 19930277/233, AN, page 5.

Turning against Prior Rules

Separate discussions on concentration often turned to (a) the contradiction between competition rules and the national champions policy and (b) how to alter, work around, or undo competition rules—French or European—in order to implement this policy.[132] Prior pro-competition policies were a direct impediment to the national champions policy, and French policymakers sought to cast them aside. One representative from academia, Jean Chardonnet, referred to the CTE as "useless" unless it supported the goals of concentration.[133]

The final report addressed how concentration could circumvent EEC competition rules.[134] Duret, a representative from organized labor (CGT), wanted to limit the applicability of the competition clauses from the European treaties.[135] By contrast, just a few short years earlier, in 1961 and 1962, France had wanted to *enhance* the EEC competition rules regarding concentration and abuse of dominant position. Separately, discussing a proposal for increasing *autofinancement* by removing price ceilings for the domestic market only—allowing French multinationals to sell at different prices domestically and internationally—they quickly realized that this violated GATT and EEC competition rules, because this was the textbook definition of dumping, a clear violation of most trade agreements.[136]

Financial Power and Technology

While the evidence presented has already shown finance and investment as the primary motivation for these changes, it should be further demonstrated that none of this was the result of, or a response to, technological changes. Earlier discussions of research and development did not have the same focus

[132] Conseil Économique et Social – Section du Plan et des Investissements, "Problèmes posés par la concentration des entreprises," July 11, 1966, 19920430/104, AN.

[133] M. Chardonnet in Procès-Verbal, Conseil Économique et Social – Section du Plan et des Investissements, October 26, 1966, 19920430/104, AN, page 16.

[134] François Lagandre, Conseil Économique et Social – Section du Plan et des Investissements, "Rapport: Problèmes posés par la concentration des entreprises," December 13, 1966, 19920430/104, AN, pages 127–133.

[135] Procès-Verbal, Section des Finances, du Crédit et de la Fiscalité – Conseil Économique et Social, November 22, 1966, 19920430/106, AN, page 9.

[136] Procès-Verbal, Section des Finances, du Crédit et de la Fiscalité – Conseil Économique et Social, March 7, 1966, 19920430/106, AN, page 17.

on firm size, scale, profits, and competitiveness. For example, a 1957 Planning Commission policy report on technology emphasizes primarily the lack of qualified research personnel and certain tax issues.[137] Conversations about technology in the *Conseil* in the early 1960s focused on the shortage of qualified researchers in France[138] or the details of public funding toward basic research.[139]

Discussions in the *Conseil* starkly show that policymakers were aware that technology was not the driver. A representative from INSEE stated that "the requirements of the concentration are probably much more at the level of the firm than at the level of the establishment."[140] Purely technical arguments about plant size generally contend that, based on economies of scale, larger plants or factories would have higher productivity because they would be able to scale up larger batches and produce more at lower cost. But French policymakers at the time did not even believe this. The INSEE representative continued that it is rather the "financial power" of a large firm, which

> is more capable than a smaller enterprise of facing a number of the problems of modern economic evolution. Problems of technical research, on the one hand, are obviously more easily solved by larger companies, being more financially powerful than smaller companies. On the other hand, larger firms are better able to adapt to changing markets, as they are often more versatile than smaller companies, but above all because the size of a company gives it a greater capacity for financing, a greater variety of means of financing, and consequently a greater freedom to pursue technical innovations that are be presented to it.[141]

[137] R. Schwob, "Note concernant les principaux problèmes soulevés par l'établissement du Marché commun dans le domaine de la Recherche technique," July 18, 1957, 80AJ/137, AN.

[138] Procès-Verbal, Conseil Économique et Social, Section de l'Adaption à la Recherche technique et de l'Information économique, February 6, 1963, 19920430/86, AN; Procès-Verbal, Conseil Économique et Social, Section de l'Adaption à la Recherche technique et de l'Information économique, November 28, 1962, 19920430/86, AN; Procès-Verbal, Conseil Économique et Social, Section de l'Adaption à la Recherche technique et de l'Information économique, January 30, 1963, 19920430/86, AN.

[139] Procès-Verbal, Conseil Économique et Social, Section de l'Adaption à la Recherche technique et de l'Information économique, May 9, 1962, 19920430/86, AN; René Goussault, Conseil Économique et Social, Section de l'Adaption à la Recherche technique et de l'Information économique, "La recherche scientifique dans le IVème Plan," May 21, 1962, 19920430/86, AN.

[140] Conseil Économique et Social, Annexe au Procès-Verbal, June 14, 1966, 19920430/104, AN, page 12.

[141] Ibid., page 12.

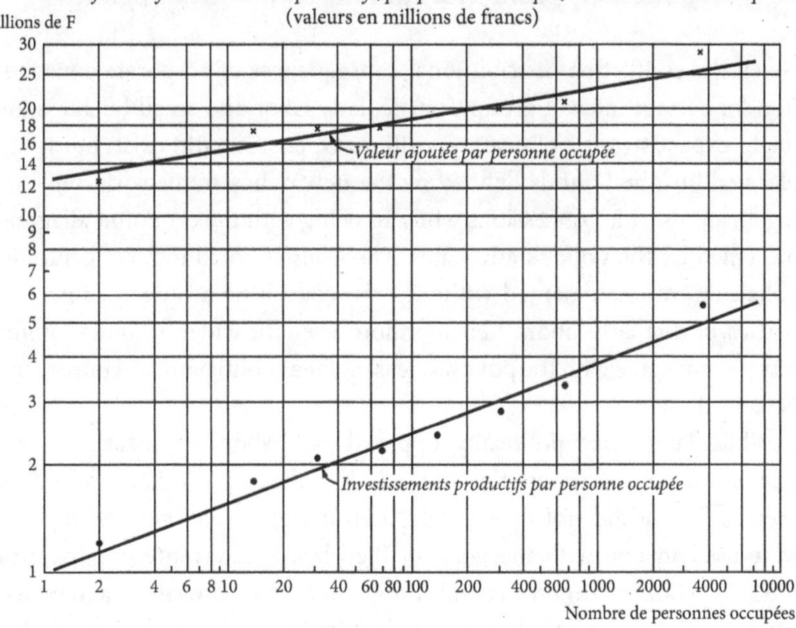

Figure 4.3 Investment Rate per Employee—Ministry of Industry[143]

French firms were at a *financial* disadvantage, and limiting competition was seen as necessary to provide resources to develop those technologies.

These arguments were reinforced by internal research. An April 1968 Ministry of Industry study on the chemical and pharmaceutical industries found that industry concentration had *declined* in the early 1960s.[142] The final section of the report, "Size and Economic Efficiency," was meant to analyze the efficiency from scale—but measured that exclusively in terms of profitability—and found larger firms had higher value-added and higher rates of investment (Figure 4.3).

[142] Direction Générale de la Politique Industrielle, "Premiers éléments pour une étude de la concentration industrielle," April 9, 1968, 19770378/103, AN; Direction Générale de la Politique Industrielle, "Annexe II: La concentration des facteurs de production dans les unités locales de production," April 9, 1968, 19770378/103, AN, page 2.

[143] This shows the marginal increases to the rate of investment from firm size (bottom line) and the marginal gains in value added from firm size (top line). Both are measured per employee. Direction Générale de la Politique Industrielle, "Annexe IV: Taille et efficacité économque," April 9, 1968, 19770378/103, AN, Graphique 1.

Political Opposition within the New Policy Regime

Given the conflicting distributional consequences of corporate consolidation for certain interest groups, particularly labor and small business, one might expect strong political opposition. Opposition did exist, but it took place within the bounds defined by the new policy framework, only asking for minor side concessions while agreeing with the economic diagnosis presented by the policy's advocates. The *Conseil* noted that concentration policies were implemented without even consulting a range of interested parties, particularly labor.[144] Furthermore, even the wider business community did not agree with the policy, at least as far as politicians and bureaucrats perceived.

While labor was politically opposed—all labor organizations voted against concentration in the *Conseil*—but that opposition was on the premise that it did not do enough to ensure that *autofinancement* funds were used in line with the goals of the plan.[145] The representative from CGT-FO (*Confédération Générale du Travail-Force Ouvrière*), agreed with concentration but requested that an "antitrust" law be implemented along with it. The CFDT (*Confédération Française Démocratique du Travail*) complained that the government had not sufficient examined past experiences with concentration that had ended badly for labor. The CGT (*Confédération Générale du Travail*) suggested nationalizing the larger firms, though agreeing that larger firms were needed.[146] To the Planning Commission, the CFDT requested social insurance policies to ensure employment for displaced or redundant workers.[147] The CFTC (*Confédération Française des Travailleurs Chrétiens*) lobbied for active labor market policies as a side concession.[148]

Similar meetings were held to quell opposition from small and medium-sized enterprises (SMEs).[149] Industry groups complained that the new procurement policies were cutting out smaller suppliers,[150] yet the *Conseil*

[144] Emile Roche to Premier Ministre, January 12, 1967, 20090342/3, AN, page 2.

[145] Roche to Pompidou, May 11, 1967, 20090342/3, AN, page 4.

[146] Roche to Pompidou, January 12, 1967, 20090342/3, AN, page 3.

[147] CFDT, "Les conséquences sociales des concentrations, fusions, mutations dans l'industrie et le commerce," February 6, 1967, 81AJ/257, AN.

[148] Commissariat Général du Plan – Mission Conversion, Compte-rendu – Entretiens CFTC, January 31, 1967, 81AJ/257, AN.

[149] Commissariat Général du Plan – Mission Conversion, Compte-rendu – Entretiens Confédération Générale des Petites et Moyennes Entreprises, January 19, 1967, 81AJ/257, AN.

[150] Roche to Pompidou, January 12, 1967, 20090342/3, AN, page 3.

itself complained about the business attitudes of family firms opposed to concentration.[151]

Conclusion

This chapter has shown that concerns about investment, specifically brought on by a decline in profits from competition, were a central concern driving the shift toward anti-competition industrial policies and that the prior pro-competition policies of the late 1940s and 1950s were primarily responsible. This contrasts with some existing literature that often frames the postwar *trente glorieuses* as a time of institutional and policy stability, highlighting the central role of the state at the expense of market mechanisms and competition. The national champions policy of the 1960s is characterized either as a continuation of or an outgrowth of prior industrial policies, external market shocks, or technological requirements. A few points are worth emphasizing to conclude.

First, this case has shown that the early decades of the *dirigiste* state coexisted with a range of pro-competition policy priorities, with no perceived contradiction between the two. Even interventionist, statist institutions like price controls or nationalized industries can and have been used to pursue pro-competition market outcomes. As this book argues throughout, the question of state intervention is orthogonal to the question of competition versus market power.

Second, the case shows quite clearly that a decline in private investment, perceived as diminishing returns from decades of pro-competition policies, was the driving motivation for a reconstitution of market power. This was even at the known risk of creating economic rents and monopoly profits at the expense of domestic consumers and competitors. Whereas it would have been possible for promoters of the national champions policy to defend it exclusively by reference to technological needs for international market competitiveness, this chapter provides direct evidence they *explicitly knew* that their policy goals and tools were designed to create monopoly power domestically and significant market power internationally.

[151] M. Chapel to Commissariat Général du Plan, "Le Plan et les industries de transformation," undated memo, 19930277/115, AN. There were two similar memos under this same title. Both memos were written in 1965 or 1966, based on 1965 being referred to as immediately recent.

Third, this also provided supporting evidence in favor of the theory of learning and bureaucratic turnover. This shift in policy was mirrored by a shift in the senior staff and advisors around de Gaulle and the prime minister in this time. Those who favored industrial policy along the lines of the national champions policy, like Jean Dromer, François-Xavier Ortoli, Jean Saint-Geours, Michel Albert, and Alain Prate became substantially more influential in the years from 1964 to 1967 (Warlouzet 2011, 446–454), while established, pro-competition advisors and policymakers were either ignored or retired in the same time, such as Louis Franck (left the Price Directorate in 1962) or Jacques Rueff (ignored as the national champions policy was developed). Similarly, the technical advisors providing the economic and intellectual justifications for national champion policies showed up later, with Lionel Stoleru only starting to advise the Industrial Development Committee in 1967—shortly after finishing his PhD at Stanford—and moving to advise the prime minister in 1969. Pierre Massé, the planning commissioner, appears to have changed his mind on the issue, with his statement at the top of the chapter capturing the pro-competition mood of 1960. Yet as noted, he was among the first in 1961 to agree with the CNPF's assessments of private investment and pushed others overseeing the plan toward similar conclusions. And by October 1964, Massé was privately defending *autofinancement* to conservative legislator Louis Vallon.[152]

[152] Massé to Vallon, October 21, 1964, 19930276/2, AN.

5

Nixon, the Chicago School, and the Trust-Busting State

> Republican philosophy recognizes that competition regulates the economy.
>
> —Department of Justice, 1969[1]

> The free-traders, the trust-busters, and the rest of them make one hell of an argument . . . but in terms of our competition around the world, they sure, in my opinion, do not hold up. I just don't think that you can do it.
>
> —Richard Nixon, 1971[2]

The American pro-competition policy regime originating in the 1930s continued and deepened through the 1960s and 1970s, with progressively stricter merger enforcement, stronger *per se* bans on a range of anticompetitive practices, prohibitions on restrictive patent licensing, progressively more open trade policy, and the pro-competition deregulation of regulated industries like airlines or trucking. Then in the late 1970s and 1980s, the United States switched course to a market power policy regime that endured for four decades, shifting to favor a "consumer welfare standard" for antitrust, an approach developed by scholars from the Chicago school of antitrust. This resulted in a permissive environment for mergers of all kinds, a range of new procedural barriers to antitrust enforcement, and an elimination of most effective rules against anticompetitive vertical restraints. Along with this, intellectual property (IP) rights were expanded to legally protect processes and technologies previously un-patentable (e.g., biotechnologies, software, and silicon chip topography) and extended internationally into

[1] "Justice Department Enforcement of the Celler-Kefauver Anti-Merger Act - 1969," October 8, 1969, Business-Economics, Box 6, Central Files, RN, pages 9–10.

[2] CAB 52a, April 8, 1971, White House Tapes, RN, 58:35.

Monopoly Politics. Erik Peinert, Oxford University Press. © Oxford University Press (2025).
DOI: 10.1093/oso/9780197789506.003.0005

trade policy through the 1994 Trade-Related Aspects of Intellectual Property Rights (TRIPS) Agreement attached to the World Trade Organization (WTO).

This chapter argues that the diminishing returns to competition manifested in part as the international competitive pressures of the 1970s and 1980s, and that the shift away from pro-competition policy followed from early policy debates about these problems in the Nixon administration. The international pressure from open trade—combined with antitrust restrictions and uncertain IP protections—put corporate profits, employment, productivity growth, and the American technological edge in peril. Despite Nixon at first aggressively supporting existing antitrust and trade policies, executive reorganizations of the White House brought in new policymakers to key positions. The newly created Domestic Council elevated antitrust as a priority in 1970, and then Peter G. Peterson, the director of the newly formed Council on International Economic Policy, brought the administration's attention to the United States' lost economic dominance and the role of antitrust and technology policy in this decline. Despite some policymakers being constrained by their prior commitments to antitrust, following some uncommitted policymakers, the Nixon administration filled courts and administrative agencies with like-minded judges and bureaucrats, aiming to weaken antitrust enforcement. The subsequent presidencies—Ford, Carter, and Reagan—continued this trend in an uneven fashion. Each was presented with evidence and the costs of diminishing returns, but different subsets of each administration had committed to continuing with the pro-competition regime of the postwar period, resulting in policy change in fits and starts over the course of the 1970s.

This case is divided into two chapters for several reasons, with this chapter covering the Nixon administration and Chapter 6 covering the Ford, Carter, and Reagan administrations. First, these changes occurred in a complex and uneven pattern across four presidencies, each with their own internal politics, and the changes occurred in parallel with related developments in Congress, the federal courts, and the antitrust profession. Second, the gradual and uneven nature of changes to anti-competition policy show strong evidence in favor of the theory, as administrations like Ford show effectively how early commitments constrained later policy action. Third and lastly, unlike some of the other cases in this book, the causes of changes to antitrust policy in the 1970s are extensively studied and debated in and outside of academic research (Berman 2022; Eisner 1991; Hovenkamp 1985;

Khan 2018; Lancieri, Posner, and Zingales 2024; Lande 1982; Leslie 2014; Philippon 2019; Stoller 2019), and this book's argument is distinct from several established explanations.

By far the most common alternative explanation is that new economic ideas from the Chicago school of antitrust persuaded antitrust professionals, judges, and legislators on the merits of their arguments (Davies 2010; Ergen and Kohl 2019; Kovacic and Shapiro 2000; Pitofsky 2008). The Chicago school argued that postwar antitrust policy was incoherent and internally contradictory, ideologically opposed to large firms with no economic basis, and prohibited a number of efficient business practices.[3] This argument is supported by the fact that Chicago school scholars like Robert Bork were heavily cited in significant court decisions in favor of the consumer welfare standard,[4] that the antitrust agencies of the Reagan administration (1981–1989) were staffed with Chicago school advocates and academics, and that the consumer welfare standard is still today the dominant approach to antitrust policy. Scholars such as Eisner (1991) and Berman (2022) make related ideational arguments that the general diffusion of microeconomic expertise into the antitrust agencies was the main driver of policy change.

Another alternative argument sees these changes more as the result of partisanship and class interests in the form of business lobbying. At the end of the 1960s and the early 1970s, business interests and the American right perceived the federal government as excessively and dangerously interventionist (Blyth 2002; Hacker and Pierson 2010; Waterhouse 2013). Bringing a plethora of new regulations, many federal agencies were created in a few short years: the Environmental Protection Act (EPA), the Equal Employment Opportunity Commission (EEOC) in 1965, the Occupational Safety and Health Administration (OSHA) in 1971, and the Employee Benefits Security Administration in 1970. In this version, the Chicago school—along with the more general mobilization of business into a network of organized lobbies and think tanks—was an ideological cover for business elites to implement their preferred policies. Elinson (2015) extends this to argue that many of these general changes were driven by a shift in business's position within the Republican coalition. With differences in timing and emphasis on different policy changes, both Philippon (2019) and Lancieri, Posner,

[3] See, in particular, Bork (1978), Posner (1976), Posner (1979), and Easterbrook (1984) as examples of Chicago school antitrust thinking.

[4] See, for example, *Continental T.V. Inc. v. GTE Sylvania Inc.*, 433 U.S. 36 (1977) and *Reiter v. Sonotone Corp.*, 442 U.S. 330 (1979).

and Zingales (2024) argue that antitrust enforcement was scaled back by business lobbying.

Accordingly, this chapter first outlines the pro-competition policy regime of the time period and its development in the decades following World War II. Then, the chapter turns to a detailed case study of the Nixon administration. Despite some hesitance, Nixon's Department of Justice (DOJ) aggressively pursued antitrust enforcement at first. However, a major reorganization of the executive offices of the White House precipitated newer, noncommitted policymakers to push for change. New policymakers brought into newly created White House offices directed the administration's attention to the United States' lost economic dominance, leading Nixon to pursue a comprehensive antitrust review that reached anti-competition conclusions across the board. Despite recognizing the problem, the administration was constrained by its prior commitments to competition and antitrust, whereas Nixon's appointments to courts and key bureaucracies were successful in revising policy in favor of market power. The chapter then details many of the arguments regarding the influence of the Chicago school of antitrust, having shown how diminishing returns to competition played heavily in internal policy debates. Rather than a novel set of ideas that dramatically changed the terms of the debate, the Chicago school served more as a conveniently available set of legal interpretations to support the protectionist and anti-competition preferences of key members of the Nixon administration.

The Trust-Busting State

The pro-competition policy regime established in the 1940s deepened in the decades between then and Nixon's inauguration in 1969, with progressive extensions of antitrust rules, merger laws, restrictions on IP rights, and increasingly open trade policies internationally.

One of the most clear changes to antitrust was that beginning in the 1940s, antitrust policy established a wider range of *per se* bans on anticompetitive activity, meaning that a given practice was prohibited in any all circumstances.[5] This is in contrast to practices adjudicated under antitrust's "rule of reason" analysis, under which only "unreasonable" restraints of trade

[5] *Socony-Vacuum Oil* established a per se prohibition on direct price-fixing. *United States v. Socony-Vacuum Oil Co.*, 310 U.S. 150 (1940). 1947's *International Salt* banned tying the purchase of a separate product as a condition of a sale, which can eliminate competition for that second product.

would be deemed illegal, and which requires lengthy factual and theoretical analysis regarding the effects of a given practice.[6]

Congress implemented several legislative updates to strengthen antitrust law, enforcement, and procedures, such as the 1950 Celler-Kefauver Amendment to the Clayton Act and the 1962 Civil Process Act. The 1950 Celler-Kefauver Amendment completely overhauled merger policy, and successive court decisions gave force to the law. The 1962 *Brown Shoe* decision established a legal precedent against vertical mergers and established that a trend toward concentration is valid grounds to block a merger.[7] The 1963 *Philadelphia National Bank* decision established that a merger to over a 30 percent market share was presumptively illegal.[8] The 1966 *Von's Grocery* decision blocked a merger where the combined from would have only amounted to a 7.5 percent market share of the *regional* grocery market.[9] The first formalized merger guidelines in the United States were published under President Johnson in 1968,[10] which outlined levels of economic concentration that should draw government scrutiny based on horizontal, vertical, or conglomerate mergers.

This entire period was punctuated by several rounds of negotiations over the General Agreement on Tariffs and Trade (GATT), at a time when they were focused on clear pro-competition tariff reductions. The initial GATT was signed in 1947 and followed by the Annecy Round in 1949, the Torquay Round in 1951, the Geneva Round in 1955–1956, the Dillon Round in 1960–1962, and the Kennedy Round in 1964–1967. All of these were pro-competition, both in the sense that they removed direct tariff barriers and in that they were *intended* to substantively promote competition: most of the GATT agreements included language against restrictive business practices and anticompetitive behavior, parallel agreements were reached through the United Nations Conference on Trade and Development (UNCTAD), and the United States was known during the postwar era to scuttle some of these agreements when other countries had insufficient competition policies to accompany them (Sell 1998).

International Salt Co. v. United States, 332 U.S. 392 (1947). 1949's *Standard Stations* banned exclusive dealing. *Standard Oil Co. of California and Standard Stations, Inc. v. United States*, 337 U.S. 293 (1949). 1967's *Schwinn* decision per se banned territorial sales restrictions. *United States v. Arnold, Schwinn & Co.*, 388 U.S. 365 (1967).

[6] The 1911 *Standard Oil* cases established the rule of reason as a legal category, but per se prohibitions expanded in the 1940s through the 1960s.

[7] *Brown Shoe Co., Inc. v. United States*, 370 U.S. 294 (1962).

[8] *United States v. Philadelphia Nat'l Bank*, 374 U.S. 321 (1963).

[9] *United States v. Von's Grocery Co.*, 384 U.S. 270 (1966).

[10] United States Department of Justice, Merger Guidelines (1968).

Antitrust policy continued to place stronger restrictions on patents and patent licensing, given the role of patents and IP in maintaining temporary monopolies and following the World War II-era antitrust campaign against patents. Through a series of antitrust cases, US government forced lead firms to license out their most important patents to their competitors. For example, this was done with IBM with reference to most of their computer machinery (Chandler 2001) and AT&T with reference to semiconductors and any important telecommunications innovations (Gertner 2012), with both consent decrees finalized in 1956. This spurred technological diffusion but often also forced research-intensive industries to face direct price competition in technologies where they had only just commercialized a series of expensive investments.

Although defined by domestic policy, these antitrust rules, and the trade system within which they operated, defined much of how multinationals were allowed to behave globally during this period. Precedent for the World War II-era antitrust cases established extraterritorial jurisdiction for antitrust enforcement, constraining what market arrangements American companies could have with foreign firms abroad.[11] Most especially, antitrust rules about patent and brand licensing applied across borders, albeit with uncertain jurisdictional boundaries.

This web of pro-competition policies were intellectually encapsulated nicely by what was referred to as the "structuralist" or Harvard School of antitrust. During the postwar era, the economic models used to justify antitrust interventions were often in the form of the "structure-conduct-performance" (SCP) paradigm.[12] Gaining popularity among economists and policymakers immediately following World War II, SCP contended that market structure—and particularly the number of firms in a given industry—largely determined competitive conduct and market outcomes. Concentrated industries were more likely to collude, regardless of the specific nature of the relationships between the firms. In expanding this thinking, vertical restraints—where a firm uses contractual restrictions on the behavior of its suppliers, vendors, or other business partners—were viewed with nearly as much skepticism as horizontal restraints (where competitors in the same market collude or merge). The DOJ and the Federal Trade Commission (FTC) opposed almost any moves toward increased market

[11] See Fugate (1958) and Townsend (1980).

[12] SCP has its origins in Chamberlin (1933) and Robinson (1933), but came to represent a broad way of thinking about competition and antitrust policy during the postwar period.

concentration or anticompetitive business practices, and often they did not feel the need to look at the details of the underlying behavior or economic effects before establishing a presumption against a business practice or a merger.

That being said, despite global economic dominance at the end of World War II, by the 1960s and 1970s a range of American industries faced harsh competitive pressures, both domestically and from abroad. This at first began in a range of labor-intensive, lower-technology industries like textiles, but then progressively traditional smokestack industries like steel, automobiles, and chemicals were challenged by international and domestic competition. Many firms were pushed to the point of bankruptcy against foreign producers, with global demand falling well short of capacity. Eventually even the most advanced industries, such as semiconductors, struggled. In many of these cases, foreign firms from Western Europe and Japan had become particularly skilled at licensing and adapting American technologies—which American antitrust policies required that they be able to license—only to produce them at lower cost and re-import them into the United States.

The Nixon Administration

Accordingly, Nixon inherited a government strongly favoring competition across policy areas, but he also entered office at a turning point with two clear alternatives, represented by the competing Neal and Stigler Reports. The first was the 1969 Neal Report, written at the very end of the Johnson administration by a group of antitrust experts to make recommendations regarding possible changes to antitrust policy.[13] It followed the structuralist Harvard school of antitrust throughout, blaming concentration for inflation, higher consumer prices, and excess profits. It recommended further pro-competition reforms, including the repeal of the Miller-Tydings Act, a pro-competition deregulation of the regulated industries (the "little NRAs" from Chapter 3), revision of portions of the Robinson-Patman Act that arguably interfered with price competition, and the addition of new statutes to limit concentration.[14] Nixon appointed his own commission, headed by the Chicago school's George Stigler, to make its own recommendations on

[13] "Report of the White House Task Force on Antitrust Policy," May 27, 1969, 115 Cong. Rec. 11, 13890.

[14] There was a single dissent in the Neal Report, that of Robert Bork.

antitrust policy in competition with the Neal Report. The Stigler Report rejected nearly all the conclusions of the Neal Report and recommended many changes to scale back existing antitrust laws in the opposite direction.[15] However, the Stigler Report was practically never mentioned in any subsequent policy discussions in the White House.

Accounts of the Nixon administration are often conflicted between two seemingly contradictory perspectives. On the one hand, many accounts focus on the scandals and drama of Nixon and his inner circle, broadly ignoring the formal policymaking processes and decisions that progressed in parallel.[16] On the other hand, Nixon's tenure coincided with some of the largest transformations in the world economy, based on decisions made in the Nixon White House. The end of the Bretton Woods institutional order of fixed exchange rates, a dollar peg, and capital controls came crashing down as a result of some of these decisions, something that social scientists are hesitant to attribute to the contingencies of a paranoid, grudge-holding president.[17] This account primarily focuses on the formal policymaking process among key advisers who showed clear policy preferences, while taking into account the moments where personal politics appear to have shifted policy conversations.

The Early Years

In contrast to Nixon's clear pro-business biases and perceptions to the contrary, his administration at first aggressively pursued antitrust enforcement, both accepting the received wisdom of the structural paradigm and extending it to new areas. Nixon appointed William McLaren as assistant attorney general of antitrust as a matter of course in 1969, and McLaren quickly made a name for himself as an aggressive enforcer.[18] Whereas previous administrations had entirely avoided the issue of conglomerate mergers (where a firm acquires other companies in unrelated industries), McLaren filed a flurry of cases challenging them, with three cases filed in 1969 alone

[15] The competition between these two reports is well known, often seeing the Stigler Commission as immediately rebutting the conclusions of the Neal Report, ending the conversation now that a Republican was in office (Hovenkamp 2009).

[16] For example, see Perlstein (2014) and Summers (2000).

[17] For example, see Gowan (1999), Helleiner (1996), and Hudson (2003).

[18] McLaren was selected because he was competent in this area of the law, and the Nixon administration saw little reason to change it. See John Mitchell to Nixon, January 21, 1969, FG17, Box 2, Central Files, RN.

against ITT Corporation's attempted acquisitions of Canteen, Hartford Fire Insurance, and Grinell. The Neal Report, advocating for stronger antitrust policies, had been secret before McLaren himself released it in early 1969.[19]

These actions were backed up by White House and DOJ policy statements. In comments in March 1969, Nixon argued that the administration would be "pro-good business," meaning "business that promotes free competition," arguing that "good business competes on the basis of quality and service and price." By contrast, it would be "anti-bad business," meaning "business that harms the entire financial and commercial community by the restrictive concentration of power."[20] Justice Department statements echoed this: "Of course, no Administration expects to increase its popularity in business circles as the result of a vigorous antitrust enforcement program. Nevertheless, historically Republican administrations have been characterized by vigorous enforcement. Republican philosophy recognizes that competition regulates the economy."[21]

The antitrust fervor against patents in fact reached its height under Nixon, with McLaren opening a patent enforcement group within the Antitrust Division. A deputy to McLaren gave a well-known 1970 speech that outlined "nine no-no's" of patent licensing, listing a range of restrictions on patent licenses that the Antitrust Division thought illegal in all circumstances.[22] In short, the antitrust division saw restrictive patent licenses as a key component of monopoly. While this was not a formal policy statement, it nonetheless represented the sorts of cases that the division brought or expected to bring, based on cases it had recently won.

The Nixon administration trade policy reflected these priorities as well. Nixon's message to Congress in November 1969 regarding his trade bill was broadly in line with pro-competition priorities: "For the past 35 years,

[19] "Antitust: Secret Formula," *Time Magazine*, May 30, 1969, https://content.time.com/time/subscriber/article/0,33009,840151,00.html.

[20] William Safire, "Suggested Remarks for Business Council Dinner: Conglomerates and Bank Holding Companies," March 20, 1969, FG85, Box 1, Central Files, RN, page 1.

[21] "Justice Department Enforcement of the Celler-Kefauver Anti-Merger Act - 1969," October 8, 1969, Business-Economics, Box 6, Central Files, RN, pages 9–10.

[22] Bruce B. Wilson, deputy assistant attorney general, remarks before the Fourth New England Antitrust Conference, "Patent and Know-How License Agreements: Field of Use, Territorial, Price and Quantity Restrictions" (Nov. 6, 1970). The nine no-no's were (1) tying the purchase of unpatented materials as a condition of the license, (2) requiring the licensee to assign back subsequent patents, (3)restricting the right of the purchaser of the product in the resale of the product, (4) restricting the licensee's ability to deal in products outside the scope of the patent, (5) a licensor's agreement not to grant further licenses, (6) mandatory package licenses, (7) royalty provisions not reasonably related to the licensee's sales, (8) restrictions on a licensee's use of a product made by a patented process, and (9) minimum resale price provisions for the licensed products.

the United States has steadfastly pursued a policy of freer world trade. As a nation, we have recognized that competition cannot stop at the ocean's edge."[23] These goals were framed specifically in terms of *price* competition, with cost, productivity improvements, and consumer prices being at the fore.[24] With trade competition and job losses on the horizon, the public zeitgeist was turning in favor of protectionism, but the administration resisted these trends (Chorev 2007, 71–76).

The intersection of these antitrust rules, existing IP and technology policy, and open trade created a series of clear competitive difficulties that would come up repeatedly over the following decade. The United States was developing the most advanced technologies in most industries at the time, and these technologies were being patented in the United States. At the same time, antitrust rules often required that those technologies be freely licensed—for example, with the 1956 consent decree against AT&T—or would require that any licenses be relatively free of restrictions, as with the nine no-no's. As a result, American companies were licensing out their leading technologies to foreign competitors, who would then make improvements to the design or develop processes to make it cheaper than the American firm could. Then, despite having invested to make the technology in the first place, the original American manufacturer would face significant import competition from its own licensees. Business interests would complain to the Nixon administration that this transfer of US technology abroad was hurting US trade balances by having US technologies come back in the form of import competition.[25]

And the United States' trade balance with the rest of the world was still declining. Concerns about this began very early on, with the undersecretary of commerce complaining that European Community trade policies were hurting US business as the American trade surplus was shrinking.[26] In March 1969, Council of Economic Advisers (CEA) Chairman McCracken reported that the trade deficit for February was the largest on record: $362

[23] President Nixon Message to Congress, November 18, 1969, FG263, Box 1, Central Files, RN, page 1.

[24] Nixon elaborated: "We have always welcomed such competition. It promotes the economic development of the entire world to the mutual benefit of all, including our own consumers. It provides an additional stimulus to our own industry, agriculture and labor force. At the same time, however, it requires us to insist on fair competition among all countries." Ibid., page 1.

[25] Minutes of the First Meeting of the Commission on International Trade and Investment Policy, May 27, 1970, Box 1, FG263, Central Files, RN, page 4.

[26] Undersecretary of Commerce Memorandum to the President, "The Businessman's Concern over EEC Trade Policies," February 20, 1969, Business-Economics, Box 29, Central Files, RN.

million.[27] The main solutions proposed at this stage were minor tweaks: tax incentives for exports, export credits for private firms, and pressure for trading partners to remove tariffs abroad.[28]

As the same time, Nixon administration officials were acutely aware that profits declined in the late 1960s. Federal Reserve data noted in 1969 that non-utility businesses were cutting back capital spending.[29] Later that year, the Council of Economic Advisers reported that profits were flat in the first half of 1969 and dropped in the third quarter. Sales were down, with plant and equipment expenditures slowing down with them.[30]

Despite any of Nixon's own early hesitancies, advisers were successful at halting any serious changes to policy, often to Nixon's noticeable frustration. Shortly after taking office, an article in *Barron's* on conglomerates and mergers prompted Nixon to direct the attorney general to "keep a very close watch on [US trustbusters]. They tend, at times, to be anti-business professionals."[31] He later asked the CEA to look into conglomerate mergers, as Nixon had been informed of reasons to doubt the antitrust cases against them.[32] In September 1969, when Nixon asked that Assistant Attorney General McLaren and Attorney General Mitchell come up with a "new approach" for antitrust enforcement,[33] a simultaneous request was made for James Lynn, undersecretary of commerce, and Hendrik Houthakker of the CEA to look into it.[34] These inquiries focused exclusively on conglomerates and amounted to very little, with gaps of months to a year passing in the Nixon administration's early years with no follow-up or discussion.

Despite these early commitments to antitrust enforcement by the DOJ, more broadly the Nixon administration had very vague economic priorities of its own upon taking office. On July 3, 1969, William Safire suggested that the administration develop a clear economic program for itself, because "in the public mind, there is not clearly defined or readily *identifiable economic*

[27] This was admittedly inflated by a dock strike on the East Coast. Paul McCracken to the President, March 26, 1969, FG6-3, Box 58, Central Files, RN.

[28] Maurice Stans to the President, "Export Expansion," December 10, 1969, Box 62, Subject Files: Confidential Files, RN.

[29] Arthur F. Burns to the President, "Prospective Trend in Business Capital Spending," August 20, 1969, Box 29, Business-Economics, Central Files, RN.

[30] Ehrlichman to President, December 2, 1969, Box 59, Business-Economics, Central Files, RN.

[31] Alexander Butterfield to Mitchell, "Notes from the President," March 25, 1969, Box 6, Business-Economics, Central Files, RN.

[32] Ehrlichman to Burns, "Conglomerates," April 28, 1969, Box 62, Special Files: Egil Krogh, RN.

[33] Ken Cole to Ehrlichman, September 22, 1969, Box 7, Business-Economics, Central Files, RN.

[34] Ken Cole to Henry Cashen, "President's Request That We Develop a New Approach to the Antitrust Issue," October 6, 1969, Box 7, Business-Economics, Central Files, RN.

philosophy of the Nixon administration."[35] Suggestions like "growth economics" or "enterprise economics"[36] were passed around in response, but the proposals had little content, and the administration was without clear economic priorities.

Executive Reorganizations

A series of reorganizations of White House offices overcame this inertia. In April 1969, Nixon created the Ash Commission under Roy L. Ash to provide recommendations for White House organizational structure. Among the implemented recommendations was the creation of the Office of Management and Budget (OMB), the Domestic Council, and the Council on International Economic Policy (CIEP). The Domestic Council was to decide what policy should be, whereas the OMB focused on how to efficiently carry out those choices.[37] The CIEP did not began until 1971. These executive reorganizations moved uncommitted newer policymakers into more influential positions over these policy areas.

With the creation of the Domestic Council, antitrust revision very slowly began to gain momentum in the fall of 1970, even as interest among top officials was vague and their substantive opposition was still rather pronounced. As the issue arose, Peter Flanigan, Nixon's main economic aide, expressed several doubts about the wisdom of an antitrust study group, particularly in light of public antitrust pressures and commitments. Richard McLaren had a positive reputation as an antitrust enforcer, and he worried that "a White House antitrust policy study, if leaked, might be viewed as an attempt by special business interests to 'turn off the heat.'" Flanigan and others in the administration also questioned whether protectionist business interests even had a legitimate say in the policymaking process, noting, "Coming in the wake of an anticompetitive trade bill, any effort to reform or modify the antitrust laws might be overly influenced by strong anticompetitive interests."[38] The plan was still vague at this stage, conflicted between a broad

[35] Emphasis in original. Bill Safire to Nixon, "The 'Growth Economics' of the Nixon Administration," June 19, 1969, Box 2, Confidential Files: Subject Files, RN, page 1.

[36] Bert Cox to Paul McCracken, July 19, 1969, Box 2, Confidential Files: Subject Files, RN.

[37] Nixon Message to Congress on Executive Reorganizations, March 12, 1970, Box 1, FG6-16, Central Files, RN; Reorganization Plan No. 2 of 1970, March 12, 1970, Box 1, FG6-16, Central Files, RN.

[38] Flanigan to Ehrlichman, "DCSM #6 – Antitrust Policy Study," October 21, 1970, Box 6, Business-Economics, Central Files, RN, page 2.

review of antitrust in its entirety[39] and a very narrow review focused on specific technical issues. Staff Assistant James Loken argued that outside of reforming Robinson-Patman,[40] "the other likely issues for study are relatively minor." He asserted that "the central core of the antitrust laws in my opinion serves the country and the private enterprise system well," and the administration should focus its energy on "reforming unsound federal regulatory schemes less consistent with Republican philosophy than the antitrust laws."[41]

So in the fall of 1970, these advisers agreed only to create a small working group to discuss the possibility of opening a real review of the policy area, focusing on the relationship between international trade and antitrust. Most among these policymakers agreed that it would be controversial and of little benefit to do anything, as "any adverse economic impact of the antitrust laws is probably attributable to misguided enforcement and judicial interpretation rather than their content."[42] Peter Flanigan again brought up that they "should not ignore the possibility that businessmen may be wrong in suggesting that the anti-trust laws unduly hinder economic growth and efficiency."[43]

Parallel to this, beginning in mid-1970, the Department of Commerce, along with Senators Robert McLellan and Hugh Scott, pushed for a revision of US patent law, in particular the antitrust rules that restricted the terms of patent licensing such that anticompetitive vertical restraints could be included in patent licenses.[44] The DOJ strongly opposed this, and both agencies stood fast to their positions. Commerce, accusing the DOJ of seeking to minimize the value of patents, invoked "the freedom of the patentee

[39] The broad review would discuss whether there should be precise limits on size, whether anti-merger enforcement works, whether Robinson-Patman (an anti-price discrimination law from the 1930s) economically was counterproductive, how overall antitrust should relate to industry-specific industrial regulations, whether the FTC Act Section 5 sufficiently informed business of its consumer obligations, and whether the antitrust laws had been made obsolete by the existence and spread of multinational corporations. Ibid.

[40] The contentious Robinson-Patman Act prohibits sellers from offering different prices to different buyers, meant to prevent powerful retailers from extorting better terms than their smaller competitors.

[41] Emphasis in original. Loken to Flanigan, "Proposed Study of Antitrust Policies," October 15, 1970, Box 6, Business-Economics, Central Files, RN, page 2. John Ehrlichman, Nixon's top aide, shared these doubts. Ehrlichman to Cole, October 9, 1970, Box 6, Business-Economics, Central Files, RN.

[42] Memorandum, "Advisability of Full-Scale Antitrust Policy Study," November 1970, Box 2, FG6-15, Central Files, RN.

[43] Loken Memorandum for the Files, "Anti-Trust Policy Study," November 6, 1970, Box 6, Business-Economics, Central Files, RN.

[44] Eugene Cowen to Tod Hullin, June 3, 1970, Box 67, Business-Economics, Central Files, RN.

to select his licensees and establish his own terms for licensing others to use his invention,"[45]

The Nixon DOJ, in contrast, framed the problem entirely in terms of competition and the risk of monopoly if patent licensing rules were liberalized:

> The resulting unwarranted extension of monopoly power would promote industrial concentration, encourage privately administered prices, and thereby increase inflationary tendencies. . . . This legislative effort is contrary to free enterprise competition which is our fundamental national economic policy. It is contrary to the interests of business and consumers alike. The legislation would be viewed as an effort to favor vested interests and would reduce public confidence in the Administration's economic policies.[46]

The DOJ emphasized that the administration had already committed itself to a position on this issue, and changing course would put the administration "in the anomalous position of having recently brought cases in the courts against patent arrangements allegedly violating the antitrust laws and then shortly thereafter adopting legislative positions that might nullify those very cases."[47]

When the White House intervened later in 1970, Peter Flanigan requested that patent enforcement cases be paused until the administration reached a position on the issue,[48] which McLaren agreed to do.[49] No clear position was taken on the issue either way for years, and White House staff often admitted they did not entirely understand it.

The Ash Commission also led to the creation of the Council for International Economic Policy (CIEP) in January 1971. The CIEP was meant to be like the National Security Council for economic policy, gathering all the high-level stakeholders on foreign economic policy.[50] Peter G. Peterson was announced as executive director of CIEP, coming to the White House after a career as a corporate executive. Nixon had offered the job to George Stigler,

[45] James T. Lynn to George Shultz, August 20, 1970, Box 67, Business-Economics, Central Files, RN.

[46] Richard Kleindienst to Robert Mayo, June 5, 1970, Box 67, Business-Economics, Central Files, RN, page 3.

[47] Ibid.

[48] Flanigan to Arnie Weber, October 14, 1970, Box 67, Business-Economics, Central Files, RN; Flanigan to Weber, October 26, 1970, Box 67, Business-Economics, Central Files, RN.

[49] Weber to Flanigan, October 20, 1970, Box 67, Business-Economics, Central Files, RN.

[50] George Shultz to Nixon, January 11, 1971, Box 1, FG6-20, Central Files, RN.

who turned it down,[51] before selecting Peterson.[52] Peterson met with Nixon and White House staff to discuss his possible appointment for the first time on January 5.[53]

The Domestic Council progressed on the antitrust question. In February 1971, Nixon created a Domestic Council Committee on Antitrust Policy, consisting of the cabinet members from the relevant agencies: Commerce, Treasury, Labor, the OMB, and the CEA.[54] Early back-and-forth over McLaren's proposed review shows Peterson (CIEP) and Lynn (Department of Commerce) asking probing questions about international competitiveness, with McLaren dismissing their points and prioritizing competition.[55]

These reorganizations did not appear to be politically motivated, as actually getting the new organizations running was a slow, arduous process with little to no specific agenda. The first Domestic Council meeting was set for July 10, 1970, then canceled and moved, at which point some advisers tried to cancel it again.[56] Early Domestic Council meetings were devoted to procedural issues with no policy agenda.[57] An early summary of Domestic Council projects focused on aging, health, drugs, and transportation policy.[58] The administrative arrangements for the new CIEP were disorganized in December 1970,[59] as White House Staff were still arguing over the type of person to hire as executive director.[60]

[51] Shultz Memorandum for the President's File, December 17, 1970, Box 80, Special Files: President's Office Files, RN.

[52] The earliest appearance of Peterson in White House records is a note to Ehrlichman on December 24, 1970, when he was still president of Bell & Howell, proposing an advisory board of philanthropic policy. Hullin to Ray Price, December 31, 1970, Box 58, Special Files: John Ehrlichman, RN.

[53] Shultz to Nixon, "Meeting with Mr. Peter Peterson," Box 1, FG6-20, Central Files, RN. However, Safire (1975, 497–8) suggests that Peterson's influence on Nixon preceded this, in 1970, but based on the content of Safire's account, and in comparison to Peterson's own account (Peterson 2009), this appears to be a typographic error.

[54] Domestic Council Study Memorandum #12, "Antitrust Policy," February 19, 1971, Box 58, Special Files: John Ehrlichman, RN.

[55] Antitrust Division Comments on Questions of James T. Lynn, Peter G. Peterson, Peter G. Peterson, Hendrik S. Houthakker, and Samuel R. Pierce, Kr., Box 1, Special Files: Peter Flanigan, RN.

[56] One adviser even commented at this point, "Is there really a Domestic Affairs Council? Are they going to meet?" Dwight Chapin to Ken Cole, July 10, 1970, Box 1, FG6-15, Central Files, RN.

[57] Memorandum for the President, Domestic Council Meeting, July 21, 1971, Box 1, FG6-15, Central Files, RN.

[58] Kenneth Cole to Domestic Council, October 19, 1970, Box 1, FG6-15, Central Files, RN.

[59] John Brown to Haldeman, December 1, 1970, Box 1, FG6-20, Central Files, RN; C. Fred Bergsten Memorandum, December 9, 1970, Box 2, FG302, Central Files, RN.

[60] Haldeman to Brown, "Committee on International Economic Policy," December 10, 1970, Box 1, FG6-20, Central Files, RN.

The April Briefing

The first meeting of the CIEP was held on April 8, 1971, at which Peter Peterson shocked Nixon and much of his cabinet with a simple slide presentation that showed that the era of unchallenged American economic dominance was over. Other countries had caught up to the United States by unfairly free-riding on the GATT trade regime and were using industrial policies to bolster their export industries, with the subtext being that the United States needed to take a tougher line. The conversation took an unplanned turn into issues of antitrust when the conversation turned to zaibatsu and Japanese industrial organization generally.

The primary point of concern was the declining balance of trade of the United States. While the US economy remained strong, inadequate increases in productivity, excess inflation, and the breakdown of international monetary adjustment mechanisms had put a strain on the United States' position as the trade balance turned against it. Peterson's presentation ran through a number of industries one by one, highlighting the ones where the United States was being caught by the competition and the ones where it remained at a significant competitive advantage. While the United States remained competitive even in agriculture, it was being caught in low-tech manufacturing, commodities, and other non-differentiable goods, whereas it was retaining a significant surplus in "technology-intensive" products (Figure 5.1).

Direct trade protectionism was immediately rejected as a policy option. While imports from foreign competitors were a key dimension of the problem, Peterson emphasized that many American firms were earning substantial fractions of their income from licensing their technology abroad.[61] Certain categories of high-technology sectors were the main places where the United States maintained a significant advantage over the rest of the world, and royalties and license fees from these technologies were a sizable portion of American export earnings at the time, as shown in Figure 5.2 (Peterson 1971b). On this very point, looking at the figures of American-owned investments abroad, one member in attendance cut in with the epiphany that this was "a major reason we can't do isolationism."[62]

More centrally, however, the conversation turned to antitrust a few minutes later. As it was the first foreign country to reach and then surpass trade

[61] CAB 52a, April 8, 1971, White House Tapes, RN, 36:30.
[62] CAB 52a, April 8, 1971, White House Tapes, RN, 37:50.

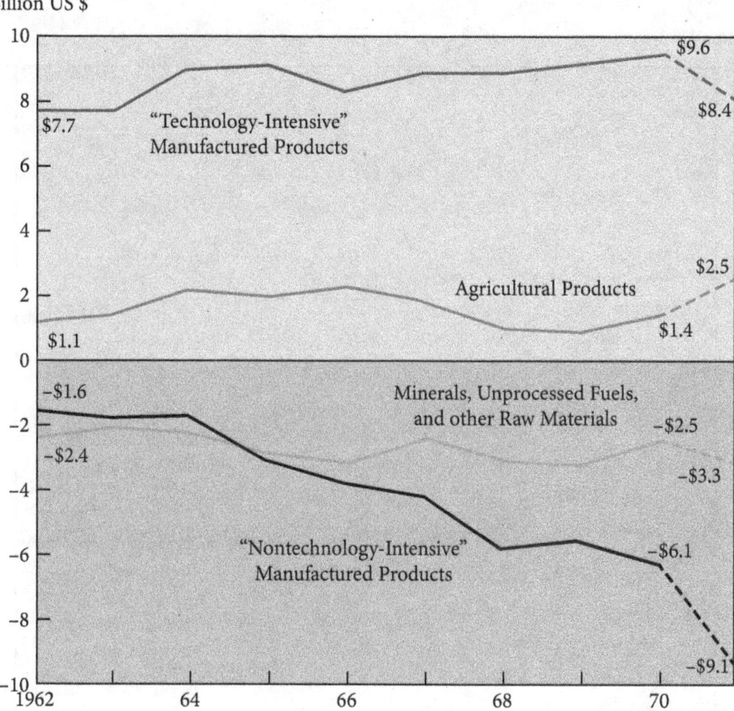

Figure 5.1 Chart 25 from Peterson's Presentation (Peterson 1971b)

parity with the United States in 1964 (Figure 5.3), Japan was a key topic of discussion. More importantly, Japan was beginning to challenge US positions even in these high-technology sectors, whereas Western Europe was a fair ways behind the United States in these areas (Peterson 1971b, 20). Peterson and others characterized Japanese industry as free-riding off of American investments, since they would invest very little in R&D compared to the United States and opt to simply license the technology from American firms (Peterson 1971b, 65).[63]

When Peterson made reference to the Japanese zaibatsu, and that they far out-scaled any of the conglomerates that domestic US antitrust authorities were contemporaneously trying to block, Nixon himself cut in:

[63] Japan had turned to the "cheap" path of R&D by simply using US technologies. CAB 52a, April 8, 1971, White House Tapes, RN, 47:25.

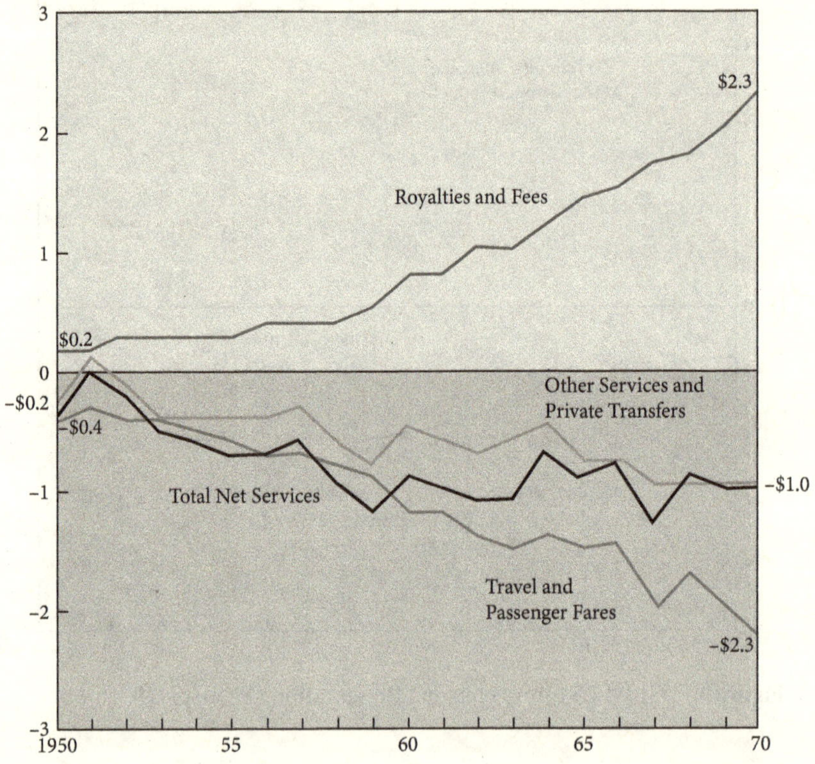

Figure 5.2 Chart 45 from Peterson's Presentation (Peterson 1971b)

> You know it's the old argument, cartelism, conglomerates, and so forth, versus the traditional Justice Department argument, that you know, that you kick big business because, only because it's big, not because it's bad. You know, this is a very fundamental point. It's a very fundamental point, and it's something that shouldn't be limited to this Council, it's something that's also in the Domestic Council. But, I think it has to be discussed.... Bill [Rogers] of course has been through it before, but I have some strong convictions, John [Connally] and I, think that our whole attitude here, that the Antitrust Division of the Justice Department is acting just like it used to act when the Sherman Act was passed, and the world has changed. The situation has changed.[64]

[64] Ibid., RN, 52:20.

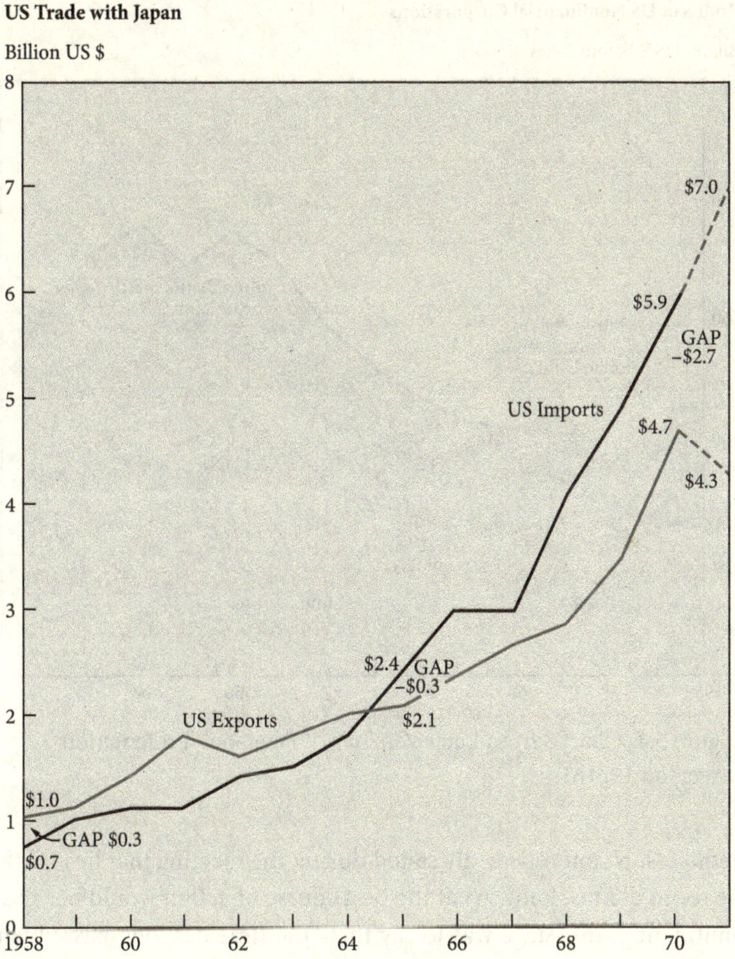

Figure 5.3 Chart 31 from Peterson's Presentation (Peterson 1971b)

Amid the conversation, Nixon elaborated that foreign competition was the main concern behind his reasoning:

> The antitrust thing, and frankly I don't know the answer, the free-traders, the trust-busters, and the rest of them make one hell of an argument that all the arguments against cartelization, conglomerates and so forth and so on, still stand, but in terms of our competition around the world, they sure, in my opinion, do not hold up. I just don't think that you can do it.[65]

[65] Ibid., 58:35.

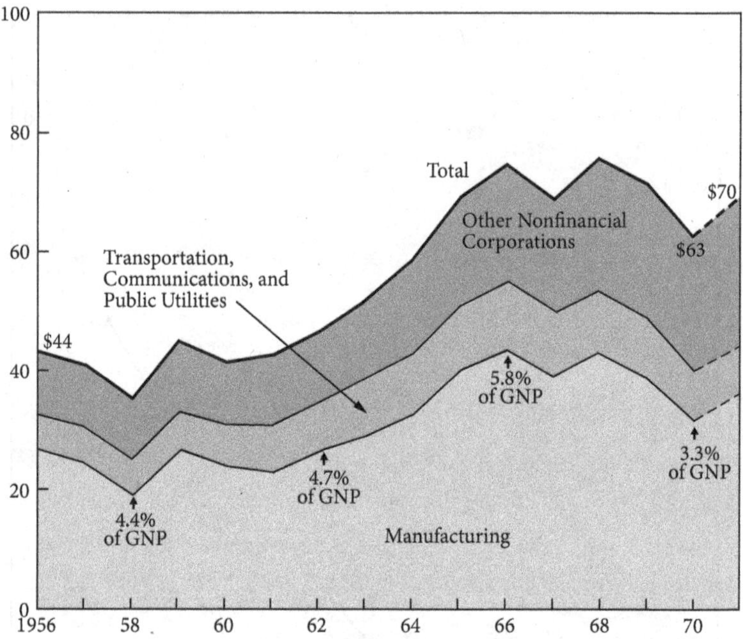

Figure 5.4 Chart 8 from Later Versions of Peterson's Presentation (Peterson 1971b)

Nonetheless, Nixon repeatedly stated during the meeting that he and those in the room did not know what the best course of action would be, and his commitment at this stage was to say that "the time has long passed where we've *got* to have a study of this antitrust thing."[66] Even without a position, Nixon himself simplified the issue to a choice between concentration versus competition.

Nonetheless, while later iterations of Peterson's presentation highlighted lagging profits as a core aspect of the problem (see Figure 5.4), the original April 8 briefing did not.[67] Profits had, nonetheless, been falling. According to Brenner (2006, 101), the rate of profit in the United States declined from 40.9 percent to 29.3 percent between 1965 and 1973. So the *rate* of profit may have been declining markedly, something Peterson himself did emphasize,

[66] Ibid., 1:01:50. Verbal emphasis in original.
[67] Compare CAB 52a, April 8, 1971, White House Tapes, RN with Peterson 1971a, 1971b.

but gross profits had no long-term trend of doing so. By contrast, disparities in investment between the United States and others were rather clear. Japan reinvested 39 percent of its GNP—despite ostensibly free-riding off of American R&D—relative to the United States' 18 percent, while most European countries invested about 10 percent more than the United States (Peterson 1971b, 4). The decline in profits at this time was a well-known and frequently debated issue among economists (Nordhaus 1974).

While Peterson's presentation was simply descriptive information, it pushed a chain of related policy conversations toward antitrust and competition policies. Desk notes from one aide who missed the briefing indicated that the primary takeaways relayed to him were "anti-trust" and "cartels."[68] A different aide retrospectively commented that "Peter Peterson's greatest and best known achievement is probably his chart presentation, which alerted the President, or rather focused him within a systematic analytical framework on a new fact of life—that the United States' economic supremacy was gone."[69]

The Nixon administration's general relation to business appears to have shifted at this time.[70] A few short days after, when meeting with Commerce Department representatives, Nixon interrupted to tell them that he had made his own aide, Peter Flanigan, the point person for business matters, with priorities to "cool the activities" in the antitrust area, prevent business from being the "whipping-boy" on environmental issues, to "take it easy" on "good" businesses, and handle IRS rulings in a "pro-business approach."[71]

For the remainder of the year, Peterson would give this briefing throughout Washington, DC.[72] Peterson, at the president's request, gave this briefing to the Chamber of Commerce, the AFL-CIO, and the Business Council.[73]

[68] John Ehrlichman Desk Notes, April 8, 1971, Box 5, Special Files: John Ehrlichman, RN.

[69] George Crawford to Peter Flanigan, January 27, 1972, Box 2, FG6-20, Central Files, RN.

[70] Elinson (2015, 54).

[71] Haldeman Memorandum for the President's File, April 12, 1971, Box 81, Special Files: President's Office Files, RN, pages 1–2.

[72] Flanigan Memorandum for the President's File, May 6, 1971, Box 81, Special Files: President's Office Files, RN; Ken Cole to Peterson, April 29, 1971, Box 51, FG6-11, Central Files, RN; Mike Johnson to the President's File, "Bipartisan Congressional Briefing," June 8, 1971, Box 82, Special Files: President's Office Files, RN; Mike Johnson to the President's File, "Bipartisan Senate Briefing, July 22, 1971, Box 82, Special Files: President's Office Files, RN.

[73] Peter G. Peterson, Draft Briefing, "The United States in the Changing World Economy," June 30, 1971, Box 17, Special Files: Subject Files, RN, page 2.

The Antitrust Revision Process

During the summer and fall of 1971, the antitrust working group reviewed a combination of what policy changes they wanted, what obstacles they faced, what their political strategy should be, and what concessions should be made. This review was undertaken entirely within these new executive offices, primarily the Domestic Council and the CIEP. Review over that summer covered nearly every issue related to competition: conglomerate mergers, foreign commerce, joint research and development ventures, failing company defense, reciprocity, territorial exclusives and franchises, patent procurement and licensing, price discrimination, oligopoly, vertical mergers, horizontal mergers, the regulated industries, and resale price maintenance. By 1972, the discussions had come to resemble a full-fledged agenda to revise antitrust policies in an anti-competition direction. Nonetheless, internal debates reveal that Nixon officials felt deeply constrained from contradicting their earlier policy commitments on patents, conglomerate mergers, and antitrust generally, considering instead less-visible approaches to policy change.

A few months later, John Ehrlichman met with Nixon to consolidate a more expansive antitrust review.[74] Throughout the meeting, Nixon indicated that politics were his primary short-term motivator:

- "I don't think there's any significant politics in it for us to be out there trustbusting. I think on the other hand that moving into this area could be extremely . . . could cause irritation among our business community friends at this time."[75]
- "I'd just as soon not give [business] any trouble between now and the [1972] election."[76]

In addition, they discussed the antitrust case against ITT, which later turned into a major scandal for the Nixon administration, which was accused of

[74] Ehrlichman had learned that Arthur Burns at the Federal Reserve was working on antitrust proposals and wanted to ensure McLaren's cooperation in the short run: "The Fed's project should be suspended for now. We will be studying cartels and foreign trade shortly in the Council on International Economic Policy. We can start it up again then. But right now the Fed getting into this seriously threatens to scare McLaren off our Domestic Council project (getting him to set out Administration anti-trust policy, in writing). That may sound silly, but I'm convinced McLaren's belief that Arthur is about to make conservative recommendations will cause McLaren to be less candid in his work with us. We will, thereby, end up with less ammunition." John Ehrlichman to Nixon, "Anti-Trust Policy," April 28, 1971, Box 59, Special Files: John Ehrlichman, RN.

[75] OVAL 497-9, May 11, 1971, White House Tapes, RN, 43:00.

[76] Ibid., 55:00.

soliciting a bribe from ITT to drop the case. There is strong evidence to support such accusations. After McLaren brought the case to trial, the White House complained to the DOJ that this put them in an "awkward" position because of "assurances" they had given the company about those cases.[77] Despite the political decision to slow down the filing of major antitrust cases, Nixon himself can be heard saying, "On the merits, I'm just not sure we ought to cool the antitrust, on the merits."[78]

The formal review was kick-started by a follow-up meeting with Peterson in late May.[79] Nonetheless, the content of the proposals reached by these review groups were anti-competition across the board, meant to either protect dominant American firms from competition, give them advantages over competitors, or allow them to use their position to control other firms. A summary of policy options toward the end of the summer considered conglomerate mergers, foreign commerce, joint research and development ventures, failing company defense, reciprocity, territorial exclusives (franchises), patent procurement and licensing, price discrimination, oligopoly, vertical mergers, horizontal mergers, competition in regulated industries, and resale price maintenance.[80] In nearly every one of these areas, the most pro-competition option considered was to change nothing, and the remainder of the options were to substantially weaken enforcement policies and to permit or encourage certain anticompetitive behaviors.

Business was ignored, excluded from, or subordinated to these discussions throughout this entire process. Officials still regarded business interests with skepticism, with internal correspondence frequently referring to a "lack of consensus within the Administration" regarding antitrust.[81] James Loken wrote that for all their complaining, businesspeople did not offer many details about what was wrong with foreign antitrust policies relative to competitiveness.[82] While noting that they needed to say something publicly, Egil Krogh wrote in June, "We should not tip our hand to the business community with regard to the antitrust laws."[83]

[77] Ehrlichman notes that the case was on the basis of "largeness" and should not be pursued. Ehrlichman to Mitchell, "Re: The United States vs. ITT," September 17, 1970, Box 38, Confidential Files: Subject Files, RN.

[78] OVAL 497-9, May 11, 1971, White House Tapes, RN, 56:55.

[79] John Ehrlichman Desk Notes, May 28, 1971, Box 5, Special Files: John Ehrlichman, RN. Richard Nordahl, "Antitrust Policy Review," Undated Memorandum, Box 19, Special Files: John Ehrlichman, RN.

[80] Engman to Ehrlichman, "Antitrust Policy Review," September 1, 1971, Box 19, Special Files: John Ehrlichman, RN.

[81] Lewis Engman to John Ehrlichman, "Antitrust Policy Review," September 1, 1971, Box 19, Special Files: John Ehrlichman, RN, page 2.

[82] Loken to Flanigan, May 10, 1971, Box 48, FO4-3, Central Files, RN.

[83] Crawford to Krogh, June 14, 1971, Box 6, Business-Economics, Central Files, RN.

Nixon officials were aware that this was politically unpopular among the general public or even business groups. With respect to the public, the review group warned that "such changes could be interpreted as 'weakening' the antitrust laws."[84] The fear of being criticized as too favorable to big business was mentioned throughout, but also that most individual companies and industries would have substantive problems with almost all of the specific plans that they had.[85] Existing antitrust rules, with both their anti-competition and pro-competition features, had created their own constituencies around them, across most major interest groups: "This kind of major initiative would be attacked as pro-business. Moreover, it would have to be balanced and objective and thus would inevitably gore special business interests (oligopolies like oligopoly pricing, labor likes its exemption, small business likes Robinson-Patman and resale price maintenance, etc.). And I doubt that antitrust reform would generate widespread interest and support from the general public."[86]

Having committed to it early on, the administration was hesitant to change their position on antitrust policy. Some advisers pointed back to early speeches and commitments to conglomerate merger policy as making it difficult to change—for example, noting that the attorney general had already publicly targeted conglomerates as a source of economic concentration in a June 1969 speech.[87] Changing policy against reciprocal buying would be a "repudiation of a key McLaren policy supported heretofore by the Attorney General."[88] Changes to territorial franchise restrictions would be limited because "any toning down of opposition to territorial restrictions would be a reversal of the cumulative policies of this and recent administrations."[89]

Political options were constrained even further. Simply relying on executive authority—"reversing the Antitrust Division's traditional independence and on persuading key FTC personnel to follow administration economic

[84] Lewis Engman to John Ehrlichman, "Antitrust Policy Review," September 1, 1971, Box 19, Special Files: John Ehrlichman, RN, page 3.

[85] Richard Nordahl, "Antitrust Policy Review," Undated Memorandum, Box 19, Special Files: John Ehrlichman, RN.

[86] Loken to Ehrlichman, "Antitrust Policy Study," August 20, 1971, Box 19, Special Files: John Ehrlichman, RN, page 4.

[87] Richard Nordahl, "Antitrust Policy Review: Conglomerate Mergers," Undated Memorandum, Box 19, Special Files: John Ehrlichman, RN.

[88] Richard Nordahl, "Antitrust Policy Review: Reciprocity," Undated Memorandum, Box 19, Special Files: John Ehrlichman, RN.

[89] Richard Nordahl, "Antitrust Policy Review: Territorial Exclusives (Franchises)," Undated Memorandum, Box 19, Special Files: John Ehrlichman, RN.

policies"—was recognized as a risk because of "adverse publicity caused by leaks, and perhaps by resignations"[90]

Legislative possibilities were already ruled out by anticipated popular opposition, but they did foresee ways to link antitrust to broader international economic problems to motivate wider support, and they did view the question in an overtly protectionist frame:

> Adequate protection of U.S. industries abroad may necessitate a fresh look at antitrust and foreign commerce, plus realistic merger policies. And ensuring the U.S. lead in new technology may require reasonable incentives through patent licensing.[91]

Legislation would only be possible if it were sold in a particular way. Loken continued, "I do not believe legislation shrinking the antitrust laws can be obtained unless it is presented as part of a sweeping Presidential program regarding 'Competition in the 70's' which would tie antitrust initiatives (legislative and otherwise) to broader economic goals."[92] So, even though built-in constituencies favored existing rules of various forms, linking those rules or policies to broader economic problems was one way to de-legitimize them.

Beginning to form the political messaging that would go with later, more successful antitrust reforms, Engman focused on more technical wedge issues that could be sold publicly but would be unlikely to provoke outrage, since they would not raise typical populist antitrust fears, such as limiting extraterritorial antitrust, permitting joint R&D ventures, and revising patent licensing rules. These issues are very low-salience to the electorate and to nonspecialists, and Engman suggested linking them to the broader issue of competitiveness, framing the new policies "as being designed to enable us to compete more effectively in the world under the rapidly changing conditions of the 1970's and 1980's."[93]

Despite all of these general anti-competition view, and aware of the political scrutiny they would likely face for potentially trying to scale back antitrust enforcement, Nixon's group still sought strong enforcement against

[90] Loken to Ehrlichman, "Antitrust Policy Study," August 20, 1971, Box 19, Special Files: John Ehrlichman, RN, page 2.

[91] Ibid., page 4.

[92] Ibid., page 4.

[93] Lewis Engman to John Ehrlichman, "Antitrust Policy Review," September 1, 1971, Box 19, Special Files: John Ehrlichman, RN, page 3.

direct, horizontal price-fixing. While they voiced agreement with the policy in substance, the *motivation* was entirely political:

> As a counterpart to any changes in the direction of specific areas of antitrust enforcement policy, whether publicly announced or internally generated, it may be advisable to also include strengthening elements to antitrust enforcement in the areas where there is general agreement as to the need for strong action, for example: Endorsement of a vigorous policy against conspiracies to fix prices, allocate territories, or suppress innovation.[94]

The opposition to horizontal collusion appears important primarily as a political counterbalance to hide or obfuscate the real priority: overt weakening of competition in almost every other area. Horizontal cartel policy was not discussed by the Nixon White House other than in the face of this political consideration.

This review was capped off by McLaren's removal from the top antitrust position at the DOJ, to be replaced with someone more willing to take the administration's direction on antitrust. He resigned in January 1972, nominated to be a federal judge in Illinois.[95] When discussing various options for who to replace him, Peter Flanigan wrote that any nominee would need to "understand the disquiet caused by the Anti-Trust Division in the past and our desire to remedy it during the coming year."[96] Thomas Kauper, McLaren's replacement for the assistant attorney general position, was nominated in June 1972.[97] McLaren was hired largely on autopilot in 1969, but he was removed for clear policy reasons.

Second Term Efforts

Based on these learned anti-competition beliefs, the Nixon administration made two legislative efforts to amend the rules around antitrust and competition in its second term: (a) a push for a major overhaul of the US patent system and (b) antitrust reforms to be inserted into the administration's trade bill.

[94] Ibid., page 4.
[95] Nixon to McLaren, February 1, 1972, Box 11, FG17, Central Files, RN.
[96] Flanigan to Mitchell, December 27, 1971, Box 19, Confidential Files: Subject Files, RN.
[97] Kingsley to Nixon, "Nominations in the Department of Justice," June 9, 1972, Box 2, FG17, Central Files, RN.

Continuing on from the Department of Commerce's efforts from the summer of 1970, the administration made several efforts for a general rewriting of the US patent code, with the antitrust rules around patent licensing as the main target. Plans among this same group of advisers—Peter Flanigan, Jim Loken, and John Ehrlichman—began in early 1972.[98] The business lobby that had pushed the issue along with the Department of Commerce in 1970 felt that the administration had been sitting on the fence about the issue for too long,[99] with that lobby also clear that "what is at issue is the ability of a patent holder to maximize his profits through licensing agreements which would ordinarily run afoul of our antitrust laws."[100] In late 1973, the administration had finally submitted a bill for general patent reform,[101] but this died in the Senate in 1974, particularly as Watergate continued to occupy the White House and the rest of Washington.

The Nixon administration also attempted to insert proposals for antitrust reform into its trade bill, developed under Nixon but signed by Ford. One priority being sought was to expand the Webb-Pomerene Act, an exemption from antitrust for export associations, with the goal of assisting with export competitiveness. In April 1973, as the White House was submitting their bill to Congress, an aide noted that the Webb-Pomerene amendments should be included in the trade bill, "with these antitrust provisions being treated for all practical purposes as a part of that bill."[102] However, very minimal changes made it into the final law. Commerce had simultaneously sought to add a provision to "provide antitrust immunity for activities designed to restrict or control the transfer from the United States of technology, information and knowledge" as a way of "promoting R&D development in the U.S. and resultant exports,"[103] though this provision was not added.

Despite the failure to change the antitrust rules related to US trade policy, the final law was far more restrictive than previous trade bills. The Trade Act of 1974 included a number of provisions meant to counteract the unfair trade practices of foreign countries, namely countervailing duties

[98] Flanigan to Ehrlichman, February 4, 1972, Box 67, Business-Economics, Central Files, RN.

[99] McClellan and Scott to Nixon, September 21, 1972, Box 67, Business-Economics, Central Files, RN.

[100] Shepard to Bush, July 15, 1973, Box 67, Business-Economics, Central Files, RN.

[101] Brooks to McClellan and Brooks to Scott, April 8, 1974, Box 68, Business-Economics, Central Files, RN.

[102] Gunning to Flanigan, "International Antitrust Bill for Trade Package," April 3, 1973, Box 6, Business-Economics, Central Files, RN.

[103] Flanigan to Letson, "Antitrust Immunity for Private Restraints on Technology Transfer," June 8, 1973, Box 6, Business-Economics, RN.

under Section 301, used to punish foreign trade practice for insufficient IP rights or unfair export systems.

While Nixon's administration was constrained by a combination of its own prior commitments and public opposition, its main victory was in the courts. In total, Nixon appointed four justices to the Supreme Court: Warren E. Burger, Harry Blackmun, Lewis Powell, and William Rehnquist. The first two of these were made prior to the administration's internal debates and learning in 1971, and such appointments are rarely, if ever, made on the basis of the nominee's opinions on antitrust specifically. That being said, the latter two appointments were likely chosen at least somewhat for their favorable attitudes toward big business, and as or after these events took place. In 1971, shortly before his nomination, Lewis Powell had written a now well-known memo for the Chamber of Commerce, "Attack on the American Free Enterprise System," discussing how the United States had become hostile to big business and outlining a strategy for conservative big business to push back (Powell 1971). He was confirmed to the Court in December 1971, at approximately the same time as Rehnquist.

Regardless of the more general motivations for their nomination, these appointments began changing the stance of antitrust immediately. The first notable rollback of strict 1960s merger policy was made with the Supreme Court's *General Dynamics* decision in March 1974. While viewed as relatively inconsequential at the time, this decision created the "weakened competitor" defense to make mergers easier.[104] The decision was five-four, with four of the five justices allowing the merger being Nixon's four appointments. The case has, nonetheless, been followed up with a chain of decisions making mergers easier more broadly.[105]

Staffing and agency appointments during this second term decisions had a mixed degree of impact. The core antitrust appointments that Nixon had made—Lewis Engman as chair of the FTC and Thomas Kauper as assistant attorney general for antitrust—were also kept in their respective positions through the Ford administration. However, in those roles, as will

[104] Under this defense, if one company can claim that it is unable to effectively continue to compete in the market into the future, the merger itself will not reduce competition and therefore is legal under the Clayton Act. The case itself dealt with two coal companies intending to merge. One of the company's coal reserves were low and already committed to long-term contracts with utility companies. Arguing it would thus not be able to bid competitively on any future contracts, the merger arguably would not reduce competition. *United States v. General Dynamics Corp.*, 415 U.S. 486 (1974).

[105] *United States v. International Harvester Co.*, 564 F.2d 769 (7th Cir. 1977); *Kaiser Aluminum Chemical Corp. v. F.T.C.*, 652 F.2d 1324 (7th Cir. 1981), and *Federal Trade Commission v. Arch Coal, Inc.*, 329 F. Supp. 2d 109 (D.D.C. 2004).

be seen below, they primarily made bureaucratic reforms or helped the Ford administration with pro-competition deregulation. Nonetheless, both Kauper at the DOJ and Engman at the FTC professionalized agency staff into industrial organization economics—to screen enforcement choices through economic analysis rather than to enforce straightforward violations of the law—which had the effect of greatly reducing the degree of antitrust enforcement in many categories.[106] Collectively, the result was to limit overall antitrust enforcement, paring it back to focus almost exclusively on direct price-fixing and adding a range of procedural barriers to enforcement of any kind.

The Chicago Critique and Consumer Welfare

At the same time, the Chicago school of antitrust had been rising as an intellectual response in the background of these discussions in the Nixon administration. The Chicago school of economics more generally is particularly associated with Milton Friedman and George Stigler's views on Keynesian macroeconomics and the regulatory state, whereas the Chicago school of antitrust represented parallel but more specific and nuanced arguments about competition and specific business practices, mainly associated with figures like Robert Bork, Richard Posner, and Frank Easterbrook. Their views came to be accepted by the federal courts and antitrust enforcement agencies, and therefore many argue that new economic ideas from the Chicago school led to the decline of antitrust enforcement in the United States (Davies 2010; Ergen and Kohl 2019; Kovacic and Shapiro 2000; Pitofsky 2008). This section argues that to the degree that the shift and scaling back of antitrust policy was carried out through the acceptance of Chicago school ideas, this occurred through a process of diminishing returns, learning, and a shift to favoring unambiguously anticompetitive policy proposals.

The Consumer Welfare Standard and the Success of Ideas?

In terms of the substance of their ideas, Chicago school figures emphasized that antitrust should follow a "consumer welfare standard," principally articulated by Robert Bork, author of *The Antitrust Paradox* (Bork 1978).

[106] Berman (2022) and Eisner (1991, 170).

Bork argued that "(1) The only legitimate goal of American antitrust law is the maximization of consumer welfare; therefore (2) 'Competition,' for purposes of antitrust analysis, must be understood as a term of art signifying any state of affairs in which consumer welfare cannot be increased via judicial decree" (Bork 1978, 51). Bork claimed that "surely, on the face of it, this meaning is consistent with everyday speech" (Bork 1978, 61), but this definition of competition is distinct from many of the everyday meanings of competition, whether understood as business rivalry, price competition, profit maximization, or marginal cost.

Nonetheless, for Chicago schoolers, the consumer welfare standard implied significant changes to antitrust policy. The Chicago approach sought to maximize allocative efficiency, rather than intuitive proxies for anticompetitive harms, such as mergers or greater concentration. So, rather than reject mergers on the basis that they would eliminate one competitor and lead to greater, harmful concentration, the Chicago school proposed instead that the greater efficiencies from economies of scale—which they argued would be passed on to consumers in the form of lower prices—should be balanced against the potential costs of lesser competition. And as a result, the Chicago school wanted to limit antitrust enforcement to only prohibiting direct, horizontal price-fixing and preventing mergers in extremely concentrated industries (only three to four firms) (Posner 1971).

The Chicago school argued that the existing approach to antitrust—the structuralist, SCP approach—was misguided at best, introducing the notion that *over-enforcement* of antitrust was harmful by arguably placing a series of unnecessary and burdensome rules on business that prohibited them from efficient practices. If economies of scale created significant consumer benefits that needed to be balanced against harms from less competition, then antitrust enforcement potentially worsened consumer welfare by, for example, blocking an efficient merger. And, by assuming that market competition would eventually undo the harmful effects of inefficient mergers, but that the harms of enforcement would endure, the Chicago school argued that the risks to over-enforcement were greater than the harms of under-enforcement (Easterbrook 1984).

There are several key pieces of evidence to the argument that Chicago ideas were responsible for the decline in antitrust, even going beyond that many of their ideas became the law of the land. The first is that higher courts in the United States heavily relied on and adopted Chicago school arguments—most especially, the *Continental T.V., Inc. v. GTE Sylvania, Inc.*

Supreme Court decision (hereafter *Sylvania*).[107] *Sylvania* overturned previous law that per se banned vertical restraints of competition (where a firm acquires, controls, or colludes with its suppliers, vendors, or any firm that is not a direct competitor), and instead highlighted the potential efficiencies from such restraints, opting that they should be analyzed under a "rule of reason" analysis that would balance their harms against purported efficiencies. *Sylvania* contributed to a wave of similar decisions thereafter.[108] Nixon had appointed Chicago antitrust scholar Robert Bork as solicitor general (the lawyer responsible for arguing the government's cases before the Supreme Court) in March 1973, a position he held for four years, up until one month before the *Sylvania* case was decided. The Supreme Court thus would have been rather familiar with his ideas. *Sylvania* cited Bork's work four times. The Court formally adopted the consumer welfare standard as the standard for antitrust in the 1979 *Reiter* decision.[109]

A second key piece of evidence is that the enforcement agencies—the DOJ and the FTC—both dramatically changed their enforcement priorities after the 1980 election of Ronald Reagan, who filled the antitrust agencies with Chicago school advocates and academics like William Baxter and Douglas Ginsberg. Under Baxter, the DOJ dramatically scaled back merger enforcement and enforcement against vertical restraints, instead focusing exclusively on horizontal collusion. Reagan also appointed Chicago thinkers to federal courts, including Frank Easterbrook, Richard Posner, Robert Bork, and again Douglas Ginsberg, among others, who then reinforced many of the earlier court wins for the Chicago perspective.

There are immediately several difficulties with this explanation, in part based on the preceding case study of the Nixon administration. First, while Chicago school figures were present at the periphery of many of these debates in the Nixon administration, their role was limited in these discussions. The author of the Stigler Report, George Stigler was a central Chicago school figure. Nixon's initial skepticism about conglomerate enforcement followed his reading of *Barron's* magazine articles by Robert Bork, another prominent Chicago school antitrust academic. Kenneth Dam, a University

[107] *Continental T.V. Inc. v. GTE Sylvania Inc.*, 433 U.S. 36 (1977).

[108] *Monsanto Co. v. Spray-Rite Svc. Corp.*, 465 U.S. 752 (1984) allowed vertical price-fixing for resale price maintenance to be under the rule of reason. Then *State Oil Co. v. Khan*, 522 U.S. 3 (1997) moved direct vertical price-fixing to be under the rule of reason. More recently, *Leegin Creative Leather Products Inc. v. PSKS Inc.*, 551 U.S. 877 (2007) then overturned a century-long precedent that direct price-fixing in resale price maintenance was per se illegal.

[109] *Reiter v. Sonotone Corp.*, 442 U.S. 330 (1979).

of Chicago law professor serving as an assistant director in the OMB in 1971, consulted on the antitrust review,[110] but his expertise was not primarily antitrust, and his input was focused more on the political calculations of *how* to implement policy changes rather than what they should be. By contrast, in the Nixon White House these conversations were dominated by aides like Jim Loken, Peter Flanigan, John Ehrlichman, and Martin Anderson, who either had no academic background or one entirely disconnected from the Chicago school. Chicago school figures like George Shultz and George Stigler were around the administration, but not these discussions.

Second, as this and the following chapter show, the Chicago school's arguments were being presented in a context where policymakers were already looking for anticompetitive and protectionist policy measures, seeking to scale back antitrust restrictions and enhance the profits and competitive advantages of American corporations. These preferences and priorities were expressed and pursued in a range of policy contexts, with and without the presence of Chicago school partisans or even knowledge of Chicago school arguments. While the Chicago school's formal ideas and arguments did received favorable rulings and stamps of approval from the courts, it is also the case that as the 1970s went on, Chicago school theories and arguments found antitrust enforcement agencies and a federal court system that were increasingly receptive to arguments against antitrust enforcement generally.

This was in part because of the general economic context and Nixon's own appointments to federal agencies and the judiciary, but it was also because the antitrust profession underwent its own learning process. Among antitrust thinkers and policymakers, the profession shifted to favor a more economic and less legal approach to enforcement, largely based on or similar to ideas from the Chicago school of antitrust, with prominent figures like Richard Posner, William Baxter, and Donald Turner openly having changed their mind. While now seen as central to the Chicago school, Richard Posner had written the 1963 *Philadelphia National Bank* decision, one of the mainstays of strict 1960s merger policy.[111] He did this, however, as a law clerk, and therefore to some degree anonymously at the time. Just a few years later, his public and academic articles favored a far more liberal merger policy, to only block mergers at extremely high concentration levels, such as three to four firms in an industry (Posner 1971). Bill Baxter, also later to be greatly

[110] Kenneth Dam to Shultz, September 28, 1971, Box 19, Special Files – John Ehrlichman, RN.
[111] *United States v. Philadelphia Nat'l Bank*, 374 U.S. 321 (1963).

associated with the Chicago school, had been one of the authors of the initially nonpublic Neal Report from the Johnson administration, which had suggested passing laws to restrict conglomerate mergers and unwind already concentrated industries. Baxter's earlier scholarly works had, following the structural antitrust school of the time, emphasized the monopoly problems associated with patents (Baxter 1966).[112] Donald Turner, the head of the Antitrust Division under Johnson in the late 1960s and who was responsible for the first formal merger guidelines, returned to academia, where his later writing adopted much of the Chicago school's framing of price theory, rejecting structural approaches to antitrust (Posner 1979).

Market Power and the Consumer Welfare Standard

Following this argument, the Chicago school's interpretation of antitrust law systematically favored market power (Khan 2018). It did so in a way that would have been evident to policymakers at the time, and some of the evidence presented here indicates that it knowingly intended to favor market power and dominant firms. This, however, conflicts with Chicago thinkers' self-representations that they were outlining a smarter, more coherent version of antitrust with a more accurate understanding of how markets work, and that they were the true defenders of economic competition and all its merits. This also conflicts with many of their critics, who argue that Chicago excessively focuses on low prices at the expense of other values,[113] as well as other academic descriptions of the Chicago school that note that it refocused enforcement priorities to other areas, most especially by focusing on enforcement against horizontal price-fixing and being more liberal with mergers and vertical restraints (Eisner 1991).

First, even at a conceptual level, under Bork's own definition of consumer welfare, clearly anticompetitive practices—or actual monopolies—could be deemed pro-competitive, as long as they arguably benefit consumers. Bork considered competition to mean a term of art where consumers cannot be made better off by a judicial intervention (Bork 1978, 51). Then, for example, if fixed capital costs were so high that a monopoly providing cheap goods

[112] Hovenkamp (2009) suggests that Baxter "kept silent" as an author on the Neal Report, but there is no reason to believe he was not wholeheartedly in agreement at the time (Schmalensee 1998).

[113] See, for example, Khan (2017).

or services (such as a utility or natural monopoly) would become more expensive with the introduction of competitors, that monopoly would meet Bork's definition of competition. Accordingly, early Chicago thinkers, as well as consumer welfare standard adherents today, frequently defend the consumer benefits from mergers that eliminate one of the last few firms in an industry by assuming significant efficiencies from scale.

Furthermore, however, Bork and others explicitly rejected competition itself as a guiding principle for antitrust. In speaking of policies that would maximize price competition, Bork argued:

> A policy of maximizing competition would . . . require the dissolution of virtually all industrial and commercial organizations. It is a prescription for the annihilation of our society and most of the individuals in it. Even a policy of pushing to a condition that a majority of economists would agree constituted pure competition would involve a vast destruction of the wealth of our society. (Bork 1967, 251–252)

Along with this assumption that the extremes of price competition were destructive and inefficient, there was a general assumption that concentration was the result of efficiency rather than market power. Bork and Bowman (1965, 368) argued that increasing concentration in an industry was prima facie evidence that there were efficiencies from economies of scale, rather than the range of plausible anticompetitive and harmful motivations. Richard A. Posner (1971, 505) likewise argued that "the antitrust laws cannot, in general, do more than temporarily retard the process by which an industry attains an efficient scale of operation."

Even more central to their ideological goals, Chicago schoolers and their policy advocates spent much more time seeking to weaken antitrust rules against a specific list of practices primarily used by dominant firms than they did on strengthening, enhancing, or streamlining enforcement in other areas. The antitrust rules they wanted scaled back, most notably, were merger limits and vertical restraints like predatory pricing, resale price maintenance, and territorial sales restrictions. This core to the Chicago mission can be seen in its intellectual origins. According to Richard A. Posner (1979), Chicago antitrust goes back to Aaron Director, a professor at the University of Chicago in the 1950s, who opposed three specific prohibitions in antitrust law: tying agreements (where a buyer is required to buy a second product in order to buy the first), resale price maintenance (where a manufacturer requires retailers to sell a product for a specific price), and predatory pricing (where a firm sells below cost to drive competitors out of business and then later price-gouges in the absence of competition). Director contended that such practices were irrational ways for a firm to acquire market power and, therefore, that antitrust enforcement against them was unnecessary. His students elaborated on the formal theories of how exclusionary practices such as price discrimination, vertical mergers, and exclusive dealing contracts arguably did not harm competition because (a) if one firm could do it, then theoretically their competitors should be able to do so, and (b) it theoretically would hurt oneself as much as one's rivals (Bork and Bowman 1965; Bork 1965a; Posner 1974).

And contrary to Chicago school claims that it favored stronger enforcement against horizontal collusion, this was effectively never a focus of their arguments or policy efforts. Private correspondence and memoranda indicate that strong enforcement against horizontal collusion was made a focus precisely to deflect and obfuscate from the fact that the remainder of the Chicago proposals favored large firms, scaled back antitrust, and undermined competition, as highlighted earlier in this chapter. Further to this point, Priest (2014) has argued that Chicago school's (and specifically Bork's) advocacy of a per se ban on price-fixing was little more than a strategic choice to sell their policy ideas. The evidence of the following chapter will show further support of this idea: that a focus on horizontal competition intended to offset the negative political image associated with the broader range of anti-competition proposals that would favor dominant firms.

To the larger point, however, policymakers were receptive to Chicago school arguments as a result of the diminishing returns to competition, in particular a declining trade balance, declining profits, and a lost technological edge for American industry.[114] The new evidence presented in these chapters shows that rising international competition and America's economic decline were central in changing minds about anti-competition policies, while Chicago school figures, theories, and perspectives were often absent from key conversations. And where key figures from the Chicago school were present or influential, many policymakers had already reached similar protectionist conclusions separately. None of this suggests that Chicago school figures were not influential, or that they thought of themselves as protectionist and anticompetitive, but the evidence from this

[114] See Christophers (2016) and Freyer (2006, 136–138).

early time lends credibility to the notion that the elective affinity between Chicago ideas and the material pressures of competition made their arguments more successful.

Consumer Welfare and Cognitive Closure

The Chicago framework for antitrust also provided—in the language of this book's argument—a simplified mental model of competition that allowed enforcers and judges to reach cognitive closure and simply decide in favor of market power, ignoring complicated details and ambiguities. By providing assumptions that consumer welfare was the only purpose of antitrust, along with a range of assumptions that certain types of mergers and many types of vertical restraints were likely to benefit consumers, the Chicago school presented simple rules of thumb that allowed policymakers to avoid wading into details, ambiguities, and trade-offs implicit in regulating competition. Rather than a parsimonious or sophisticated model of antitrust law and policy, Borkian Chicago school thinking provided a range of reasons to quickly decide in favor of corporate antitrust defendants. This manifested in multiple ways.

This can first be seen in how the Chicago school itself prioritized simple theory, showing disdain for empirical debates by deriving arguments from hypotheticals of price theory:

> Economic analysis does away with the need to measure efficiencies directly. It is enough to know in what sorts of transactions efficiencies are likely to be present and in what sorts anticompetitive effects are likely to be present. The law can then develop objective criteria, such as market shares, to divide transactions likely to be predominantly favorable to consumers through the creation of efficiency from those likely to be predominantly injurious through their suppression of competition. (Bork 1965a, 411)

Additionally, in rejecting alternative economic goals for antitrust, Bork (1965b, 832) argues that promoting innovation is not a valid goal of antitrust "because there exists no science or set of meaningful criteria which indicates how much competition or elimination of competition is most effective in reaching the goal," something that is equally true in an empirical sense for wealth creation or consumer welfare maximization.

Similarly, Chicago thinkers derided the structuralist Harvard school of antitrust as economically illiterate precisely for its sometimes complicated and ambiguous empirical content. Richard A. Posner (1979, 931) criticized the Harvard school for "doing studies of competition in particular industries—airlines, tin cans, aluminum, rayon, Douglas firs, etc." He elaborated:

> These studies exemplified the particularistic and non-theoretical character of the field. The powerful simplifications of economic theory-rationality, profit maximization, the downward sloping demand curve-were discarded, or at least downplayed, in favor of microscopic examination of the idiosyncrasies of particular markets. The "kinked demand curve," "workable competition," "cutthroat competition," "leverage," "administered prices," and the other characteristic concepts of the industrial organization of this period had this in common: *they were not derived from and were often inconsistent with economic theory, and in particular with the premises of rational profit maximization.*

As Christopher Leslie has argued, Bork "is influential because his explanations of complex economic phenomena were so simple," presenting "an unnuanced view of economics without any shades of gray, where economic issues are black-and-white and probabilities were replaced by 'always' and 'never'" (Leslie 2014). The consumer welfare standard satisfied the need for cognitive closure, oversimplifying "how markets work and offered easy answers to complex questions, answers that relieved judges of the burden of wrestling with complicated facts" (Leslie, 2014, 934). To many, including judges, Bork's Chicago school views "sound unimpeachable precisely because they assume away the troublesome points in the analysis" (Silkenat 1978). Rather than grapple with the difficulties that allocative efficiency and economies of scale are hard to measure or predict, that the antitrust statutes themselves prioritized a range of goals alongside (and often before) efficiency, or that his economic theory did not match how many specific markets operated, Bork provided judges with a simple decision rule to ignore all of those concerns. The result was an array of justifications and possible efficiencies that largely give pretenses for judges to get complex, confusing antitrust cases off of their docket, primarily by deciding in favor of the corporate defendant.

Notwithstanding this general critique and characterization of the Chicago school of antitrust, policymakers were well aware of surging imports from Western Europe and particularly Japan, job losses associated with many long-standing firms going under, and the capital scarcity of the 1970s. And while the Chicago school generally did not emphasize issues such as international competition, technology, extraterritorial antitrust, or patent licensing as core points in their arguments, the Chicago arguments about vertical restraints would also extend to allow for more restrictive patent licensing.[115]

Conclusion

This chapter has shown how the Nixon administration's original commitment to strong antitrust enforcement initially resisted policy change despite evidence of diminishing returns to competition, only for executive reorganizations and the introduction of uncommitted policymakers to spur a rethinking of antitrust and IP policy. While the Nixon administration internally revised its stance about antitrust and made a series of executive and judicial appointments in line with those new preferences, it resisted direct advocacy for legislative changes, constrained to maintain consistency with past policy commitments.

Likewise, this account shows how these policy conversations and decisions paved the way for the Chicago school to later succeed in court. In the economic and political context of the 1970s, the Chicago school appears less as a novel set of ideas that dramatically changed the terms of the debate and more as a conveniently available set of legal interpretations that justified, in simple and unambiguous terms, the protectionist and anti-competition preferences of key members of the Nixon administration and policy circles more broadly. This is explored further in Chapter 6, which continues this story in the second instance, showing how the successive administrations of Ford, Carter, and Reagan either pursued policy change or were constrained by early commitments by key policymakers.

[115] See Peinert (2023).

6
The Return of American Monopoly Power

I am determined to return to the vigorous enforcement of antitrust laws.

– Gerald Ford, 1974[1]

Many hallowed principles of antitrust are silly . . . especially with regard to vertical restraints and modest-sized horizontal mergers.

—Richard Posner and George Stigler to Martin Anderson, 1980[2]

Despite the Nixon administration's policy rethinking, as well as its judicial and executive appointments, substantial policy changes only occurred later over the course of the 1970s and 1980s, across the presidential administrations of Gerald Ford (1974–1977), Jimmy Carter (1977–1981), and Ronald Reagan (1981–1989). Enforcement priorities for the antitrust agencies slowly evolved over the course of the 1970s, federal courts began accepting the Chicago school's scaled-back version of antitrust in the late 1980s, and merger enforcement was suddenly and dramatically decreased by the Reagan administration in the early 1980s. Intellectual property rights were expanded and strengthened in various qualitative ways beginning in 1980—despite significant pro-competition legislative changes in the 1970s pushed by both the Ford and the Carter administrations.

This chapter shows that even as policy began and continued to change through the mid-1970s, executive and legislative policymaking was still often dominated by patterns of commitment, with policy change moving or halting based on the prior policy commitments of key policymakers. Policy problems already recognized in previous administrations, such as the United States' declining technological edge, would either be relearned by

[1] President Gerald R. Ford's address to a joint session of Congress on the economy, October 8, 1974.

[2] Posner and Stigler, "Throttling Back on Antitrust: A Practical Proposal for Deregulation," received December 15, 1980 (received), Box 2, Martin Anderson Files, WHSOF, RR.

Monopoly Politics. Erik Peinert, Oxford University Press. © Oxford University Press (2025).
DOI: 10.1093/oso/9780197789506.003.0006

uncommitted policymakers in a new administration or would be ignored by committed policymakers. However, as the years passed, the executive branch, the legislature, and the courts coalesced around a policy regime favoring large, vertically integrated corporations with strong intellectual property protections, planting the seeds for the pharmaceutical and technology giants that are today at the heights of the American economy.

With Nixon's resignation in August 1974, the Ford administration entered office in a moment of high inflation, and in response it doubled down on antitrust as a tool to fight it. Ford strengthened antitrust law multiple times, oversaw the beginnings of deregulation of the regulated industries, and eliminated the anti-competition "fair trade" laws. And having committed to pro-competition policy and maintaining a stable set of advisors through its tenure, the Ford administration tended to downplay or ignore incoming evidence, complaints, and information about declining American competitiveness, as well as a significant shortage of capital and investment—despite some of Nixon's appointments to important antitrust positions continuing in their roles.

Next, the Carter administration faced a series of internal tensions over antitrust and market power. On the one hand, committed antitrust enforcers and deregulatory officials sought to strengthen antitrust enforcement and competition based on public promises made early in the administration. On the other hand, a new set of science and technology advisors identified problems of international competitiveness that they connected to technology, patent, and antitrust policies. This group pushed for industrial policies and anti-competition changes to patent and technology policy, helping to strengthen private patent rights with the passage of the 1980 Bayh-Dole Act.

The Reagan administration, however, came into office with the established goal of scaling back antitrust. The administration was staffed with newly committed converts to the Chicago view on antitrust and competition (or even more extreme views). The Reagan administration changed the executive branch's enforcement policy to match this new vision for antitrust, installing officials who adhered to Chicago school economic philosophy to key antitrust positions and making several legislative attempts to weaken or remove antitrust rules. Chicago school language about competitiveness, efficiency, and consumer welfare was used throughout the Reagan administration to justify these policies, but other executive offices in the administration openly saw these policies as protections for American corporate interests, sometimes openly acknowledging that Chicago antitrust arguments were nonsense or that certain antitrust exemptions served functionally as political and economic alternatives to direct protections like tariffs.

The Ford Administration

Following Nixon's resignation in the wake of the Watergate scandal, Gerald Ford was sworn in as president in August 1974. Despite being a Republican and having been in the Nixon White House, Ford entered office uncommitted to the Nixon administration's policy thinking.[3] Committing to vigorous antitrust enforcement as a strategy for containing inflation, the administration later would refer back to these early commitments when ignoring various problems arguably stemming *from* competition, such as depressed profits and lagging investment, and then continued with an agenda to eliminate antitrust exemptions and pass additional enhancements to antitrust law.

Early Commitment to Antitrust and Competition

Ford and his staff were not initially familiar with antitrust and related areas. In mid-September 1974, about six weeks after taking office, Ford asked staff to assemble "a briefing paper for him which sets forth the current policy in the area of anti-trust."[4] Public reporting reflected this lack of knowledge, with the *National Journal Reports* commenting that "Ford has no antitrust experience and his White House is not well organized.... But neither [White House Counsel Phillip] Areeda nor anyone else inside the White House is directing or coordinating antitrust policy."[5]

However, at the end of September, the White House put together a list of recommendations to fight the unprecedented levels of inflation, based on the suggestions out of an economic summit of economists and policy

[3] Neither Ford nor practically any of his core advisors were involved in the Nixon conversations about competition, antitrust, or patent reform.

[4] Geoff Shepard Memorandum for the Deputy Attorney General, "Current Administration Anti-Trust Policy," September 12, 1974, Box 33, May Files, GF.

[5] Louis M. Kohlmeier, "Ford Leaves Antitrust to Justice," *National Journal Reports Regulatory Focus*, November 30, 1974.

experts. The list of highest-priority recommendations included "general enforcement of the anti-trust laws," "force increased price competition in airlines now regulated by [the Civil Aeronautics Board]," support for free trade, "pass Surface Transportation Act and seek greater anti-trust enforcement," "repeal of the Anti-trust Exemption of Agricultural Cooperatives with Annual Sales Exceeding $10 Million," and "repeal of the Jones Act governing coastal shipping."[6] Ford publicly incorporated these priorities into his October 8, 1974, "Whip Inflation Now" speech.[7]

Ford signed the Antitrust Procedures and Penalties Act (the Tunney Act) in December 1974, which greatly increased fines for certain Sherman Act violations, converted some violations from misdemeanors to felonies, and lengthened the possible criminal penalties. Ford even successfully pushed Congress to increase penalties more than initially proposed.[8]

In November, the administration filed a monopolization case against the telecommunications giant AT&T, a case that led to the breakup of the company in 1982. Media commentary saw this as Ford keeping his antitrust promises and turning away from Nixon's coddling of big business.[9] This was not a costless action to take. Treasury Secretary Simon was infuriated when he found out, the day of, that the Department of Justice (DOJ) would be filing the case, highlighting that the suit could have significant negative effects on the bond market, as AT&T was the highest-valued company in the world.[10]

Deregulation

As part of this pro-competition push, the Ford administration pushed hard to deregulate the regulated industries, which it conceptualized primarily as the elimination of immunities and exemptions from the antitrust laws. Despite only making limited progress, the Ford administration illustrates

[6] Sidney L. Jones Memo, "Economic Policy Recommendations," September 28, 1974, BE Box 17, Central Files, GF, pages 1–10.

[7] President Gerald R. Ford's address to a joint session of Congress on the economy, October 8, 1974.

[8] Tom Korologos to William Timmons, "Anti-Trust Penalty Increases," November 3, 1974, JL Box 17, Central Files, GF.

[9] See, for example, "Suit to Split Up AT&T Bears Out Ford Pledge of Antitrust Firmness: Justice Agency Is Viewed as Shucking Nixon Image of Coddling Big Business," *Wall Street Journal*, November 21, 1974.

[10] William Simon to President, "Government Antitrust Action against American Telephone and Telegraph," November 22, 1974, JL Box 17, Central Files, GF.

many of the theoretical arguments of the book: the over-reliance on simple mental models in the face of complexity, the generalization of pro-competition mental models to all industries all at once, and the lock-in effects of early commitments.

In February 1975, the Economic Policy Board requested a comprehensive examination of antitrust immunities across all industries.[11] The task group reviewed "agriculture, defense, energy, export trade associations, insurance, labor, newspaper joint operating arrangements, ocean carriers, small business concerns, and professional sports."[12]

Both this group and the administration's broader agenda on regulatory reform emphasized across-the-board motivations to deregulation, without much of any focus on the details of what individual policies may have been or what other trade-offs may have been present. Ford's Domestic Council Review Group on Regulatory Reform grouped a range of industries under the same banner, including rail deregulation, natural gas, financial institutions, retail (via resale price maintenance policies), trucking, airlines, and cable TV.[13]

When discussing particular industries, the administration ignored substantive objections and generalized, with little basis, the reasoning applied in one industry into another. Regarding motor carrier deregulation, which removed rate-making authority and antitrust exemptions, James Lynn wrote regarding industry's opposition to the changes, "The claims made by both groups that the legislation will produce 'market chaos' are similar to those of the airline industry regarding the Aviation Act. After serious investigation, we concluded that while more competition would reduce rates and profits of those in protected positions, competition would not disorganize markets."[14] The concerns of those in the regulated industries were largely those expressed by the theory of this book: with unmitigated competition, price wars and bankruptcies ("market chaos") might ensue. But internally, the Ford administration simply dismissed these concerns as inconsistent with their own theories around competition and deregulation, under which more competition just means lower prices.

[11] L. William Seidman Memorandum to White House Staff, "Task Group on Antitrust Immunities," February 20, 1975, Box 40, Seidman Files, GF.

[12] Roger Porter and Thomas Kauper, "Report on the Activities of the Task Group on Antitrust Immunities," July 11, 1975, Box 40, Seidman Files, GF.

[13] Rod Hills to Economic Policy Board, "Domestic Council Review Group on Regulatory Reform," July 16, 1975, Box 55, Seidman Files, GF.

[14] James T. Lynn to the President, "Reform of Motor Carrier Regulation," October 30, 1975, Box 55, Seidman Files, GF.

That said, the administration's concrete results were limited. The administration's work socialized the idea of deregulation for future administrations, with significant DOJ reports on both antitrust immunities (touching on exemptions in agriculture, defense, energy, export trade associations, government enterprise, insurance, labor, professional associations, marine insurance, newspapers, resale price maintenance, small business, sports, state action, airlines, ocean shipping, and railroads),[15] but few changes were passed. Most concretely, Ford signed the Consumer Goods Pricing Act in December 1975, which repealed Miller-Tydings and prohibited resale price maintenance, a form of vertical price fixing that eliminated retail price competition.

Profits and Capital Formation

Separately, the problem of "capital formation" was brought to the attention of the Ford administration almost immediately. Capital formation is the net addition of capital stock to an economy, and with lagging investment, many argued that the United States was not adding enough new capital stock. After the National Association of Manufacturers wrote to the White House in August 1974 regarding "the limited availability of funds for capital expansion,"[16] the White House Economic Policy Board was tasked with examining the problem, spearheaded by Treasury Secretary Simon.[17]

Simon summarized the capital formation the next year, emphasizing that both (1) the needs for capital formation were expected to increase over the following decade and (2) there were fewer financial resources, with low corporate profits being a key problem.[18] Per Simon, "Many qualitative reports are being received from private companies indicating increasing uncertainty about future capital investments and even cutbacks in current outlays."[19] Per the policy group:

[15] Department of Justice, Report of the Task Group on Antitrust Immunities, January 1977.

[16] Doug Kenna to Kenneth Rush, August 7, 1974, BE Box 31, Central Files, GF, page 2.

[17] Statement by William E. Seidman before the Senate Finance Committee, May 7, 1975, Box 45, Seidman Files, GF, page 5.

[18] William Simon to President, "Tax Measures for Capital Formation," July 21, 1975, Box 42, Seidman Files, GF.

[19] William Simon to President, July 1975, Box 45, Seidman Files, GF, page 3.

> It is well known that corporate profitability has declined in recent years—especially in the 1968–1974 period. The rate of return on corporate investment, moreover, appears to have dropped sharplyespecially over the last few years.[20]

Increasing competition was mentioned intermittently in reports as an explanation for low profits, but usually only as one among many issues, as Simon tended to highlight broader issues like the United States' traditional emphasis on consumption over investment, the costs of government fiscal policies, and distortions in the tax code.[21]

The proposed solutions, however, were modest in nature. The Economic Policy Board's report focused purely on tax and financial reforms, taking for granted that profits and investment had fallen.[22] The main legislative proposal was the Capital Recovery Act of 1975, which comprised a minor adjustment to depreciation allowances, and even that did not pass in Congress.

The Final Antitrust Push

The Ford administration continued its antitrust push through to the end, locked by its early commitments to the policy. In December 1975, White House Counsel Phil Buchen wrote that the administration "appear[s] passive and damage limiting, with respect to antitrust," but referred back to the October 8, 1974, "Whip Inflation Now" speech and highlighted the administration's regulatory reform, elimination of fair trade laws (which had permitted resale price maintenance), and successful budget increases for both antitrust agencies.[23]

In July 1976, six months before Ford left office, the administration needed to reappoint a new assistant attorney general for antitrust, with Donald

[20] Economic Policy Board, Draft Report of the Task Force on Capital Formation, Growth, and Job Creation, Revised April 15, 1975, Seidman Files, Box 45, GF, page 7.

[21] Simon Statement before the Senate Finance Committee, May 7, 1975, Box 45, Seidman Files, GF.

[22] White House Economic Policy Board, "Task Force Report: Capital Formation, Growth, and Job Creation," Draft October 20, 1975, Box 46, Seidman Files, GF.

[23] Phil Buchen, "Administration Anti-Trust Policy," December 1975, Box 6, Schmults Files, GF, pages 1–2.

Baker viewed as the most aggressive enforcer among the options. One Ford aide summarized their political situation in terms of these past commitments:

> There is a growing concern among Ed Levi, Phil Buchen and Ed Schmults that if Baker is not nominated, it would be an indication that your position on antitrust enforcement is very "soft" and that politically this could work very much to your disadvantage. This would also be perceived as a position contrary to your previous statements respecting strict enforcement of the anti-trust laws placing you in an extremely sensitive and politically difficult position.[24]

The aide urged a rapid nomination of Donald Baker "to avoid a possible flap respecting an appearance of your softening on anti-trust matters," worried that negative press highlighting the contradiction would appear within days if they did not move.[25] Ford nominated Baker that day.

Most significantly, Ford signed the landmark 1976 Hart-Scott-Rodino Antitrust Improvements Act (HSR Act), expanding antitrust enforcement with a sophisticated premerger notification system and new rights for state governments to recover on behalf of consumers. Despite disputes over technical details, the Ford administration supported the general outlines of the bill. Opinions across the federal agencies in the Ford administration were rather mixed, with Treasury Secretary Simon opposed,[26] and Attorney General Edward Levi opposed,[27] but Assistant Attorney General for Antitrust Thomas Kauper in support.[28]

The opposition was significant. Republican senators lobbied against HSR, as did corporate law firms, whereas consumer groups and unions were strongly in support.[29] A September 1976 tally of the business opposition by the administration showed that all were opposed to the bill.[30]

[24] Douglas Bennett to President, "Assistant Attorney General, Anti-Trust Division - Donald Baker," July 21, 1976, FG Box 91, Central Files, GF.

[25] Ibid.

[26] William Simon Memorandum for the President, September 22, 1976, BE Box 6, Central Files, GF.

[27] Edward Levi Memorandum for the President, September 27, 1976, BE Box 6, Central Files, GF.

[28] Testimony of Thomas Kauper in S. 1284 before the Senate Subcommittee on Antitrust and Monopoly, May 7, 1975, Box 33, May Files, GF.

[29] Letter from Senators Strom Thurmond, Roman Hruska, Henry Bellmon, James McClure, James Allen, Jesse Helms, Paul Laxalt, Dewey Bartlett, PaulFannin, Carl Curtis, William Lloyd Scott, and John Tower to President Ford, September 17, 1976, BE Box 6, Central Files, GF; Coalition letter to Ford in support of H.R. 8532, September 21, 1976, BE Box 6, Central Files, GF.

[30] Ed Schmults to Jack Marsh, "Reaction by the Business Community to Antitrust Legislation," September 23, 1976, Box 5, Schmults Files, GF.

The Ford administration was under pressure from Democrats to live up to its previous antitrust commitments, with the administration having to deny that it was weakening its antitrust position or shirking on previous promises, all while Secretary Simon publicly opposed the passage of the HSR.[31] In April 1976, the administration's internal summary of their antitrust position relative to the criticism over HSR was as follows, in a private memorandum to Ford: "The Administration has in the past been the champion of vigorous antitrust enforcement and reducing government regulation while Congress has largely been playing 'catch-up' ball. Recently the Administration's positive antitrust policy has been criticized by Members of Congress and others because of our position on antitrust legislation before the Congress."[32]

Written by the DOJ, the internal draft of the speech for Ford to sign the HSR Act as of September 14, 1976, was pro-competition through and through. It highlighted their previous enforcement of the antitrust laws, noted their passage of the 1974 Tunney Act, and outlined their initiatives to deregulate the regulated industries and introduce competition.[33] One special assistant for legislative affairs showed surprise that Ford had signed the bill in the face of opposition from business and his own party: "P.S. Well how about that . . . he signed it!"[34]

The Carter Administration

In contrast to other administrations around this time, the Carter administration shows two divergent sets of policy conversations. One chain of conversations regarding science and technology policy went in an anti-competition direction, driven by uncommitted policymakers who were exposed to the problems of international competition, insufficient investment, and their relationship with intellectual property rights. Those officials pushed for both patent reforms and a formal industrial policy in the United States, the main result of which was the 1980 Bayh-Dole Act, which shifted patent protections for government technologies to the private sector. At the same time, the antitrust agencies and deregulation advocates came in with

[31] Robert M. Smith, "Administration and Critics at Odds on Antitrust Laws," April 26, 1976.

[32] Edward Schmults, "Meeting to Discuss Administration's Position on Antitrust Legislation," May 19, 1976, Box 5, Schmults Files, GF, page 1.

[33] Stan Morris to Ed Schmults enclosing DOJ first draft of signing statement, September 14, 1976, Box 5, Schmults Files, GF.

[34] See margins of Joseph Jenckes to Senator Robert Morgan, September 30, 1976, BE Box 6, Central Files, GF.

strong commitments to a pro-competition agenda, including the deregulation of the regulated industries, the passage of a conglomerate merger control law, and the legislative rolling back of anti-competition decisions by the Supreme Court, now comprising a number of Nixon appointees.

Carter Antitrust: Committed but Inattentive

In the specific domain of antitrust, the Carter administration committed itself to pro-competition policies, pushing for multiple pieces of antitrust legislation paired with its deregulatory agenda, albeit most unsuccessfully. Despite this commitment, however, no senior advisors in the Carter administration engaged significantly with antitrust: the administration did not appear to even notice the federal court system's adoption of the consumer welfare standard, though it did attempt to reverse those decisions when it noticed or understood them.

In December 1977, Carter established a National Commission for the Review of Antitrust Laws and Procedures to examine litigation procedures, legal remedies for violations, and existing antitrust immunities and exemptions.[35] This was deeply paired with the administration's deregulatory agenda, as Associate Director for Domestic Policy Simon Lazarus wrote at the time:

> The body will really be as much a "regulatory reform" commission as an antitrust commission; this is because its substantive responsibility is mainly concerned with looking at antitrust immunities and exemptions—i.e., anti-competitive regulatory schemes in transportation, insurance, banking, and communications.[36]

After the Commission's report over a year later, the administration, through the DOJ Antitrust Division, moved forward with many of its proposals. The Antitrust Procedural Improvements Act of 1979 was moved through Congress, which gave the DOJ greater powers in pre-litigation investigation, increased some antitrust penalties, and expanded jurisdiction for antitrust

[35] Executive Order 12022—National Commission for the Review of Antitrust Laws and Procedures, December 1, 1977.

[36] Stu Eizenstat to Si Lazarus, "Antitrust Commission," November 11, 1977, Box 227, Eizenstat Files, JC.

enforcement. Among the Commission's other recommendations were to strengthen Section 2 of the Sherman Act to lower the bar for bringing charges for attempts to monopolize and to add a "no-fault" monopoly provision.[37]

The most notable industry deregulation of the Carter administration was the Airline Deregulation Act of 1978,[38] which eliminated the Civil Aeronautics Board. The Civil Aeronautics Board had been assigning routes to airlines and setting rates and fares for the industry since the 1930s, when it had been created to rein in the "destructive competition" in the industry at the time. The Airlines Deregulation Act was justified in Congress for its aim of introducing competition into air travel, and the law itself includes a range of competition provisions intended to ensure that outcome.[39]

Having seen the Nixon administration's failures to block conglomerate mergers, the DOJ under Carter sought new conglomerate merger legislation, which had gained interest once again with a new wave of conglomerate mergers in the late 1970s. Assistant Attorney General for Antitrust John Shenefield proposed changing legal presumptions to require that the larger merging companies prove the merger will enhance competition, rather than requiring the government to prove it will harm competition.[40] While the Federal Trade Commission (FTC) and DOJ wanted to move on this issue and with this position, Senator Ted Kennedy wanted to simply prohibit mergers above a certain size.[41]

Others in the Office of Management and Budget (OMB) and the Council of Economic Advisors tended to disagree, and uncommitted policymakers were lost as to the reasoning for conglomerate legislation. Spelling out a list of pros and cons for such a law in January 1979, Carter's main domestic policy advisors Stuart Eizenstat and Robert Malson noted that "the economic evidence is at best neutral so that we are likely to be left with the 'bigness is bad' justification."[42]

[37] Report to the President and the Attorney General of the National Commission for the Review of Antitrust Laws and Procedures, 1979.

[38] For more on that act and deregulation more generally, see Derthick and Quirk (1985).

[39] See House Report 95-1779, filed with S. 2493, Airline Deregulation Act, 95th Congress, February 6, 1978.

[40] John Shenefield to Bert Carp, "Possible Conglomerate Merger Legislation," December 8, 1978, BE Box 2, Central Files, JC.

[41] Bob Malson to Stu Eizenstat and Frank White, "Talking Points for the Conglomerate Merger Meeting," December 21, 1978, BE Box 2, Central Files, JC.

[42] Bob Malson and Stu Eizenstat to Carter, "Conglomerate Merger Legislation Proposed by the Department of Justice," January 21, 1979, BE Box 2, Central Files, JC, page 6.

Furthermore, the Carter administration appears to have barely noticed the judicial winds already turning toward the Chicago school's version of antitrust, with the weight of four Nixon Supreme Court appointees rebalancing the scales. Five days after Carter was inaugurated in 1977, the Supreme Court's *Brunswick* decision added a new procedural barrier to antitrust enforcement.[43] The Supreme Court's 1977 *Sylvania* decision was only a few months later, endorsing the Chicago school's views about vertical restraints, efficiency, and consumer welfare, citing Robert Bork's work multiple times.[44] Yet the Carter White House and DOJ barely appear to have noticed these cases at all. The sole mention of *Sylvania* found in the Carter archives was to *approvingly* look upon it as a pro-consumer antitrust decision, and even then it was only mentioned as a side-comment years later in 1980 in the context of a separate legislation about soft drink bottlers.[45] Also seemingly outside of the Carter administration's awareness, the Supreme Court's 1979 *Reiter* decision formally ruled that the legislative history "suggest[s] that Congress designed the Sherman Act as a 'consumer welfare prescription,'" citing Bork's broadly incorrect reading of the Sherman Act's history.[46]

The Carter administration did, however, focus on the Supreme Court's 1977 *Illinois Brick* decision, which prohibited "direct purchasers" from making antitrust claims, meaning that only buyers who directly bought from a part violating the antitrust laws could recover damages in court.[47] Carter advisors saw bills to repeal the *Illinois Brick* as "the major consumer efforts for the remainder of the Session and . . . we should do all we can to get them passed."[48] However, no federal *Illinois Brick* repealer has ever been passed, though many individual states have passed laws to circumvent the ruling.

[43] *Brunswick Corp. v. Pueblo Bowl-O-Mat, Inc.*, 429 U.S. 477 (1977). *Brunswick* required that plaintiffs show proof of an "antitrust injury," meaning they must prove not just that they themselves were harmed by the defendant's illegal actions, but that competition itself was harmed by those actions. Sensible on its own terms, procedural barriers like this serve to simply reduce the chances of an antitrust case succeeding.

[44] *Continental T.V. Inc. v. GTE Sylvania Inc.*, 433 U.S. 36 (1977).

[45] The Carter administration characterized the bottlers' bill as "a special antitrust exemption" for bottlers to establish exclusive territories. Even recognizing that this was consistent with *Sylvania*, they nonetheless saw no justification for a special antitrust exemption. Ky Ewing, "Soft Drink Bottlers Bills," received June 9, 1980, Box 10, Malson Files, JC.

[46] *Reiter v. Sonotone Corp.*, 442 U.S. 330 (1979).

[47] Otherwise, those violators face "double recovery" from direct buyers and potentially multiple layers of indirect buyers down the supply chain. *Illinois Brick Co. v. Illinois*, 431 U.S. 720 (1977).

[48] Bob Malson to Bill Cable and Bob Thompson, "'Illinois Brick' Legislation S. 1784; H.R. 11942," May 26, 1978, Box 227, Eizenstat Files, JC, page 1.

The Battle for the FTC

In 1978, the authority of one of the main antitrust regulators, the FTC, was challenged in an intense lobbying debate, in an episode that is marshaled as evidence that business lobbying was centrally responsible for the rollback of many 20th-century economic policies (Hacker and Pierson 2010). The story is well-documented (Pertschuk 1982), but it was primarily an issue of consumer regulation and provides no evidence that antitrust policy was even affected. At no point in the debate were issues of competition, antitrust, concentration, or other related topics ever raised. While the business lobby was successful in significantly constraining the FTC's consumer protection powers, its antitrust authorities were untouched and unchallenged.

As background, in 1974, the Magnuson-Moss Warranty Act gave the FTC greater powers over several areas of consumer protection, and within two years the FTC had undertaken eighteen major consumer protection rule-makings across different sectors (Baer 1988). In 1977, Congress was considering expanding its mandate further with the FTC Amendments of 1977, legislation vehemently opposed by business interests, with both the Chamber of Commerce and the National Association of Manufacturers staunchly against.[49]

However, when the FTC turned its eyes to the issue of children's advertising in 1977 and 1978—looking to limit the volume of commercial advertising aimed at children as an "unfair act or practice" under the FTC Act—this was met with immediate controversy and reproach, with the FTC quickly becoming the face of the over-intrusive "nanny state." A very public fight over the FTC's reauthorization occurred in 1979, with bills introduced to eliminate the FTC's jurisdiction over advertising.[50] The eventual FTC reauthorization came with the Federal Trade Commission Improvements Act of 1980, which limited certain uses of FTC funds in the short term but left its power intact. Carter objected to some concessions, but he actively supported requirements that FTC rules be based in economic analysis and be the least burdensome of regulatory alternatives.[51] Antitrust itself was never

[49] James Carty, NAM Director of Regulatory and Consumer Affairs, Letter to Congress, June 9, 1977; Milton Davis, Chamber of Commerce Legislative Action Vice President, Letter to Congress, July 11, 1977; both in Box 41, Lazarus Files, JC.

[50] Si Lazarus to Dan Tate, "FTC Authorization Bill," November 21, 1979, Box 54, Lazarus Files, JC.

[51] Office of the White House Press Secretary, Statement of the President, May 28, 1980, Box 54, Lazarus Files, JC.

seen as the core of this fight, though the final bill did limit the FTC's ability to investigate farm cooperatives under the antitrust laws.

This, however, was not an antitrust or competition issue, and the archival record indicates that the administration viewed the fight as a defense of regulatory authority against resurgent special interests. In September 1979, Ed Cohen, a deputy special assistant, wrote to Eizenstat regarding the conflict over the FTC: "This particular action, however, demonstrates so vividly how Congress is dominated by the special interests. The proceedings halted by this action effect everybody's least favorite industries—oil, used cars, funeral homes, health spas, to name a few."[52]

Trade, Competition, and Technology

Trade competitiveness—particularly in relation to policy around technology, patents, and licensing—continued to come up as an issue during the Carter administration. Despite earlier administrations' fears over the absolute size of the trade deficit, the Carter White House came to the conclusion early on that the trade deficit itself was almost entirely a result of export surpluses from OPEC countries since the oil embargo. As of 1977, the US deficit was to be $27 billion, and was entirely accounted for by the deficits in oil, gas, coal, and nuclear fuel.[53] In the administration's view, "so long as OPEC has substantial trade surpluses, the rest of the world must have substantial trade deficits."[54]

However, a group of technology advisors did became increasingly concerned about the competitiveness and technological position of the United States and the role that technology transfers played in this process. In particular, American firms would often develop new technologies for commercial or industrial use, only for foreign firms to quickly license and adopt the technology, implementing it faster and more effectively than the American firm that developed it. While this dynamic only occasionally received dedicated attention on its own, it was addressed frequently throughout different policy issues and areas. For example, in a report on tax policy, the Economic Policy Group noted:

[52] Ed Cohen to Stuart Eizenstat, "Congressional Assault on the FTC," September 14, 1979, FG Box 189, Central Files, JC.

[53] Stu Eizenstat and Bob Ginsberg to Carter, "The Trade Deficit (At Your Request)," August 4, 1977, Box 227, Eizenstat Files, JC.

[54] Richard Cooper to Zbigniew Brzezinski, November 14, 1977, TA Box 1, Central Files, JC.

> The relationship between R&D and trade is complicated by the fact that the location of the R&D and the location of production may be different. For example, the Video Tape Recorder (VTR) was originally developed in the U.S., but is now produced exclusively in Japan and is being imported in large quantities. If U.S. consumer electronics firms are further motivated to increase R&D, this may well increase imports instead of stimulating exports.[55]

A 1980 joint budget proposal from the Commerce and Labor Departments made similar arguments with respect to yet more technologies:

> Although the U.S. has always been the leader in developing new products and processes, it has clearly not been the most successful at using this technology in the forms of patents and licenses has given other countries the opportunity to put that technology to work when we ourselves would not–usually to our ultimate disadvantage. A classic example of this is the use of continuous casting in making steel. Although this cheap and efficient process was developed in the U.S., American steelmakers use it for making only 16 percent of their steel, Japan and Germany use it to make 50 percent and 38 percent respectively. On the product side, another example in the home videotape player. Although U.S. firms developed the technology, a Japanese firm (Sony) turned it into a marketable product. The U.S. is the world's leading exporter of technology, and Japan is its leading importer.[56]

Another memo from Carter staff to Congress in May 1978 discussed the same issues again:

> The steady increasing positive U.S. trade balance in sales of technology, through foreign direct investment, licensing, and joint ventures, is both an indicator of U.S. past and present technological superiority and a source of concern that the U.S. is failing to develop exports of finished products by prematurely transferring its technical know-how to foreign subsidiaries

[55] "Tax Policy toward Research and Development in the U.S.," Economic Policy Group Meeting, November 14, 1978, Box 109, CEA Files, JC, page 6.

[56] "Departments of Commerce and Labor Joint Budget Proposal for FY 1982 Paper #4: Financing Industrial Development," 1980, BE Box 14, Central Files, JC, pages 2–3.

> and foreign-owned firms. There is evidence of a shift from product exports to foreign investment and licensing by high technology U.S. companies.[57]

Generally speaking, under the United States' relatively open intellectual property (IP) regime at the time, which included a series of antitrust requirements about IP licensing, American firms were frequently choosing to, or were required to, transfer technology to their foreign competitors.

The Ford administration had touched on these issues, but with its antitrust commitments continued to support the position of the Antitrust Division on the patent issue, even as representatives from industry and its own Commerce Department pushed for anti-competition reforms to strengthen and deepen patent rights.[58]

When complaining to the Ford administration about the unreliability of patent protections—for example, that from 1953 to 1963, 57.5% percent of patents were ruled invalid, which increased to 68.2% from 1964 to 1974[59]—proponents of reform directed their ire at the Antitrust Division.[60]

Patents and the Office of Science and Technology Policy

However, these policy conversations changed under Carter, albeit showing a stark conflict between committed and uncommitted policymakers. The Office of Science and Technology Policy (OSTP) was created by the National Science and Technology Policy, Organization, and Priorities Act, passed in May 1976 under the Ford administration. The OSTP was a new White House office to serve as an executive advisory office on technology policy. Frank Press, an uncommitted geophysicist who had previously held research

[57] Steve Merrill to Howard Cannon, "Hearings and Proposed Activities on Industrial Innovation," May 24, 1978, SC Box 1, Central Files, JC, page 2.

[58] Immediately after Ford took office, the General Council from the Department of Commerce wrote to the White House that the administration desires to increase the percentage of valid patents, suggesting a single, consolidated patent court. Bernard Parrette to F. Lynn May, August 28, 1974, Box 3, May Files, GF.

[59] Gausewitz, Carr & Rothenberg PC, "Patent Law Section 103 and Its Proposed Amendment," BE Box 96, Central Files, GF.

[60] For example, at some point during these debates in 1974 and 1975, Arthur Whale, president of the American Patent Law Association, gave a statement accusing a small group within the antitrust division of being the "locus of the infection" of views opposing strong patents, noting that "this group has trouped the country giving speeches and leveling threats to implement its views." Whale contended that that the administration's patent was written by the Antitrust Division. See Statement by Arthur Whale, Reference Tab "B," BE Box 96, Central Files, GF.

positions at California Institute of Technology and the Massachusetts Institute of Technology, was hired to be the first director of the OSTP.[61] In May 1977, shortly after being appointed, Frank Press wrote to Carter about trends in the US international position in technology, presenting an image of the United States as losing its edge, with other countries gaining in the rate of new technological development and R&D spending.[62]

Simultaneously, Hyman Rickover, a well-decorated Navy admiral, made inquiries at the White House regarding government patents. Having personally been Carter's commanding officer in the Navy when Carter served in the 1950s, Rickover had the president's ear. Rickover had long been well-known for his dislike of military contractors, holding them to high standards for quality and safety. In June 1977, Rickover met with the White House to address the issue of government patents. Rickover objected to "license policies" for government patents, in which government-funded research would hand off the patent rights to the contractor who conducted the research, arguing strongly pro-competition positions to the White House that license policies "result[] in large companies, who get the lion's share of the Government contracts to develop monopoly positions at Government expense."[63]

Rickover's stance was met with an administration poorly informed on the issue. Carter expressed the primary concern as the government losing money by giving away the patent rights.[64]

However, in contrast to Rickover's long-held views, others expressed their skepticism and eventual disagreement, even if they were initially uninformed as well. Staff for the OMB and OSTP were unconvinced by the presentation from Rickover's staff.[65] Discussions between Stu Eizenstat and Frank Press led to different conclusions that "contrary to the view expressed

[61] Bert Lance Memorandum for the President, "Dr. Press' letter to you on the Science and Technology Advisor's Office," February 21, 1977, FG Box 91, Central Files, JC.

[62] Frank Press to Carter, "Trends in US International Position in Technology over the Past 10–15 years: Preview of an NSB Report," May 24, 1977, Box 1, OSTP Files, JC.

[63] Stu Eizenstat, Bo Cutter, and Frank Press to Carter, "Patent Policy," July 25, 1977, Box 233, Eizenstat Files, JC.

[64] Bob Malson, "Opening Memorandum: Patent Problem," June 10, 1977, Box 15, Malson Files, JC.

[65] Bob Malson to Stu Eizenstat, "Patent Policy," July 18, 1977, Box 233, Eizenstat Files, JC. Phil Smith of the OSTP wrote about a meeting with Tim Foster (of Rickover's staff) in July 1977, "I found Foster's arguments very circular and very narrow. The spectre of corporate 'rip off' demanding a drastic change in policy is viable only if one can postulate an alternative system of government development that would seem to offer superior advantages from the standpoint of innovation, and I don't think Foster discussed this issue at all well." Phil Smith to Bob Malson, "Patent Policy Meeting July 14, 1977," July 15, 1977, Box 15, Malson Files, JC.

at the Cabinet meeting, students of patent policy believe that far from a 'give away' the general situation is one of underutilization [of government patents], inconsistency in policy, lack of incentive for agencies and their employees to stimulate patent usage, and probably inadequate safeguards against international use of patents at the expense of domestic innovation."[66] In short, while the government was paying for the development of new technologies, many of them required additional investment to commercialize, and companies were often unwilling to make those expenditures if one of their competitors could free ride on those investments. Therefore, many government patents sat unused under government ownership. Some preliminary research showed that government patents were, generally, quite underutilized relative to those developed elsewhere, particularly by private funds at universities.[67]

As they had been for years, business interests were lobbying on the same issue. Fred Bucy of semiconductor manufacturer Texas Instruments wrote to Frank Press in May 1977 about patents and the problems stemming from insufficient protection abroad. He pointed to changing policies in Mexico, the Philippines, Canada, Argentina, and India, which were all reforming their patent regimes to facilitate greater technology transfer to their own economies.[68] Passing these concerns on to Stuart Eizenstat, Carter's chief domestic policy advisor, Press wrote that "though biased, it is a point of view we should know about."[69]

Bernard Martin of the OMB and others saw no rush to resolve the patent issue.[70] Action was again slow-walked against Carter's request, with Charles Goodwin of the OMB writing, "The concerns expressed to the President are cogent but not urgent or startling and are not supported by recent experience or hard data."[71]

A retrospective summary years later from the associate director for domestic policy, Bob Malson, gives a frank summary:

[66] Stu Eizenstat to Frank Press and W. Bowman Cutter, "Patent Policy," June 20, 1977, Box 15, Malson Files, JC.

[67] Bob Malson, "Talking Paper on Patent Policy," June 27, 1977, Box 15, Malson Files, JC, page 6.

[68] J. Fred Bucy to Frank Press, May 10, 1977, Box 15, Malson Files, JC.

[69] Frank Press to Stu Eizenstat, July 15, 1977, SC Box 1, Central Files, JC.

[70] Bernard Martin to Bob Malson, "Government Patent Policy," July 19, 1977, Box 15, Malson Files, JC; Stu Eizenstat, Bo Cutter, and Frank Press to Carter, "Patent Policy," July 25, 1977, Box 233, Eizenstat Files, JC.

[71] Charles Goodwin to Robert Malson, "Government Patent Policy," July 18, 1977, Box 15, Malson Files, JC.

> Early in 1977 Admiral Rickover met with us in an effort to persuade the President to adopt a patent policy which would strengthen the ability of the government to retain patent rights developed by government contractors. Following a three month study in which I participated with OMB and Frank Press' office, we sent a memorandum to the President in which *we essentially came out on the other side of the issue but watered down our recommendation.* Rather than tightening the controls desired by Rickover, we concluded that the current lack of an overall federal patent policy contributed to an underutilization in the commercial sector and, further, we agreed that greater access to patents developed by the private sector through government contracts was in order. The President agreed with our recommendation for additional study *but with noted reluctance.*[72]

In short, a policymaker committed to pro-competition views, Rickover, presented the issue to a relatively uninformed White House, only to have uncommitted policymakers on Carter's staff independently look into the issue and come to the opposite conclusions, which in this case were the anti-competition views that more private patent protections were needed.

Industrial Innovation and the Bayh-Dole Act

This grew into a protracted debate about industrial policy, with Carter commissioning a review of "industrial innovation" policies in 1978. Carter requested the domestic policy review of industrial innovation in May 1978, after Frank Press wrote the proposal for one and wrote to Carter with a series of articles addressing the loss of the American technological and innovation lead.[73]

Over the next year, the Domestic Policy Review solicited comments from various agencies, and the final report itself included recommendations across trade policy, competition and industrial organization, patent and technology policy, and federal procurement.[74] Most observers at the time, in business or otherwise, found the overall proposals to be lacking relative

[72] Bob Malson to Stu Eizenstat, "Patent Policy," September 25, 1979, BE Box 24, Central Files, JC. Emphasis added.

[73] Frank Press to Carter, "Productivity and Innovativeness in U.S. Economy," April 24, 1978, Box 1, OSTP Files, JC.

[74] Final Report of the Advisory Committee on Industrial Innovation, September 1979, available at https://babel.hathitrust.org/cgi/pt?id=mdp.39015031272316&view=1up&seq=8.

to the scale of the problems.[75] With respect to patents, it recommended a universal "title" policy for government patents, but where the government keep the patent but with exclusive licensing to the contractor introducing the product commercially. In all but name, this was a license policy, in which the patent is transferred to the private contractor. It also recommended a single appellate court for patent litigation in order to provide stronger a more consistent protections for patent holders.

This industrial innovation review helped to set the stage for legislative change with the 1980 Bayh-Dole Act, which settled the previous decade of debates over government patents by transferring government patents to small businesses and nonprofits (i.e., research universities), but with the government retaining "walk-in" rights to use the technology itself. The Carter administration opposed the bill not because of what it did but because it did not go far enough. The administration, led by the Commerce Department and the OSTP, wanted the bill to transfer government patents to large firms as well, in order to create a uniform policy for all contractors. These offices viewed large firms as playing a central role in innovation (Stevens 2004).

Despite their earlier conflicts, and the robust commitment to competition in other parts of the government, Carter's industrial innovation review came out strongly in favor of both stronger patent rights and innovation driven by larger firms. In December 1979, the administration's patents proposals were "uniform patent policy, voluntary reexamination, modernization of the Patent Trademark Office, and the patent court of appeals."[76] This was, however, not without recognizing the foreseeable costs to competition. In October 1979, an internal issue paper noted that "exclusive rights by definition foreclose competition in the marketing of the invention covered by the patent and might serve to enhance the recipient's market power."[77]

Getting the rest of the executive branch on board with these patent reforms required negotiation, primarily over competition concerns from the antitrust agencies. A conflict broke out in 1980, where the DOJ wanted to retain the right to have a "second look" for antitrust considerations before patent exclusivity would be granted to a contractor. The DOJ threatened to

[75] For contemporary commentary, Wade (1979) commented "elaborate bureaucratic exercise produces small-scale program."

[76] Phil Smith and Frank Press Memorandum for Stu Eizenstat, "Implementation of the Industrial Innovation Agenda," December 10, 1979, BE Box 5, Central Files, JC, page 1.

[77] Issue Paper on Federal Patent Policy, October 16, 1979, BE Box 24, Central Files, JC.

not support the administration bill if second-look rights were not included. Prior pro-competition commitments were raised to try to steer the policy change, with one advisor writing that "deletion of the [second look] provision will create the impression that the President is not concerned with anticompetitive forces."[78] When the Bayh-Dole bill ended up not have any of these public interest considerations, Kai Ewing of the DOJ noted that the DOJ "had finally altered their position of 30 years to allow for a limited, government-granted monopoly conferred by a patent and paid for by taxpayer research to small business and universities in order to achieve a uniform patent policy. . . . They indicated that they would feel betrayed if only S. 414 passed and would testify against it."[79] Nonetheless, the Bayh-Dole Act was signed by President Carter during the lame duck session in December 1980, after Carter had already lost his reelection against Ronald Reagan.

With the exception of the Bayh-Dole Act, the Carter administration left only a limited mark on antitrust policy and related domains, but the events of the administration nonetheless provide support for this book's argument. Even though antitrust policy was not a priority at the highest levels, a committed group of aides and policymakers in and adjacent to the antitrust agencies nonetheless pushed for stronger antitrust policies and pro-competition deregulation. The policy change that did occur during this time was away from the purview of this group, whether in the courts or in technology policy, where uncommitted policymakers faced oppositions from antitrust staff and other committed policymakers like Admiral Rickover.

The Reagan Administration

In contrast to the internal conflict in the Carter administration, the policy content of the Reagan administration (1981–1989) was decidedly anti-competition across antitrust, intellectual property, and trade. That being said, the Reagan administration is not an example of uncommitted policymakers learning from diminishing returns: the Reagan administration came into office committed to dramatically scaling back antitrust policy and enhancing intellectual property rights, as it was staffed and informed by

[78] Dick Meserve to Al Stern, "Government Patent Policy," January 23, 1980, BE Box 24, Central Files, JC.

[79] Al Stern to Stuart Eizenstat, "Patent Policy Bill," September 15, 1980, BE Box 3, Central Files, JC.

Chicago school thinkers and recent converts to the Chicago antitrust view. The Antitrust Division ceased enforcing of a number of antitrust rules, and IP rights were used as a concerted industrial strategy to protect American corporations, with both being seen as complements or alternatives to trade protectionism. Even as these policies were sold using rhetoric about international competitiveness and free markets, this section shows primarily how Chicago's views on antitrust were consistent and mutually reinforcing with directly anti-competition and protectionism views.

Chicago and Opposition to Competition

Reagan antitrust was informed directly and indirectly by the Chicago school. To begin with, George Stigler and Richard Posner, two figures central to the Chicago school, wrote to the Reagan transition team with an outline for how to dramatically scale back antitrust policy via executive action without changing the law.[80] Re-summarizing many points from a 1971 article by Posner (Posner 1971), their recommendations included appointing a head of the Antitrust Division who would modify the merger guidelines to be more permissive of mergers, intervene in FTC proceedings to *oppose the FTC*, halt increases in antitrust appropriations, and appoint favorable commissioners to the FTC.[81] Their views were clear, arguing that "many hallowed principles of antitrust are silly . . . especially with regard to vertical restraints and modest-sized horizontal mergers."[82]

Every proposal for policy change was to reduce enforcement of pro-competition rules and policies, save one. They proposed adding in minor pro-competition advocacy specifically to politically hide the overall shift in intent of policy:

> Partially to offset the dyspeptic tone of 1 above, the Assistant Attorney General could and should affirm his commitment to act as a vigorous spokesman of the competitive interest throughout the federal government, and especially before other government agencies—the ICC, FCC, FERC, International Trade Commission, etc.[83]

[80] Richard Posner and George Stigler, "Throttling Back on Antitrust: A Practical Proposal for Deregulation," December 15, 1980 (received), Box 2, Martin Anderson Files, WHSOF, RR.
[81] Ibid., pages 3–4.
[82] Ibid., page 2.
[83] Ibid., page 4.

As during the Nixon administration, the stated motivation for retaining certain pro-competition policies was to politically hide the overall anti-competition shift, given expected political opposition.

Accordingly, with notable exceptions like the breakup of AT&T in 1982, the Reagan administration's DOJ was reliably in favor of market power in almost every arena. Bill Baxter, who converted to the Chicago school of antitrust at some point in the 1970s, was appointed as assistant attorney general for antitrust and promptly revised the merger guidelines, raising the level of concentration necessary for a merger to be scrutinized and giving far more deference to the ostensible efficiencies gained from economies of scale.[84] The guidelines were revised again in 1984 to create separate, more permissive guidelines for vertical mergers.[85] Under Baxter, the Antitrust Division also ceased enforcing antitrust laws against vertical restraints or patent license violations, even though the law still prohibited them, and went so far as to file briefs pushing courts to overturn existing policy. The only area it did retain strong pro-competition enforcement was against direct, horizontal price-fixing agreements, most common in local and regional markets among actors with little to no market power to speak of.

Legislative proposals were meant to simply weaken enforcement or reduce the penalties for antitrust violations, even those where the Chicago school formally would support enforcement. One White House proposal was to "provide an affirmative defense in all antitrust cases that would reduce the plaintiff's claim for damages by the share of those damages fairly allocable to any person released from liability,"[86] a legal technicality favoring defendants and making antitrust violations cost less, even for the horizontal price-fixing that the Chicago ostensibly abhored. In 1985, the Cabinet Council Working Group on Antitrust unanimously agreed to (a) seek "detrebling" legislation (reducing the penalties antitrust violations), (b) amend the Clayton Act to codify the new 1982 merger guidelines into law, (c) allow antitrust exemptions as a form of relief from trade competition, and (d) weaken the rules against interlocking directorates (competing companies sharing board members) in Section 8 of the Clayton Act.[87] Strom Thurmond, a close White House ally, introduced a bill in 1981 to substantially

[84] United States Department of Justice, Merger Guidelines (1982).
[85] United States Department of Justice, Merger Guidelines (1984).
[86] Minutes of Joint Session of Domestic Policy Council and Economic Policy Council, November 20, 1985, Box 50, Ralph Bledsoe Files Series I, WHSOF, RR.
[87] Ibid.

lessen the penalties for naked price-fixing agreements.[88] The administration supported this, despite it being contrary to Chicago doctrine.

This policy coexisted and thrived with a range of other, more directly anticompetitive policy ideas in the administration (e.g., the idea to provide selective exemptions to antitrust rules for firms facing acute import competition). This, like many policies at this time, was openly seen as a functional substitute for direct protectionism: "Antitrust exemption relief would be available only as an alternative: protectionist relief could not be obtained concurrently, nor for a period of 10 years thereafter."[89] The proposal was suggested many times over the decade.

Other groups of economic advisors, however, did not believe these arguments. Instead, they supported the policies *precisely because they were anti-competition*. The 1985 antitrust talking points of a joint Domestic Policy Council / Economic Policy Council (DPC/EPC) meeting supported the Antitrust Working Group's recommendations to use antitrust as a form of import relief because "this will provide an alternative to protectionist measures," and "there is little threat to competition in the U.S. since these are industries already facing a great deal of foreign competition." The EPC acknowledged the falsity of the Chicago school's core claims, saying, "Inability to merge does not greatly hinder our ability to compete in international markets. Unexploited economies of scale rarely, if ever, are the problem U.S. industry faces in world markets."[90] The idea for an merger exemption for trade was dropped because the 1982 merger guidelines were deemed to have already permitted these sorts of mergers.[91]

Nonetheless, when passing on the recommendations to Reagan himself, the talking points for these more permissive merger policies were amended to use Chicago-style arguments about efficiencies and consumer welfare: "big is no longer viewed as necessarily bad and most mergers are supported as pro-competitive, helping businesses to achieve greater efficiency and consumers to enjoy lower prices."[92]

[88] Heritage Foundation Issue Bulletin, "The Antitrust Equal Enforcement Act of 1981 (S. 995)," August 31, 1981, Box 1, Barbara Honegger Files, OA8278, WHSOF, RR.

[89] Working Group on Antitrust Review to Domestic and Economic Policy Councils, "Proposed Changes in the Antitrust Laws," Undated Draft Memorandum, Box 50, Ralph Bledsoe Files Series I, WHSOF, RR, pages 6–7.

[90] Talking Points on Antitrust, Joint DPC/EPC Meeting, November 20, 1985, Box 13, Beryl Sprinkel Files, OA17747, WHSOF, RR.

[91] Charles Rule to McAllister and Bledsoe, November 14, 1986, Box 51, Ralph Bledsoe Files Series I, WHSOF, RR.

[92] Memorandum for the President, "Antitrust Review," December 16, 1985, Box 50, Ralph Bledsoe Series I, WHSOF, RR, page 3.

Intellectual Property and the Reconstruction of Market Power

Separate from narrower conversations in the antitrust arena and debates over the merits of Chicago antitrust, a series of temporary committees and working groups focused on issues related to competition and market power such as high-technology industries, antitrust, telecommunications, semiconductors, research and development, and IP rights. Building on some changes by earlier administrations, the Reagan administration sought to dramatically expand IP protections for American corporations, expanding the anti-competition protections that patents provided for new or marginally improved technology and allowing American companies to maintain higher profits. Through a combination of executive action, notable legislative tweaks, and the eventual internationalization of IP protections through the Uruguay Round of GATT negotiations, the American government put in place a market power policy regime conducive to the growth of the vertically integrated and IP-intensive corporations that dominate the economy today.

The administration did face an acute perceived problem, as one working group emphasized that "previously it was nearly always the declining 'smokestack' industries that sought trade-law protection from import competition. Now, some of our presumably most competitive, high-tech industries are asking that we use the trade laws to help overcome unfair advantages enjoyed by their foreign competitors."[93] In 1982, the Working Group on High Technology "concluded there has been a relative decline in U.S. competitiveness in high technology industries as measured by trade flows among our major trading partners, in particular Japan, West Germany and France."[94]

Nonetheless, these working groups were highly repetitive in their nature, always appealing to similar themes and questions about how antitrust restricted American competitiveness or how insufficient IP protections abroad were a barrier to US entry. Working groups were created to review the position of high technology industries,[95] research and development,[96]

[93] Office of Policy Development, "Unfair Trade Practices: New High Tech Industries Seek Help," June 21, 1985, Box 8, OA16242, Michael Driggs Files, WHSOF, RR.

[94] Minutes of the Cabinet Council on Commerce and Trade, June 23, 1982, Box 31, Ralph Bledsoe Files Series I, WHSOF, RR.

[95] Dennis Kass to Martin Anderson, "CCCT Consideration of the Outlook for U.S. High Technology Industries in the World Economy," September 14, 1981, Box 4, OA18533, Economic Policy Council, WHSOF, RR.

[96] Minutes Cabinet Council on Commerce and Trade, December 17, 1982, Box 1, Becky Dunlop Files Series I, WHSOF, RR.

antitrust reform to "identify antitrust barriers to the competitiveness of U.S. businesses in world markets,"[97] IP,[98] and a range of others.

IP rights in particular were used to advance the competitiveness and profits of American industry. A 1983 memo from Attorney General William French Smith, "Antitrust and Intellectual Property Improvements to Enhance International Trade Opportunities," laid out many of these priorities, all of which limited antitrust's intervention into patent arrangements, sought more or greater antitrust exemptions, or otherwise limited antitrust enforcement.[99] This grew out of a DOJ task force to examine antitrust laws—not IP—which had recommended four proposals in 1982: to detreble antitrust damages for antitrust violations under the rule of reason, to require IP licensing to fall under the rule of reason, to require that courts find an actual harm to competition prior to voiding IP rights based on antitrust concerns, and to expand offshore IP protections for owners of process patents.[100]

In many of these committees developing policy, despite all the talk of free trade, competition, competitiveness, and free markets, whenever the issue of technology, patents, IP rights, innovation, or research came up, it was nearly always paired with discussion of "protection." In July 1983, the Cabinet Committee on Commerce and Trade asked a number of questions: "Should they prohibit copyright licensees from copying material?" "Should semiconductor chip designs be protected and, if so, how?" "Should the United States devote greater attention and resources to obtain better protection abroad for the intellectual property rights of U.S. industry?" "Should greater protection be provided for computer software?" "Should copying the size, color, and shape of a competitor's drug tablet be permitted?"[101]

The administration looked to expand these IP rights internationally. Outlining a "trade based approach to improve IP protection," the Advisory

[97] Ibid.

[98] James Baker Memoranda for the Economic Policy Council, "Intellectual Property and Competitiveness," "Research and Development and Competitiveness," and "Human Capital and Competitiveness," all November 15, 1985, Box 97, BE005, WHORM Subject File, RR.

[99] William French Smith to Cabinet Council on Commerce and Trade, "Antitrust and Intellectual Property Improvements to Enhance International Trade Opportunities," July 11, 1983, Box 3, Geoffrey Carliner Files, OA10697, WHSOF, RR.

[100] Ibid. Those policy proposals were simultaneously being resubmitted to Congress with a fifth provision, to allow joint R&D ventures under antitrust, as Congress communicated the bill would be more likely to pass that way.

[101] CCCT Working Group in Intellectual Property Issue Papers, July 1, 1983, Box 5, Wendell Gunn Files, OA9642, WHSOF, RR.

Committee for Trade Negotiations from the Task Force on Intellectual Property highlighted the costs to US industry in lost sales and lower exports as a result of "counterfeiting" and "piracy."[102] They were also clear that they were not seeking fairness according to existing rules, but rather to expand rights that had only been recently created even in the United States:

> Where protection has been extended to new forms of technology—as with semiconductor chips—foreign countries have been slow in clearly recognizing these rights under their existing laws or in adopting new laws for their protection.[103]

This statement from October 1985 was in reference to "mask work" rights for semiconductor chips (the topography and physical layout of a silicon chip design). Despite complaining about other countries not protecting such rights, these rights were created in the United States by the US Semiconductor Chip Protection Act of 1984, passed and effective a mere eleven months earlier. This was not a matter of pushing countries to adopt standard, efficient policies, but instead as just locking in newly gained protections for American industry.

A common argument in favor of these policies was that the violation of American IP rights (which did not exist in the foreign jurisdictions in question) was "a barrier to American companies selling their products, and to establishing plants."[104] This argument—that inadequate IP protections are an impediment to market access—is a veiling of anticompetitive policies in seemingly pro-competition language. Even with weak IP rights, firms would be free and able to enter foreign markets barrier-free. They just might choose not to if competitors would be able to use their technologies or know-how and they did not have legal recourse against it.

The result of the Uruguay round of GATT negotiations (1986 to 1993) was the 1994 TRIPS (Trade-Related Aspects of Intellectual Property Rights) Agreement, a minimum-standards agreement annexed to the newly created World Trade Organization (WTO).[105] With it attached to the WTO Treaty,

[102] Summary of the Phase I: Recommendations of the Task Force on Intellectual Property to the Advisory Committee for Trade Negotiations, October 1985, Box 98, BE, WHORM Subject File, RR, pages 1–2.

[103] Ibid., page 2.

[104] Trade Strike Force to Economic Policy Council, "Strengthening Protection for Intellectual Property," Undated Memorandum, Box 13, Beryl Sprinkel Papers, OA17747, WHSOF, RR, page 1.

[105] For more background, see Sell (1998, 2003) and Drahos and Braithwaite (2002).

countries were required to adopt the minimum standards for IP protections or be blocked from membership in the WTO, and thus from access to open global trade. Copyright was to last at least fifty years, with software categorized as "literary works" under copyright, patents were to last twenty years, with limited exceptions to exclusive rights (e.g., antitrust licensing rules), and TRIPS attached all of these rules to the WTO. The minimum IP requirements were far beyond what most countries had at the time and beyond what the United States had in place even a few decades earlier.

Conclusion

This chapter has examined the policy changes related to antitrust and competition across the Ford, Carter, and Reagan administrations, highlighting many of the conflicts between policy commitments by core groups of advisors and the role of newer, uncommitted policymakers willing to change their views. The Ford administration similarly committed itself to strong antitrust enforcement almost immediately, and to a far greater degree, with Ford himself strongly advocating for strong antitrust penalties and for reviews of antitrust exemptions and deregulatory possibilities. Despite opposition from Republicans and business interests, and repeated concerns about low profits and insufficient capital formation, the Ford administration pushed ahead with stronger antitrust laws, more enforcement, and deregulation. The Carter administration saw this conflict play out between the antitrust agencies and advisors, who almost always favored stronger enforcement and pro-competition deregulation, and newer science and technology advisors concerned about the United States' technological position in international markets. The Reagan administration, with its Chicago school proponents and converts, executed a clear, anti-competition policy agenda, after a decade of deliberation across administrations and policymaking bodies.

This new market power policy regime created the market conditions and regulatory ecosystem that favored the likes of the digital giants of the late 2010s. With a policy mix of extensive protections for patent holders of advanced technologies, weak enforcement against vertical restraints, an increasingly tolerant posture toward economic concentration, and a set of trade rules to institutionalize these practices globally, the result has been an American economy led by technology giants with vertical control over networks of transnational supply chains. Even though technological change has progressed in ways that could not have been predicted at the time of these policy changes, these changes were designed to ensure that new technologies could be encoded and enforced as sources of market power for lead firms.

7
The Cartelized Economy and the End of Statism

> Unable to sell abroad at truly profitable prices, the profits of exporting companies is actually earned from their sales in France. This approach is reinforced by the non-competitive nature of the French market, which allows them to obtain top prices significantly higher than if there were active competition on the national market.
>
> —Ludovic de Montille and Bruno Lafont, 1977[1]

> More than a series of punctual and dated provisions, above all this is in effect a radical modification of the economic rules of the game.
>
> —Minister of the Economy Édouard Balladur when passing a new competition law, 1986[2]

During a similar time period as the United States' shift from competition to market power, French policy moved in the opposite direction. France's policy regime of national champions continued unabated through the 1970s and the early 1980s even under a Socialist government, but policy changed course in 1985 and 1986. The government refused support for national champion firms, allowing key companies to fail in the face of competition. The competition agency within the Ministry of the Economy[3] was reorganized in 1985, a new competition law was passed in 1986 to add stronger independent enforcement powers and merger control, and all remaining price controls—commonly used as a reference price for collusion in French industry—were simultaneously abolished. France then supported the implementation of stronger European competition policies.

[1] Ludovic de Montille and Bruno Lafont, "Cartellisation des marchés et structure des prix industriels," Présentation de l'étude – Principales conclusions, April 1977, 19780640/1, AN, page b.

[2] Press Conference of Édouard Balladur, November 26, 1986, 543AP/83, AN, pages 1–2.

[3] The Ministry of Finance was renamed the Ministry of the Economy in the time since the 1960s.

Monopoly Politics. Erik Peinert, Oxford University Press. © Oxford University Press (2025).
DOI: 10.1093/oso/9780197789506.003.0007

Following the general argument of diminishing returns, commitment, and learning, this chapter argues that the national champions policy was undone by limits intrinsic to itself—the diminishing returns to market power. As the 1970s and 1980s wore on, investment resources were misallocated by state direction or noncompetitive corporate strategies, and the French domestic economy became increasingly cartelized. These facts were known but ignored in the late 1970s in the Ministry of Industry and the Ministry of the Economy. The left-wing governments of the 1980s slowly relearned these problems, as certain newer actors turned to favor competition policies and moved to the Ministry of the Economy, where new competition policies were developed and proposed, above the opposition of key business groups.

Many existing accounts agree that the statist system of policymaking France was reaching its own internal limits. Levy (1999, 38) writes, "The crisis of *dirigisme* had its roots, then, in its own institutional logic," and Loriaux (1991) argues that France's "overdraft" economy had been running on bought time since World War II. Learning is also emphasized. Levy (1999, 51) highlights that the Socialists "underwent a genuine conversion" in their turn toward market-based policies, and both Schmidt (1996) and Abdelal (2007) argue that the Socialists learned through their first years about the difficulties of business to become better advocates for the market than the conservatives. The turnover in established officials, particularly from Mitterrand's first to second government and the decision to remain in the European Monetary System (EMS) in 1983, fits with the overall contours of the argument presented here. However, like others, Levy (1999) sees the system's collapse as the result of a mix of financial, microeconomic, and macroeconomic forces, meaning that despite many existing accounts that change was driven endogenously, it is less clear that it was diminishing returns *to market power specifically* that caused them.

Foremost, many argue that the financial costs of industrial policies caused the shift to favor market-oriented policies (Loriaux 1991, 220–227). Having dramatically increased a range of social benefits like pensions, family allowances, and other social transfers, a rapidly increasing capital flight out of the country shook the Socialist policy elite to cut government spending, including industrial policy.[4] Schmidt (1996, 95, 107) argues that after the expensive nationalizations by Mitterrand and the expansion of social

[4] See also Abdelal (2007).

spending, "there was no longer any money left" to fund social or industrial investments and that the nationalizations exacerbated problems by "depleting the coffers of the state." In response, austerity was implemented beginning in 1983 in order to remain in the EMS, and industrial policies were cut over the same years. Hall (1986, 211) argued, "The principal factor that pushed the Government away from its initial industrial strategy . . . was the financial constraint implicit in its austerity program."[5]

Others suggest that European integration drove these changes, in that France's adoption of competition policies was simply derivative of the wave of European integration in the 1980s. In particular, Mitterrand's decisions to remain in the EMS in 1983 and the Single European Act (SEA) of 1986 both laid the groundwork for European merger rules in competition policy in 1989. In this view, as Gerber (1998, 403) argues, France was "the first country to respond to the developments of the mid-1980s by changing its competition law system to bring it closer to that of the Community." Warlouzet (2018, Chapter 8) characterizes competition policy was among the first "neoliberal" European policies, driven largely by supranational disputes over state aid.

This chapter shows these alternatives to be incomplete or missing key points of evidence, beginning with an account of how the national champions policy persisted in the 1970s, despite signs that industrial supports were helping uncompetitive French firms sell at a loss abroad, only to make up their losses by gouging the domestic French market. Second, the chapter details how President Mitterrand deepened the national champions policy through a series of nationalizations, only to switch course as national champions firms failed to control their own prices and remained unwilling to invest in productive new opportunities. This persuaded a cadre of younger and newer policymakers to push for a revision in industrial policy and an expansion of competition policies in 1985 and 1986. Crucially, the internal debates to shift toward competition, and even the formal decisions to do so, preceded the Single Europe Act and were considered separately. Furthermore, with a deficit of only 3 percent of GDP in 1983, France could afford expensive industrial policies, and it did: industrial policies were not cut in the main wave of austerity in 1983, even as social benefits were slashed.

[5] Moravcsik (1998, 341–342) largely agrees with this assessment.

Competition and Industrial Policy in the 1970s

The national champions policy, established beginning with the Fifth Plan in the 1960s, endured through the 1970s, albeit via the French government frequently rebranding it under new labels: a policy of industrial redeployment (*rédeploiement industriel*), the policy of niches (*politique de créneaux*), reconquering the internal market (*reconquête du marché intérieur*), or supply chain policy (*politique des filières*).

Industrial Policy in the 1970s

This rebranding of the national champions policy began after the first OPEC oil shock in 1973, which prompted a "new" industrial policy, announced as "industrial redeployment" (*redéploiement industriel*) by President Valéry Giscard d'Estaing in 1975. On the understanding that France's industry was poorly adapted to the new international division of labor, the government opted for an active industrial policy to move into new market "niches" (*politique de créneaux*) (Schmidt 1996, 53).[6] As much as these were often framed as new policies, Giscard admitted in 1975 that this "development program does not mark a break with previous policy," but a renewal and expansion of the same policies.[7] Concretely, it entailed support for productive investment combined with price and credit controls to limit inflation (i.e., similar policy to the 1960s).[8] In line with Berger (1981), the policy of redeployment actively included support for declining firms to reduce the social tension implied by the necessary industrial adjustment,[9] and it effectively became industrial policy in favor of incumbent firms: for economic reasons to favor expanding industries, and for political reasons continued support for declining industries.

The government used the same criteria and metrics to assess these policies as it had used in the 1960s: investment, *autofinancement*, and

[6] GRESI, "Le cadre du redéploiement industriel," February 1975, 19890448/1, AN; Direction générale de l'industrie, "Programme préparatoire de travail pour la Définition et la Mise en Oeuvre d'une Politique de Redéploiement Industriel," undated document, 19890448/1, AN.

[7] "Le programme de développement de l'économie française," September 27, 1975, 1A-0000313, CAEF, pages 2–3.

[8] Ibid.

[9] Conseil de planification sur le redéploiement industriel, "Projet de relève de décisions," April 14, 1975, 19890448/1, AN, page 13.

concentration. The Ministry of Industry frequently reduced problems to a question of investment: notes among the Ministry of Industry leadership in 1975 emphasized "the financial situation of companies" and "the profitability of investments" as the most important indicators for to assess policy success.[10] Even employment would be reduced to profits and investments; the Ministry of Industry argued, "The increase in the number of employed workers in industry depends on profitability."[11] This attitude lasted through to the very end of the 1970s.[12]

These industrial policies of the 1970s fell under even more labels despite staying largely similar. "Reconquering the internal market" (*"reconquête du marché intérieur"*) referred to recapturing domestic market shares lost to foreign competition by (a) prohibiting localities from purchasing from foreign suppliers, (b) enforcing preferences for French firms in public procurement, and (c) coordinating orders among large firms and the state.[13] At the same time, the economic concept of *filières* arose in policy circles. *Filière* means supply chain, but the term came to refer to an industrial policy (*politique de filières*) centered around large vertically integrated firms to control large sections of their respective industries. The director general of industry outlined many of these priorities in 1975:

- "creation of jobs per unit of investment with a view to eliminating unemployment;"
- "the effect of *filières*, that is to say the ripple effect on sectors belonging to the same production process;"
- "the critical mass effect, in particular of investments to enable the sector considered to reach the threshold of competitiveness (example of IT);"
- "the downstream effect on sectors not belonging to the same *filière*;"
- "the *reconquering of the internal market*, that is to say the contribution of development of the sector to the elimination of a significant import deficit;"

[10] Ornano to Director General of Industry, January 1975, 19890448/1, AN.

[11] Henri Tezenas du Montcel, "Note pour le Ministre: L'industrie et la création d'emplois," July 25, 1978, 19880199/20, AN, page 1.

[12] Minister of Industry and Secretary of State for Small and Medium-Sized Industry to Minister of the Economy, August 9, 1979; "La situation de l'industrie au début des années 1980," undated document, 19880199/21, AN.

[13] "Reconquête du marché intérieur," undated document, 19800301/1-3, AN. The document is almost assuredly from early 1975, since it is an industry retrospective on the results from 1974.

- "the mobilizability of industrialists and their degree of motivation to carry out investments according to incentive or encouragement from the State."[14]

Accordingly, the Ministry of Industry created redeployment plans for each sector, focusing on the "*aspect filière*" (supply chain aspect), viewing the prospects of a sector according to how economically concentrated it was and focusing on their ability to reconquer the internal market.[15]

Through the 1970s, major interest groups for labor and business remained supportive of the national champions policy. In 1979 meetings with the Ministry of Industry, organized labor pushed for these policies even without the government's prompting:

> The GSC [*Garantie Sociale du Chef d'entreprise*][16] and the CFDT [*Conféderation française démocratique du travail*] spontaneously stated the principle of selective support for industry: sectoral recovery program focused on advanced technologies and energy savings for the GSC, while the CFDT states the need for a horizontal industrial policy (research, technology, foreign trade) and wants to maintain two axes of dialogue between the state and businesses: competitiveness in the international environment and the relationship between technological progress and employment.[17]

In similar meetings, business leaders from Conseil National du Patronat Français (CNPF) and CGPME (*Conféderation Générale des Petites et Moyennes Entreprises*, the small business association) highlighted the lack of willingness and resources to invest as a core economic problem.[18] Distributional conflict remained, but it was confined within an understanding of industrial policy centered around concentration, market power, and international competitiveness.

[14] Ministry of Industry and Research, "Interprétation des résultats de l'analyse multicritères et élaboration des premiers éléments d'une politique industrielle," April 11, 1975, 19890448/1, AN, page 2.

[15] Various documents labeled "Fiche sur les secteurs prioritaires dans l'optique 'redéploiement,'" 19800301/4-6, AN. These covered the following sectors: organic synthesis, plastic materials, fertilizer, rubber and textiles, paper and cardboard products, and apparel.

[16] GSC is and was an employers' union, providing unemployment coverage and representing the interests of managers and business owners, primarily proprietors.

[17] Ministry of Industry, "Rencontre avec les confédérations syndicales," September 1979, 19880199/20, AN, page 2.

[18] Ibid., pages 3–4. See also Ministry of Industry, "Entretien accorde par le Ministre à la CNPF," September 11, 1979, 19880199/20, AN; and Ministry of Industry, "Entretien accorde par le Ministre à la CGPME," September 13, 1979, 19880199/20, AN.

Barre Law

The endurance of some competition rules and enforcement—including the creation of a new competition law in 1977—complicated this picture, but these were neither meaningful impediments to industrial policy nor did they serve as effective pro-competition policies. In July 1977, Prime Minister Raymond Barre passed a competition law, a law sometimes seen as the first step in a move toward real pro-competition policy in France (Brault 1987; Gerber 1998). However, this law was intentionally limited in scope, motivated primarily by price liberalization that would allow private firms to *raise* prices in order to fund investment. The pro-competition intent present in initial proposals was progressively watered down by successive rounds of deliberations and debates over the decade, particularly as the question was framed in terms of mental models of international competitiveness.

In 1972, the Sixth Plan Competition Committee proposed a decree to strengthen the Cartel Committee (CTEPD) into a formal competition commission (*Commission Technique de la Concurrence*) in 1972, giving it independent authority to initiate investigations. Even this did not pass, and it would not have changed much if it had.[19] From 1974 to 1975, the issue bounced around between the legislature, the prime minister's office, and the Cartel Committee with few tangible results.[20] In May 1975, Prime Minister Chirac announced the development of a new competition law (Brault 1987, 30), with internal documentation justifying competition reforms by citing rising merger rates in France in the late 1960s and early 1970s and the disappearance of many small firms.[21]

[19] "Projet de Decret instituant une Commission technique de la Concurrence," April 17, 1972, B-0065839/1, CAEF.

[20] After the 1973 passage of the Royer law—a law to target and limit the size of large retailers—left-wing legislator Jean Poperen proposed a law to create a Competition Commission to strengthen the rules around individual restraints on competition and to add merger control (Brault 1987, Appendix 8). This went nowhere, and another major competition overhaul was proposed in June (Brault 1987, 29). Claude Villain, the director general of the Competition and Price Directorate (*Direction Générale de la Concurrence et de la Consommation*, or DGCC), and Finance Minister Fourcade put the issue to the CTEPD. (The *Commission technique des ententes, CTE,* had been renamed the *Commission technique des ententes et des positions dominantes* in 1963.) The CTEPD's report, published in February 1975, made pro-competition proposals almost across the board: more severe financial penalties for cartel infractions, lest companies or businesspeople be able to profit even having been caught, and the addition of merger control, which still did not exist. Commission Technique des Ententes et des Positions Dominantes, "Rapport au Ministre de l'Économie et des Finances sur certaines mesures propres à renforcer le dispositif de prévention et de répression des pratiques anticoncurrentielles," February 1975, 20000007, AN.

[21] "Perspectives de la politique de la concurrence," May 1975, 20030502/8, AN.

However, as the issue bounced around this way, it was frequently reframed into the mental models of the national champions policy, with the issue of ensuring international competitiveness hanging heavily over conversations. When discussing the need to harmonize French legislation with European Community (EC) competition rules, the commission was hung up on the possible difficulty if France adopted stricter rules than those of other member states,[22] pushing to ensure that the French rules were on the lax side. Accordingly, the conclusions from this commission advocated a preregistration system for cartels, like existed in Germany and for the European Community.[23] This is in contrast to France's position during the negotiations for European Regulation 17/62 in 1962, where France opposed such a system for pro-competition reasons.

When Raymond Barre became the prime minister in 1976, he made minor revisions to the proposal (Brault 1987, 30), and the law passed on July 19, 1977, alongside a series of significant price liberalizations to accompany it. This 1977 reform renamed the CTEPD as the *Commission de la Concurrence* and gave it a much larger budget as well as a permanent staff (Gerber 1998, 191). The law added formal merger controls to French competition rules, but otherwise it did little to nothing to add to or more clearly specify the scope of which practices were more or less permissible.[24]

Internal memos regarding the 1977 law did appear to defend it as a pro-competition move, at least within the Ministry of the Economy. While the conservatives were still in power from the passage of Raymond Barre's law through 1981, communications from and among the prime minister and the minister of the economy indicate they genuinely intended to enforce the new law as a way to strengthen competition, bring prices down, and benefit consumers.[25] Other memos from the *Direction Générale de la Concurrence et de la Consommation* (DGCC) around 1980 indicate that the 1977 law, and the associated price liberalization, were more openly pro-competitive, lauding the merger control, the new enforcement powers, and the new full-time staff.[26]

[22] Minutes of Commission de Révision du Code Pénal, June 19, 1975, 20000007/2, AN, page 1.

[23] Commission de Révision du Code Pénal, "Note sur le problème des ententes illicites et des abus de positions dominantes," July 1975, 20000007/2, AN, page 2.

[24] Decret portant application de la loi no. 77-806 du 19 juillet 1977, 19880001/8, AN.

[25] Finance Minister Monory to Prime Minister Barre, November 9, 1978, 20030502/8, AN; Barre to Ministers and Secretaries of State, May 31, 1978, 20030502/8, AN.

[26] Service de la Concurrence et de la Formation des Prix, "L'Action menée en matière de concurrence 1974-1980," B-0065840/1, CAEF; Direction Générale de la Concurrence et de la

However, the more likely motivation for the Barre government was price liberalizations, not competition. These were the first attempts to remove price controls from sections of the French economy since World War II, and the competition law was presented as a necessary complement to this. Documents from the Ministry of Industry and the prime minister's office show that the goal of the combined package was to allow businesses to *raise* prices and increase investment. In 1977, the minister of industry, René Monory, defended plans to liberalize prices specifically, solely and publicly on the basis that doing so was necessary to allow businesses to raise prices, such that they will be able to restore their cash reserves and invest.[27] While Raymond Barre's competition law and liberalization of prices was sincere in many respects, the leadership of the Ministry of the Economy, the Ministry of Industry, and even the prime minister's office consistently defended it not in market-making, competition, or liberalizing terms, but rather neo-mercantilist ones, in order to "expand the margin for maneuver of firms" as an element of industrial policy.[28]

The Ministry of Industry's timeline for price liberalization likewise indicated this desire to avoid competition. It was to begin with firms already facing competition, which meant that the liberalization would have no effect, since prices were already below the ceilings. The second wave of liberalizations was to apply to "sectors where a rapid reconstitution of profit margins is particularly necessary to enable them to finance their development,"[29] hearkening back to the original justifications for the national champions policy. Only as an afterthought was price liberalization seen as a way to restore competition or market forces in order to bring prices down for consumers.[30]

Barre himself made clear that he did not see the competition policy as a change: "There is no reason to modify in principle the mechanism for controlling restrictive practices and dominant positions which has now been in operation for more than twenty years."[31] Barre likewise told the Special

Consommation, "Évolution de la politique de la concurrence depuis 1970," undated document, B-0065840, CAEF.

[27] Le Quotidien de Paris, "Monory au Quotidien: la liberté des prix industriels est indispensable," November 14, 1977, found in 19780640/1, AN.

[28] Director General of Industry to Minister of Industry, "Libération des prix industriels," May 19, 1978, 19880199/20, AN, page 1.

[29] Ibid., page 2.

[30] The Minister of Industry passed these priorities to the minister of the economy. Minister of Industry to Minister of the Economy, "Libération des prix industriels," undated letter, 19880199/20, AN.

[31] "Chapitre Premier: La Politique de la Concurrence," dated December 6, 1976, B-0065839/1, CAEF, page 11.

Commission reviewing the prosed law that it was to be lenient on the mergers implicit in France's established industrial policy:

> It is not a question of going back on the policy of strengthening industrial structures pursued for several years by the public authorities. For social reasons, technical efficiency or international competitiveness, it is necessary that our country has a modern industrial apparatus, and that therefore the necessary mergers are made.[32]

While qualified with some pro-competition language, Barre's defense of the law, and his stated motivations for it, took so many tenants of the national champions policy as given: that concentration is necessary for competitiveness and that concentration is necessarily a source of technical efficiency.[33]

The firsthand account of Brault (1987, 34) similarly notes that the place of the bureaucracy, at this point hostile to market competition, was not displaced at all by the 1977 law. From 1977 to 1986—the entirety of its existence before being replaced in 1986— only one merger was blocked, and even that was annulled on procedural grounds.[34]

Early Signs of Sclerosis

Evidence began to mount that the lack of competition was a problem and that the national champions policy was exacerbating the problem. However, just as actual policy proposals were watered down, so was economic reporting that contradicted the dominant understandings of industrial policy. When mental models of competitiveness were raised in discussions, evidence of policy problems or arguments for more competition would be omitted or ignored.

Historical and political economy accounts—as well as politicians at the time—consistently highlight an investment crisis. Internal reports about declining investment all focused on the question of *autofinancement*, as it had been discussed in the mid-1960s, focusing on the insufficient profitability, insufficient income, and price controls that prevented firms from having

[32] Ibid., pages 15–16.
[33] Ibid., page 16.
[34] Déchery to Balladur, "Contrôle des concentrations," January 28, 1988, 543AP/83, AN.

sufficient resources to invest.[35] Hall (1986, 197) cites that private investment fell by 14 percent from 1973 to 1981, with the rate of *autofinancement* falling as corporate debt rose. Loriaux (1991, 232) notes that from the 1970s to 1981, the rate of *autofinancement* had declined from 70 percent to 51 percent, and then to 40.3 percent at the beginning of 1982.

But the track record of *autofinancement* from this period is not nearly as bleak this presentation implies, and there was not a clear, secular decline in investment and *autofinancement*. It should be emphasized, as before, that if corporations are taking on more debt to finance greater investments and their own investment spending stays the same, their "rate" of *autofinancement* will fall, mechanically as a matter of accounting. Furthermore, a 1981 statistical bulletin from the Ministry of Industry showed that the decline cited over this time period was far more a result of choosing particularly high and low years—1973 and 1980 or 1981, respectively—for the start and end points (Figure 7.1).

Additionally, some French policymakers knew this at the time, and they would often point to a lack of demand—and the lack of productive investment opportunities—as a more pressing economic problem than the lack of finances with which to invest. A 1979 report from the Ministry of Industry—regarding yet another proposed expansion of investment aid to industry—wrote that business groups knew that they had overinvested from 1971 to 1973. In contrast to the policy obsession over productive investment, French

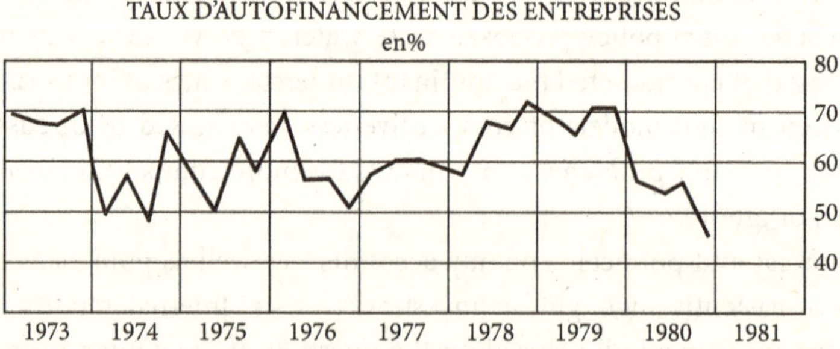

Figure 7.1 *Autofinancement* in the 1970s[36]

[35] L'insuffisance en fonds propres des entreprises françaises, July 1976, 19800301/4-6, AN.

[36] Direction Générale de l'Industrie, "La conjoncture industrielle en mars 1981," April 25, 1981, 19880199/21, AN, Annexe I.

output was sufficient to meet demand. But the national champions policy aimed to exceed it, and the focus on investment was ignoring the real constraints of demand.[37]

Businesses similarly complained that investment was limited more by a lack of profitable opportunities and low domestic demand.[38] Successful firms were primarily doing so off of exports, partially because domestic demand had been falling.[39]

Another example of watering down economic reporting was a report, "The Cartelization of Markets and the Structure of Prices," written for the Ministry of Industry and the Paris Chamber of Commerce in 1977 by two business students, Ludovic de Montille and Bruno Lafont.[40] Their conclusion, based on a new system of weighting wholesale prices,[41] was that most French firms were in practice dumping on foreign markets: exporting increasing quantities of products abroad at a loss and then trying to make up the losses by price-gouging in an increasingly cartelized domestic economy.

The conventional wisdom in the state and among business at the time was that price controls "strangled" firms and suppressed profit margins. Instead, de Montille and Lafont found—confirmed by conversations with business associations—that under normal conditions, price ceilings did not interfere with profits or exports. Price ceilings did, however, prevent firms from offsetting losses from economic downturns by charging higher prices in boom years. As a result, French firms would not revise their prices down in bad times or in response to competition.[42] And, accordingly, they suggested that that price controls had become an implicit cartel coordination device.[43] They argued that this system is only possible because the French domestic market was particularly noncompetitive:

[37] J. Maire to Director General of Industry, "Plan exceptionnel de renforcement industriel," February 13, 1979, 19890448/2, AN, page 2.

[38] L'insuffisance en fonds propres des entreprises françaises, July 1976, 19800301/4-6, AN.

[39] Compte-Rendu, Réunion "Investissements" No. 8: Entretien avec MM Joly, Ferry, Forgeot, Loygues et Gautier, undated document, 19800301/1-3, AN.

[40] Ludovic de Montille and Bruno Lafont, "Cartellisation des marchés et structure des prix industriels," October 1977, 19780640/1, AN.

[41] INSEE had been calculating its wholesale price index based on a series of weights and coefficients to bundle different products of the same industry together, but had not changed or updated these weights since 1962. Ibid., pages 16–18. They obtained an alternative measure by aggregating invoices for more specific products that the Ministry of Industry had been collecting for separate survey purposes for several years. Ibid., page 18. Their new measure was simply $Price = \frac{Invoicing}{Quantity}$ relative to the invoices from the Ministry of Industry surveys. Ibid.

[42] Ibid., page 100.

[43] Ludovic de Montille and Bruno Lafont, "Cartellisation des marchés et structure des prix industriels," Présentation de l'étude – Principales conclusions, April 1977, 19780640/1, AN, page b.

> Unable to sell abroad at truly profitable prices, the profits of exporting companies is actually earned from their sales in France. This approach is reinforced by the non-competitive nature of the French market, which allows them to obtain top prices significantly higher than if there were active competition on the national market.[44]

Normally the existence of a study like this would be little more than a curiosity, but it persuaded enough Ministry of Industry staff such that its conclusions were eventually put in front of the minister of industry.

Nonetheless, as it made its way up the Ministry of Industry, progressively more of these implications were left out. First sent from the *Direction Générale de l'Industrie* to the minister of industry's office,[45] most of the arguments remained unchanged.[46] But then Didier Maus, a technical director to the minister of industry, René Monory, passed many of these conclusions on in a similar fashion, but he left out some of the most direct conclusions and arguments about the lack of domestic competition.[47] These points were watered down even further as Minister of Industry René Monory wrote to Raymond Barre, noting primarily that competition stopped French firms from selling at higher prices abroad and that domestically "price controls have led to a sharp deterioration in profit margins or even repeated losses, and, as a result, penalized new investments," and where "recovery in the situation in these sectors seems possible from a proactive industrial policy, the pricing policy of which can be a determining factor."[48] The original concerns—that price controls were facilitating collusion in an already uncompetitive market—were entirely translated into concerns about competitiveness and insufficient investment.

The same argument is made in the full report at Ludovic de Montille and Bruno Lafont, "Cartellisation des marchés et structure des prix industriels," October 1977, 19780640/1, AN, page 100.

[44] Ludovic de Montille and Bruno Lafont, "Cartellisation des marchés et structure des prix industriels," Présentation de l'étude - Principales conclusions, April 1977, 19780640/1, AN, page b.

[45] Hors to Stutzmann, Ministère de l'Industrie et de la Recherche, undated note, 19780640/1. This was attached to the report, dated October 1977.

[46] R. Stutzmann, "Politique des prix et politique industrielle," November 7, 1977, 19780640/1, AN, page 2.

[47] Didier Maus, "Politique des prix et politique industrielle," October 21, 1977, 19780640/1, AN.

[48] Monory to Barre, "Évolution du régime des prix industriels à la production," March 2, 1978, 19780640/1, AN, page 2.

Mitterrand's Industrial Socialism

The victory of Socialist François Mitterrand in the 1980 presidential election—and a corresponding sweep of legislative elections by the left—led to a deepening of these trends rather than a break from them. While promising and delivering on plans for a policy of nationalizing most key industries, the detailed plans for industry were primarily to "reconquer the domestic market" (*reconquête du marché intérieur*) through a series of vertically integrated *filières*, led by the main nationalized firm under the tutelage of the relevant government ministry. The goal was to avoid competitive market mechanisms and establish France's economic autonomy from the rest of the world. As Brault (1987, 37) says, "In the early years of President Mitterrand's seven-year term, competition ceased to be fashionable." This sections shows how these policies were initially implemented and met their limits and how committed policymakers clung to them while others learned from their failures.

The Policy of *Filières*

At the beginning of the 1980s, France was in particularly bad economic health. The slowdown in economic growth, high unemployment, high inflation, along with the Volcker shocks from the US Federal Reserve, created a difficult environment. When Mitterrand took office in 1981, the governing coalition was broken largely into two groups. One was a left-wing group associated with Jean-Pierre Chevènement, favoring large-scale nationalizations and state-led growth with outright protectionist tariffs. Another group, associated with Michel Rocard, opposed these plans, favoring a more decentralized socialism (Hall 1986, 193). Nonetheless, the disagreements in these early years rarely touched on competition, and for the first several years, Chevènement's side won the policy battle, as the government carried out a series of large-scale nationalizations of most major industrial sectors.

Most of the nationalizations were enacted by the law of February 11, 1982, save for the steel industry, nationalized in December 1981. The nationalizations of the Mitterrand government are best understood in terms of the ideas of some of his main advisors, namely Alain Boublil and Jaques Attali. Boublil (1977) primarily characterizes the world economy as now dominated by non-price competition, largely in terms of innovation and technological advances among large vertically integrated firms. His main recommendations focus on supply-side policies in terms of investment and output, emphasize the vertical integration of industry to allow coordination between different stages of production, aim to reduce the level of imports, and to generally limit the French economy's exposure to the international economy and specifically to international competition. Boublil argued that vertical integration would reduce the vulnerability of French intermediate products from exposure to international competition and ensure that there were enough profits for *autofinancement* at every stage of production.

The Mitterrand government rapidly went through ministers of industry from various wings of the coalition, with Pierre Joxe, Pierre Dreyfus, Jean-Pierre Chevènement, and Laurent Fabius all switching in and out of the role in the first few Mitterrand years (Hall 1986, 204). Jean-Pierre Chevènement took over with the merger of the Ministry of Industry and the Ministry of Research in June 1982, and he held this position only until the spring of 1983. It was during his time there when most of the details of industrial policies were elaborated, many of its limits exposed, and the beginnings of open doubt about its wisdom appeared. As Levy (1999, 45) says, "Chevènement incarnated the *dirigiste* spirit of the early Mitterrand years." Jean-Pierre Chevènement's correspondence within the Ministry of Industry reveals that he was a strong believer in the technological constraints of the era, in that the new economy required large firms, extensive state-business coordination, and industrial supports in the era of new technologies like IT. He argued that leaving the direction of the French electronics industry to a laissez-faire, market-based approach would result in the collapse of the industry in France. At the same time, he argued that the technological requirements of the industry favored "technological, financial, and industrial integration." He thought IT particularly, but not exclusively, was defined by large investment requirement and "rents which are attached to the dominant positions, gradually concentrating the market in the hands of a very small number of multinational companies."[49]

The policies for the nationalized industries were coordinated through a series of contracts negotiated separately with each of the nationalized firms (*contrats de plan*), normally coordinated with the Ministry of Industry. The contracts were to cover some combination of output, price policies,

[49] Chevènement Speech at Forum de l'expansion, September 16, 1982, 19940139/1, AN, pages 8–9.

investment, goals for productivity gains, quality improvements, employment plans, reduction of working hours, and cooperation with subcontractors in their supply chain or *filière*.[50] According to Jean-Pierre Chevènement, the *contrats de plan* had somewhat different priorities by sector: to modernize basic industries (steel, glass, commodities), to improve competitiveness of transformation industries (cars, chemicals, manufacturing), to revive investment and research, and to maintain full employment.[51]

While there were some differences between the Mitterrand government's industrial policy and that of Giscard d'Estaing's in the 1970s, both were general continuations of the same priorities of the national champions policy. As Jack Hayward argues, "The firms that were nationalized in 1982 were already national champions and although a few president/managing directors were replaced, they [had] not been subjected to the Plan or their firms dismembered, their strategic and managerial autonomy ha[d] scarcely been challenged and their internal power structure seem[ed] untouched" (Hayward 1986, 229). Likewise, the *contrats de plan* were treading similar ground as the *contrats de programme* from the 1960s, which provided certain exemptions from price restrictions to lead firms as long as they hit certain targets from the plan, including mergers.[52]

However, despite being framed as productivity improvements and industrial upgrading, much of this remained straightforwardly anti-competition and protectionist. Chevènement outlined the policy of reconquering the internal market in terms of inter-firm cooperation and vertical controls.[53] The Ministry of Industry internally advocated for preferential buying for domestic producers to reconquer the internal market by cutting out foreign competitors.[54] Indirect barriers or safety and product regulations were overtly justified not on safety or regulatory needs but based on their ability to by exclude foreign imports.[55]

[50] Commission de Reforme de la Planification, Groupe No. 4 – Sous Groupe 3: Contrats de Plan, May 1982, 19940139/3, AN, pages 14–20.

[51] Communication de M. Chevènement au Conseil des Ministres, February 9, 1983, 19940139/3, AN, pages 4–5.

[52] See Hall (1986, 149) and Commissariat Général du Plan, La Concurrence et la Formation des Prix – Notes Annexes, August 1969, 19890575/23-24, AN, pages I–4.

[53] Intervention de M. Chevènement devant les présidents des entreprises nationales, November 19, 1982, 19940139/1, AN, page 8.

[54] "Introduction: les axes et les moyens de notre politique de reconquête du marché intérieur," undated document, 19940139/2, AN. Document in a folder dated November 1982; Noël Imbert-Bouchard, "Proposition d'orientation sur les marchés publics," undated document, 19930139/2, AN.

[55] "Stratégie de défense du marché intérieur," undated document, 19940139/2, AN, and attached Texte no. 82-S-75 du 11 juin 1982, "Contrôle à l'importation des produits industrialisés présumés

These policies yet again contradicted European rules on competition and state aid,[56] which is why they were implemented as indirect barriers to trade: standardization and technical barriers, exchange controls, preferential credit, public aids, price regulations, tax benefits,[57] and using safety clauses in public procurement to favor French firms.[58]

There were some preexisting contrary opinions at the top, but their attention was usually more on other issues. Minister of the Economy Jacques Delors openly had been calling for more market-based competition policies from very early on, with Delors himself saying that "the enforcement against anticompetitive practices, and in particular price-fixing, will be more determined than before"' (Brault 1987, 38). Nonetheless, Delors's priorities appeared elsewhere, as he helped Chévénement push the prime minister for even more government aid to industry in 1982. Their interpretation focused on the supply side and mitigating competition, emphasizing the following:

> This endowment will be used on the one hand to support the investment of companies operating in crisis sectors at the global level—steel, chemicals—on the other hand to encourage the realization of new investments in strategic sectors where competition is particularly lively—automotive, IT.[59]

Additionally, commentary from aides to Chevènement in January 1983 stated, "The [Ministry of the] Economy is divided between its solidarity with us [on industrial policy] and the visible concern of Delors not to leave to [Prime Minister] Fabius the monopoly of budgetary rigor."[60] Delors's priorities were mostly about fiscal policy, and he was willing to break with it for the sake of industrial expenditures.

dangereux ou non conformés aux normes techniques ou de sécurité," June 11, 1982, 19940139/2, AN. For the use of standardization policy for the same, see Ministry of Industry, "Projet de plan d'une communication sur la normalisation," undated document, 19940139/2, AN.

[56] "Quelques orientations pour une politique d'importation pouvant contribuer à la reconquête du marché intérieur,"' August 27, 1961, 19890448/1, AN, pages 1–3; Note pour le Ministre, "Conseil Restreint du 4 août; reconquête du marché intérieur : compatibilité avec les Traités communautaires," August 3, 1982, 19940139/2, AN.

[57] "Quelques orientations pour une politique d'importation pouvant contribuer à la reconquête du marché intérieur,"' August 27, 1961, 19890448/1, AN, pages 3–4.

[58] Note pour le Ministre, "Conseil Restreint du 4 août; reconquête du marché intérieur : compatibilité avec les Traités communautaires," August 3, 1982, 19940139/2, AN, page 2.

[59] Jacques Delors and Jean-Pierre Chevènement to Pierre Mauroy, November 8, 1982, 19890448/3, AN, page 1.

[60] Babusiaux to Chevènement, "Réunion du 12 janvier sur les contrats de plan," January 2, 1983, 19940139/3, AN.

To the degree that proposals for new or amended competition policies were proposed during these early years, they were vague, limited, and still focused on particularistic rules from the 1950s and 1960s. A memo from January 1982 noted that Delors had made specific proposals for competition policy and how responsibility should be divided between the administration and the *Commission de la Concurrence*, but the actual proposals were framed around the rules of fair competition (*concurrence déloyale*) and production-distribution disputes,[61] and the ministry saw competition as a necessary sacrifice to competitiveness or stability:

> Competition policy is also part of a whole. . . . Compromises are therefore often necessary . . . between the activation of competition, the fight against inflation, the defense of employment, agricultural policy or industrial policy.[62]

While at points highlighting competition as a mitigating factor to inflation, it otherwise focused on issues of manufacturer-retail disputes and practices.[63] Admittedly, some legislative changes were being prepared in the Ministry of the Economy at this time in November 1982, with new provisions to strengthen merger controls from the 1977 law, to prohibit additional anti-competitive practices, to expand the number of members on the *Commission de la Concurrence*, and to expand the scale and number of sanctions available for violations."[64]

Even the Competition Authority accommodated the *filière* policy. The DGCC highlighted the benefits to growth of the *filière* policy: rationalizing activity, achieving economies of scale, diversifying firms, financing future investment, rescuing firms in difficulty, and "assuring control of the market to give an advantage over the competition."[65] The DGCC would not stand in the way of concentration:

> The public authorities, through their voluntary action in the field of industrial restructuring and the organization of filières favor certain groupings

[61] "La politique de la concurrence, January 1982, B-0065840/1, CAEF.

[62] Ibid., page 2.

[63] "Orientations pour une politique d'action sur les facteurs structurels de l'inflation," November 29, 1982, 20020380/1, AN, page 8.

[64] Ibid.

[65] Direction Générale de la Concurrence et de la Consommation, "Motifs des concentrations en France," undated document, B-0065834/2, CAEF. This memo was undated, but based on its location within the DGCC records, it was written between May 1980 and February 1983.

> and certain concentrations necessary to maintain our international competitiveness. . . . This is why the DGCC does not at all envisage its role in terms of concentration as having to result in a systematic opposition—or at least hostility—to the projects which would be submitted to it.[66]

Commitment, Limits, and Learning

As in other cases, these new policies entailed or coincided with a series of reorganizations and bureaucratic changes. The managements of the newly nationalized companies were not put together until the summer of 1982, with the administration councils (*conseils d'administration*) to oversee them not nominated until June, and the presidents of the firms not put in place before July.[67] Chevènement's appointment as minister of industry coincided with the merger of the Ministries of Industry and of Research, combining hundreds of regional offices and the combination of two ministries at an already tumultuous time,[68] on top of the new staff needed to oversee the newly nationalized firms.

Among these newer bureaucrats to the Ministry of Industry was Christian Babusiaux, who would later become the director general of the DGCC in the Ministry of the Economy and was one of the central figures in the drafting and development of the 1986 competition law.[69] Babusiaux moved on to the Ministry of Industry shortly after Mitterrand was elected, and he was responsible for helping to negotiate the *contrats de plan* and the loans attached to them for about seven months, dispensing billions of francs worth of loans to the newly nationalized firms in chemicals, steel, pharmaceuticals, electronics, and others.[70] As such, he was intimately involved in financing

[66] Ibid., page 4.

[67] Comité interministériel du 1er février 1982, "Contrats de plan," January 31, 1983, 19930139/3, AN.

[68] Serge Ravanel, Expose des Motifs, undated, 19940139/1, AN; Serge Ravanel, Note de Réflexion no. 1, "Disposition à prendre pour l'organisation des nouvelles Directions régionales de la Recherche et de l'Industrie," July 29, 1982, 19940139/1, AN.

[69] For background, Babusiaux did not have a particularly strong education in economics or economic policy. Like many bureaucrats he graduated from the *École National d'Administration* (ENA), and then went to work in various bureaucracies, beginning with the *Cour des comptes*, which is responsible for auditing finances of government institutions. He moved on to the Ministry of Equipment and Transport (*Ministère de l'Équipement et Transports*), where he was first exposed to issues of competition in public procurement industries where cartels were very common. Author interview with Babusiaux, January 24, 2020. Conf. Christian Babusiaux CV, 1982, 19940139/1, AN.

[70] Babusiaux Interview.

and *contrats de plan*[71] and in coordinating these policies with the Ministry of the Economy.[72]

Likewise, at this moment, as the newly nationalized firms were being organized, many of the intrinsic failures of the national champions policy were beginning to make fundamental economic adjustments impossible. The system of providing across-the-board industrial support for national champions to continue making massive investments meant that resources—capital or otherwise—were insufficiently or barely redistributed from declining industries to growing ones. Industries in decline, such as steel, coal, textiles, chemicals, were continuously given state aid and protection from foreign competition, keeping labor, capital, and other physical resources there. Many of those industries were still given state-directed goals to try and capture as much market share as possible by continuing to invest in physical capacity, leading them to sell at a loss abroad but not experiencing any consequences for doing so as a result of the implicit guarantee of the state at home.[73] National champion firms had little incentive to meet many of the plans the state made for it, whether expanding exports or seeking new markets, because the state had developed them in sheltered domestic markets, provided them with reliable public procurement contracts, or arranged foreign contracts for them: "rather than export, they milked the protected home market" (Levy 1999, 36). Oft-quoted from Cohen (1989, 230–231) is that the subsidies to some of these firms were so great that it would have been cheaper in some cases for the government to pay workers to not produce.[74] Even with ambitious incentives, the market power the national champions was given in the domestic market prevented them from undertaking expansionary business strategies.

Discussions within the Ministry of Industry recognized this in late 1982, seeing how these state guarantees created perverse incentives: the financial guarantee of the state, effectively made possible by France's commitment

[71] Babusiaux to Chevènement, "Possibilité de financement de la restructuration de la chimie par un système analogue à celui mis en place pour le financement de la sidérurgie (FIS)," February 1, 1983, 19940139/3, AN; Babusiaux to Chevènement, "Contrats de plan," January 28, 1983, 19940139/3, AN; Babusiaux to Chevènement, "Journées de politique industrielle - éléments de cadrage financier," November 12, 1982, 19940139/2, AN.

[72] Babusiaux wrote to Chevènement on November 30, 1982 to coordinate planning with Delors for the financing of industry, particularly for high-risk venture capital. Babusiaux to Chevènement, "Votre déjeuner du 1er décembre avec M. Delors," November 30, 1982, 19940139/2, AN.

[73] For more on this overall, see Schmidt (1996, 119–121) and Cohen (1989).

[74] See Levy (1999, 48) and Schmidt (1996, 120).

to its national champions and by their own political power, created an irresponsibility that "won over business managers dependent on the state, and who come back every year for an inevitable bailout."[75] Not only was this industrial policy expensive, but it conditioned the national champion firms into a malaise.

Behind the scenes, Babusiaux, having been the one to brief Chevènement for these meetings,[76] found deeper problems. The plans initially submitted by the newly nationalized firms were inconsistent with the economic goals of the government, primarily relying on continuous domestic price increases to make up for losses elsewhere. When originally negotiating their *contrats de plan*, most of the newly nationalized firms planned for price increases that would macroeconomically make it impossible for inflation to be held in check,[77] and Babusiaux suggested that they needed to redo their projections and plans.[78]

Christian Babusiaux took a few conclusions from this overall experience in the Ministry of Industry, after dispensing billions of francs in loans. First, that the state in not capable of doing everything. Second, the economic concentration of large firms with the amount of economic and political power they had, even under conditions of nationalization, led to state capture by the largest firms, as their managers frequently bypassed the Ministry of Industry entirely and went directly to the president or prime minister to address their problems. Lastly, Babusiaux concluded that competition and international openness were good and necessary to discipline and compensate for the failures of this economic system.[79]

Chevènement resigned in March 1983. In the fall of 1982 and spring of 1983, prices and wages needed to be frozen in order to control some of the pressures created by the government's economic and social policies, which led to his removal from the government. Chevènement wanted to continue both the same industrial policies and massive social spending. Policy did not change immediately, but plans made under Chevènement either slowly languished or were abandoned after his departure. For example, the Ministry

[75] "Le financement des entreprises industrielles du secteur public," August 3, 1982, 19930139/2, AN, page 3.

[76] Babusiaux to Chèvenement, "Conseil restreint sur le financement des entreprises nationales," November 10, 1982, 19940139/2, AN.

[77] Sauzay Note, "Hypothèses macroéconomiques sous-jacentes aux différents Plans des Entreprises Nationales," December 15, 1982, 19940139/3, AN.

[78] Babusiaux to Hennekinne, "Contrats de plan," December 21, 1982, 19940139/3, AN.

[79] Babusiaux Interview.

of Industry had begun drafting a new law for industrial development,[80] but this work appears to have ended when Chevènement resigned.

Austerity and Industrial Policy

Chevènement's resignation was likewise tied to a major policy shift in March 1983, when the Mitterrand government turned to austerity and fiscal rigor (*politique de rigeur*). This U-turn is often argued to be at the core of all the liberalizing changes in policy at this time, whether in financial, tax, competition, or regulatory policy. Having expanded social spending upon taking office by increasing wages, shortening the workweek, lowering the retirement age, and so on, inflation once again rose dramatically in the early 1980s, and pressures to address this began very early on in Mitterrand's presidency. In late 1981, with inflation already at 14 percent, Mitterrand devalued the franc by 8.5 percent relative to the German mark, and prices on basic products were frozen again (Schmidt 1996, 109). Mitterrand first announced some austerity policies in June 1982, as the unsustainability of their spending had become clear by the previous fall (Hall 1986, 199–200). Wages and all prices were frozen that summer, along with more reductions in social benefits and tax increases (Schmidt 1996, 110).

The key point of reckoning was the decision of whether to remain in the European Monetary System (EMS). The EMS, having begun 1979, was initiated among European states to coordinate monetary policy to attain exchange rate stability by holding each of their currencies within an agreed-upon band of +/− 2.25 percent (the "currency snake"). While bringing the financial benefits of currency and exchange rate stability, it placed significant constraints on member states that typically had higher inflation and had previously relied on devaluations to remain competitive. Not only would devaluations not be possible within the snake, but inflation would need to be held in check by other means, and high government spending, like that carried out by the Mitterrand government, was likely to make inflation worse. So if France failed to contain inflation—which any further reflationary spending would preclude—it would not be able to maintain the exchange rate bands required by the EMS (Schmidt 1996, 110–111). The Mitterrand government had expected—based on, among others, a faulty

[80] "Assises Nationales de l'Industrie française," undated, 19940139/2, AN.

OECD projection[81]—that the United States would exit recession in late 1981 and begin a reflationary policy, and therefore expected its own reflationary spending to be accommodated by this and enable them to take advantage of it (Schmidt 1996, 109). Instead, the United States remained in recession, and this largely succeeded in generating domestic inflation in France.

Through 1982 and early 1983, the Mitterrand government was unsure of what to do, both in terms of its domestic policy and its ability or desire to stay in the EMS. Pierre Bérégovoy, Michel Rocard, Pierre Chevènement, and Laurent Fabius had all initially opposed strict cooperation with the EMS, instead favoring a more radical French monetary policy. Delors and Pierre Mauroy were the primary opposition (Loriaux 1991, 231–231), but several of these advisors changed their position when faced with the economic and political calamity of exiting the EMS, particularly Mauroy and Bérégovoy. In March 1983, Mitterrand made the final decision to remain in the EMS, undertaking a dramatic austerity program (*politique de rigueur*) to contain inflation, cutting social spending across the board and increasing taxes.

However, these pressures were not what they may seem and did not, at the very least, constrain spending on industrial policy. Askenazy (2015, 80) shows that as a result of austerity measures by the state undertaken by the Barre government in the late 1970s, the French state was comparatively debt-free relative to its neighbors, even if many French firms were debt-laden as a result of those fiscal cuts. Levy (1999, 29) also points out that the French government's deficit in the decades since the early 1980s have been reliably higher than the 3 percent deficit in 1983. To emphasize how minor this was, in 1980, 1981, and 1982, France's budget deficit was 0.1 percent, 2.2 percent, and 2.8 percent of GDP (Askenazy 2015, 80). This was hardly a massive fiscal drain, and certainly enough to maintain the industrial support for firms. The primary concern with spending was its propensity to drive inflation, not its cost to government coffers. There was money.

More directly, however, with this fiscal space and despite deep austerity cuts into other areas, the Mitterrand government *expanded spending on industrial policy*. This U-turn moment of 1983 explicitly exempted spending on industrial policy. Aid to industry actually *increased* even following the macroeconomic U-turn, going from 35 billion F in 1981 to 86 billion F in 1986 (Levy 1999, 44). As Peter Hall noted, France "was trimming both defense and social spending to pass public resources into industrial

[81] Askenazy (2015, 77) notes that most international observers and economic forecasters were predicting a world economic expansion in 1982.

investment" (Hall 1986, 203). State aids to industry in France had increased from 1981 to 1983, gone flat in 1984, and then progressively declined only thereafter (Warlouzet 2018, 165). It was not until a year later, on March 29, 1984, that a new industrial policy was announced (Warlouzet 2018, 165).

From Industrial Socialism to Market Liberalism

Following this experiment with nationalized industrial policy, France shifted to adopt competition policies and more completely pull back from industrial supports. A new competition law was passed in December 1986, driven by lessons learned following years of learning from the failures and costs of previous anti-competition policies and the opinions of uncommitted policymakers in the DGCC. Whereas the law was passed after the Socialists had lost the legislature in 1986, the record clearly shows that most of the development of the ideas behind the law had been under the Socialist government in 1983 and 1984.

The Rise of Competition Policy

The earliest shift in public positions came in the form of a series of pronouncements in favor of competition by Jacques Delors on November 9 and December 21, 1983, at the *Conseil des Ministres* (Brault 1987, 53), focused on using competition to combat the "structural factors of inflation," again before significant changes to industrial policy had been made. The earliest available draft of these communications, drafted by Jean-Michel Maury in Delors's office, highlights the need to fight inflation, the lack of competition in France, and the role of the state in restoring it along two main dimensions: changing the rules of competition to meet the changes in the economy and to better apply the existing rules.[82] The drafting pointed to competition beyond just exposure to the international competition:

> The choice of an open economy means that some of our businesses are subject to international competition, in particular our industry, but that is not enough. There are still many phenomena that are hindering competition.[83]

[82] Jean-Michel Maury to Delors, "Projet de communication sur la concurrence," October 27, 1983, 20030502/8, AN, page 1.

[83] Ibid., pages 2–3.

It then goes on to explain some of these impediments, such as regional concentration of retailers, cartelized industries, or market-sharing arrangements among oligopolistic industries that had become common.

Among these well-known issues were the *supercentrales d'achat.* The macroeconomic conditions of the early 1980s, the austerity policies in particular, had resulted in a massive crisis among large retailers. In response to the inflation driven by Mitterrand's expansionist policies, the decline in household consumption, and the general rise in costs, large retailers in France underwent an unprecedented merger wave. The number of retailers declined, but the more important change was the creation of *supercentrales d'achat,* groupings of several independent retailers under one legal entity (Billows 2017, 51–52). These were, in effect, purchasing cartels, and the mergers and the creation of the *supercentrales* was motivated by a desire to gain bargaining power over smaller suppliers. The seven *supercentrales* that remained in 1985 controlled 40 percent of all retail and over 80 percent of the food market. But the situation was worse than this even implies, since the number of competitors in a given regional or local market of large retailers was appreciably less.

Thus, some early conversations about merger control had focused especially on retail and distribution, particularly because of the problem of the *supercentrales.* In the conclusions from an interministerial meeting on August 2, 1982, the section on merger control read:

> The application of the 1977 law on the control of the concentration of companies poses a specific problem for the distribution sector. The criteria adopted by the law of 1977 is not well adapted to wholesale enterprises. It is important to find new legal means to control the concentration of these distribution companies.[84]

This was particularly because the existing merger rules created in 1977, even weakly enforced, did not even apply to regional economic concentration—the relevant market for brick-and-mortar retail—and instead regulated concentration based on their national market share.[85]

Accordingly, as work on competition policy within the Ministry of the Economy expanded rapidly in response to these communications, though

[84] Relève de conclusions de la réunion interministérelle du 2 août 1982, August 2, 1982, B-0065841/3, CAEF, page 3.

[85] See Décret n°77-1189 du 25 octobre 1977 - art. 4.

the Ministry had been making clear plans for this for nearly a year. Reports from the DGCC from as early as February 1983 made the same points: that premerger notification was necessary, that the thresholds were too low, and that the *Commission de la Concurrence's* powers were too limited.[86]

And, following Delors's pronouncements, Director General Jouven of the DGCC wrote to the Director of the Treasury on November 28, 1983, regarding revisions to the 1977 law. He noted that very high merger thresholds and the reference points by parts of the national market made the law ineffective: it excluded practically all services and distribution, and it had no premerger notification system.[87] Her wrote, "Indeed, after 6 years of experience, it appears that the current legislation has not produced the expected results. The structural aspect of competition policy, which should be based on merger control, remained secondary."[88] Other reports reviewing the record of the *Commission de la Concurrence* agreed that the 1977 law, as recent as it was, was already not a good law and woefully inadequate. It had, in total, received ten merger notifications: one in 1981, three in 1982, and six in 1983.[89]

Others listed off all the ways in which concentrations were actually bad, in generalized, theoretical terms:

> Under an oligopoly, the adoption of a pricing policy creates an unstable situation which can lead to the disappearance of certain competitors. In fact, in the event of a price war, the competitors with the weakest financial capacity will be declared bankrupt and ultimately a monopoly situation will result.[90]

On December 26, 1983, the DGCC sent the minister of the economy a draft series of letters to be sent from the prime minister to the rest of the *Conseil des Ministres*, as well as secretaries of state. It highlighted the new policy

[86] Chargé de mission auprès du Directeur Général, "Finalité du contrôle des concentrations économique," "Inadaptation de la loi du 19.07.1988," and "Caractères du projet établi," February 10, 1983, B-0065834/2, CAEF; DGCC, "Modifications de la loi de juillet 1977 relative au contrôle des concentrations," B-0065834/2, CAEF.

[87] Jouven to Director of the Treasury, "Modification de loi no. 77-806 du 19 juillet 1977 relative au contrôle de la concentration économique et son application aux opérations boursières," November 28, 1983, B-0065834/2, CAEF, pages 1–2.

[88] Ibid., page 1.

[89] Direction Générale de la Concurrence et de la Consommation, "Argumentaire sur l'intérêt d'une réforme de la loi sur les concentrations," undated copy, B-0065834/2, CAEF, page 2.

[90] DGCC, "Les aspects négatifs des concentrations," undated document, B-0065834/2, CAEF, page 1.

priorities set out by the minister of the economy. This was framed particularly against inflation over other goals, but it was in terms of broader pro-competition mechanisms and motives:

> Competition is the main driver of innovation, increasing productivity and the competitiveness of our businesses because it is the only objective means of rewarding dynamism. However, its operation in France is far from satisfactory: French companies too often tend to make profits more by protecting themselves from competition than by creating it; administrations frequently neglect the importance of competition in their various interventions.[91]

The letters directed ministers to take a series of bureaucratic actions: for regional and local governments to more seriously report anticompetitive practice or violations, for ministries to more strictly surveil the dependent nationalized firms they oversaw, for all of them to make use of and consult with the *Commission de la Concurrence* and the DGCC, and to ensure competitive bidding in public markets. It likewise highlighted the legislative plans for a new competition law, which would (a) add new merger controls, (b) strengthen the enforcement powers of the *Commission de la Concurrence*, and (c) set clearer rules for production-distribution relationships (vertical restraints).[92]

In this time, Christian Babusiaux had moved from the Ministry of Industry to the DGCC as the chief of the service, the second position within the DGCC, beginning in September 1983. Even this early in his time at the DGCC, Babusiaux was clearly one of the main influences in the area. A December 28, 1983, draft argument for the need of a reinforcement of merger control—amended by Babusiaux—argued that "the necessary counterpart to price liberalization is the strengthening of competition policy."[93] In justifying the need for stronger merger control, the memo said that

> a poor functioning of competition does not only result from the behavior of companies. It can also come from the structure of the market (existence of

[91] Draft of Delors to Ministers, Ministers délégués, and Secretaries of State, December 26, 1983, B-0065840/1, CAEF.

[92] Drafts of Delors to Ministers, Ministers délégués, and Secretaries of State, Delors to Minister of the Interior and Decentralization, Delors to Minister of Urbanism and Housing, December 26, 1983, B-0065840/1, CAEF.

[93] Projet d'argumentaire sur l'interêt d'un renforcement du contrôle des concentrations, December 28, 1983, B-0065834/2, CAEF. Also found in 20030502/8, AN, page 1.

> dominant positions, oligopolies, etc.) which can naturally carry rigidities (price parallelism in the case of an oligopoly, for example) or even create situations of irreversible economic domination, definitely distorting the competition in a sector.[94]

Drafts and comments about competition from different ministries frequently cite back to Babusiaux's position on various issues.[95]

Ideas for reform were produced exceptionally quickly. Delors sent a proposed competition law to the *Commission de la Concurrence* on January 2, 1984, for their opinion, as the government was planning to introduce the new law that spring.[96] The DGCC and the Ministry of the Economy appeared to have already decided to push for competition generally, hashing out the details of what merger thresholds should be, how to define the relevant market for those thresholds, how exactly to define the Commission's expanded powers, and so forth.[97] Competition proposals continued in 1984 despite no law submitted in the legislature.

Business interests did try to intervene to stop this policy shift. In January 1984, Director General Jouven of the DGCC met with a representative of the CNPF, the main business association, regarding this proposed merger control law. The CNPF representative Sarre immediately made it clear that "the position of the CNPF was very strongly negative on the very concept of merger control,"[98] and proceeded to inundate Jouven with arguments against it, many of which were aligned with the recently accepted national champions policy:

1. National merger control made no sense because the relevant market was European.
2. Merger control in distribution would prevent distributors from expanding abroad.

[94] Ibid.

[95] Argumentaire sur les suites du seminaire de Strasbourg sur la distribution selective, exclusive, et la franchise, December 28, 1983, page 1.

[96] Minister of Finance to President of the Commission de la Concurrence, January 2, 1984, 20030502/8, AN; DGCC, Note d'information, January 2, 1984, 20030502/8, AN, page 1.

[97] The commission likewise singled out vertical integration as a main culprit in the relationship between concentration and collusion, in contrast to Chicago assumptions. President of the Commission de la Concurrence to Minister of Finance, "Avis de la Commission de la Concurrence sur un avant-projet de loi," January 10, 1984, B-0065840/1, CAEF, page 1.

[98] "Projet de loi sur les concentrations, Réunion du 22/184 avec M. Sarre, CNPF," January 22, 1984, B-0065834/2, CAEF, page 1.

3. Concentrations expanded the competitiveness of firms with economies of scale.
4. If the government really liked competition it would start by liberalizing prices.
5. Nationalized firms were monopolies or dominant firms, making merger control for private firms not credible.
6. There were already too many regulations.
7. Premerger notification was dangerous because mergers require speed and confidentiality.
8. The CNPF doubted the government was competent enough to assess a merger.
9. Mergers are necessary for economic adjustment and particularly for firms facing difficulty.
10. It was not clear that the proposed law conformed with European regulations.
11. The German model (on which this proposal was based) was not appropriate for France.[99]

The memo of the conversation simply summarizes that "the Director General then refuted all of the arguments presented by Mr. Sarre."[100] Over the following month, business interests—including the CNPF and the Paris Chamber of Commerce—were sending articles and memos to the Ministry of the Economy about merger control, particularly highlighting Chicago school arguments from the United States for how mergers were, in fact, efficient. They cited Robert Bork and the Chicago critique of the 1968 American merger guidelines and the need to continue mergers to remain internationally competitive in the face of aggressive and protectionist industrial policies of many competitors.[101]

As part of this moves toward competition—but a year after the austerity policies implemented in order to stay in the EMS—the government finally decided to cut their financial supports and guarantees to some of the national champion firms. In 1984, Usinor, one of the largest steel companies—and a national champion created by state-directed credit and

[99] While not exact quotes, these are the actual enumerated points from the conversation summary. Ibid., pages 1–2.

[100] Ibid., page 3.

[101] Henri Lepage, Institut de l'entreprise, "Faut-il avoir peur des concentrations? L'exemple américain," February 13, 1984, B-0065834, CAEF.

mergers in the 1960s—was refused a needed loan and, along with the rest of the steel industry, was told it needed to fend for itself entirely by 1988. The new industrial policy in March 1984 required several industries—coal, steel, and automobiles—to cease trying to exceed domestic demand and instead cut capacity and streamline operations.[102] A few months later, on June 28, 1984, the steel and engineering conglomerate Creuset-Loire filed for bankruptcy after being refused state aid by Chevènement's replacement, Laurent Fabius.[103]

By chance and despite his young age, Babusiaux became the director general of the DGCC within a year after moving over to the Ministry of the Economy, starting in August 1984. The previous director general, Jouven, had taken a position as the president of *Crédit Commercial de France* several months after Babusiaux arrived, so at a surprisingly young age and largely through the circumstance of mundane staff and organization turnover, Babusiaux became the top competition policy official in the Ministry of the Economy, appointed by the new minister of the economy, Pierre Bérégovoy.[104]

In this new position, Babusiaux worked to liberalize prices rapidly and entirely, a necessity for competition to function. However, when Babusiaux had first arrived in the Ministry of the Economy, the DGCC as an organization was still primarily concerned with maintaining the web of price controls that permeated the French economy. Bérégovoy and Babusiaux together developed an unwritten plan between the two of them to liberalize all prices within a year. This took the form of agreements between the Ministry of the Economy and individual firms that prices would be liberalized in a year if they maintained prices and wages as agreed in the meantime.[105]

At Bérégovoy's request, in 1985 the DGCC was fused with the *Direction de la Répression des Fraudes* (from the Ministry of Agriculture) to become the *Direction Générale de la Concurrence, de la Consommation, et de la Répression des Fraudes* (DGCCRF),[106] giving the Direction about 1,800 more staff. While administrative in nature—not to mention that the responsibilities from agriculture were only tangentially related to competition—Bérégovoy and Babusiaux used this reorganization to convert most of the

[102] Schmidt (1996, 121) and Warlouzet (2018, 165).
[103] See Schmidt (1996, 128) and Cohen (1989, Ch. 1).
[104] Babusiaux Interview.
[105] Ibid.
[106] The documentary evidence indicates that Babusiaux himself was the origin of reorganization. "Réorganisation de la DGCCRF," July 10, 1987, B-0074082, CAEF.

new and existing staff of the DGCCRF away from maintaining price controls and into an administration focused on fair trade, product quality, and consumer protection, along the lines of what the Federal Trade Commission (FTC) does in the United States.[107]

Lastly, on December 30, 1985, the Socialists passed a minor amendment to French competition laws, meant as a first step in broader reforms.[108] This law did not go very far, in part because with elections coming up, the Socialist government felt pressure to maintain distinct policy positions from the conservatives. If they went too far in favor of competition, there was concern that their position would begin to look indistinguishable from those of the right.[109]

Nonetheless, the March 1986 elections changed the political landscape in France. Despite Mitterrand remaining president, the conservative parties swept the legislative elections and assembled a majority. Jacques Chirac took over as prime minister and appointed conservative politicians to most ministries. France thus entered one of its few periods of split government—referred to as "cohabitation"—when the president and prime minister were from different parties. This created complications for lawmaking, as Mitterrand generally refused to sign *ordonnances* (which only require the prime minister, president, and relevant minister to sign), forcing Chirac to go through the entire legislative procedure for any new policies. The conservative coalition that won the 1986 legislative elections ran on three primary economic policies: (1) tax and government spending cuts, (2) deregulation, and (3) privatizations (Levy 1999, 63). While their platform did include the removal of price controls and the institution of a competition law, the new right government was not entirely sold on competition or full liberalization.[110]

La Loi Balladur

Mitterrand made one exception to his refusal to sign *ordonnances* during this period: on December 1, 1986, he signed an *ordonnance* to create the *Conseil de la Concurrence*, replacing the *Commission de la Concurrence* and

[107] Babusiaux Interview; Note: rôle et rattachement du Service des Fraudes aux Finances," August 4, 1986, 543AP/83, AN.

[108] Law no. 85-1408 of December 30, 1985.

[109] Babusiaux Interview.

[110] Levy (1999, 66–9). Conf. Babusiaux Interview.

giving it legal independence from the Ministry of Finance. This divided the enforcement powers of competition rules between the new *Conseil* and the DGCCRF, which remained within the Ministry of the Economy. The law expanded the independence and enforcement authority of the competition regulatory, maintained clear bans on collusion and abuse of dominance, specifically banned predatory pricing, and liberalized all prices.

Even before the election, the conservatives had said in their platform that they would abolish price controls and pass a competition law. They had already assembled a commission, headed by former commissioner to the *Commission de la Concurrence* Jean Donnedieu de Vabres, to review possible competition law proposals and make a series of recommendations. The commission consisted of business executives, industry association presidents, and academics,[111] at the exclusion of bureaucrats and or political leadership. As a generality, the commission of Donnedieu de Vabres favored the German competition model, with a Federal Cartel Office as an administrative agency (Gerber 1998, 403–408).

Additionally, Donnedieu de Vabres's commission's recommendations were in many ways anti-competition. First, the commission was planning to weaken the prohibitions on restrictive practices like price discrimination or refusal to sell by prohibiting them only if specific negative effects could be shown,[112] akin to how such practices are assessed under the "rule of reason" in the United States. This would give more power to mass distributors (who had consolidated into a series of collective purchasers) and less to industrial producers (who had used the law against price discrimination as one of their only defenses against these anticompetitive practices).[113] Likewise, it was entirely focused on the *Commission de la Concurrence*, with investigations, sanctions, and injunctions all being put under its control, with no connection to civil law or the regular court system.[114]

In addition, however, the conservatives also wanted to clear out perceived or actual political opposition in the bureaucracy, and this spelled

[111] Babusiaux Interview.

[112] "Premières réactions sur les travaux de la Commission de réforme du droit de la concurrence," July 23, 1986, 543AP/83, AN, page 2.

[113] Villain to Balladur, "Rapport de M. Donnedieu de Vabres – Ordonnance sur la Concurrence," August 12, 1986, 543AP/83, AN, page 3.

[114] "Premières réactions sur les travaux de la Commission de réforme du droit de la concurrence," July 23, 1986, 543AP/83, AN, page 2. Conf. Babusiaux interview. Babusiaux, in fact, explicitly drew on the American model of dividing powers between the DOJ, the FTC, and so on, since it avoided "putting all your eggs in one basket." This resulted in the eventual form of the DGCCRF, *Conseil de la Concurrence*, and the Paris Appellate Court having separate authority. Babusiaux Interview.

disaster for any hopes of continuing any existing policy projects begun under Socialist leadership. Before the election, they had published a list of "100 heads that must fall" in *Le Point*, consisting of bureaucrats they planned to fire upon winning the election.[115] Babusiaux, now director general of the DGCCRF, was on the list. Eight days after the election, Babusiaux was told that he had fifteen days to resign. Instead, Babusiaux wrote Balladur, the incoming minister of finance, with a plan for price indexation—another way to limit wage increases without anyone noticing—to try and save his job, and he successfully convinced Balladur to keep him on.[116]

As of April 1986, the important questions left for a new competition law were (a) whether the state should maintain any power to intervene in prices, (b) whether decisions should be made in special tribunals or in civil court, (c) how should power be divided between the *Commission de la Concurrence* and the Ministry of the Economy, (d) whether to maintain the distinction of anticompetitive practices between individual practices (discrimination, predatory pricing, resale price maintenance) and collective practices (cartels, abuse of dominant position), and (e) what the rights of defendants should be.[117] In the policy space between encouraging mergers and competition, these were incredibly minor differences.

Throughout 1986, in anticipation of the new competition law, the DGCC began a series of comprehensive reviews of competition in different sectors, as well as how to best introduce competition into them. In June, Balladur asked Babusiaux to put together a more comprehensive list of noncompetitive sectors, and the DGCCRF "identified approximately 70 sectors where competition is limited by legislative or regulatory texts and established, on each of these sectors of first files analyzing the problem and proposing solutions."[118] Then in August, based on a DGCCRF assessment that about one-seventh of the French GDP was covered by either monopolistic or sheltered sectors, an aide to Balladur wrote that "the challenge of these reforms is less in terms of the effects to be achieved on prices, which will be generally modest, but on the development of competition and the in-depth evolution

[115] Le Point, 1986. Conf. Babusiaux Interview.

[116] Babusiaux Interview.

[117] DGCCRF, Note pour le Ministre, "Les principaux choix à effectuer pour la réforme du droit français de la concurrence," April 16, 1986, 543AP/83, AN.

[118] Babusiaux to the attention of Friedmann, "Réformes à apporter aux textes législatifs et réglementaires restreignant le jeu de la concurrence sur divers marchés," August 5, 1986, B-0074074, CAEF.

of the mentalities of economic actors."[119] By the end of the year, the DGC-CRF had drawn up detailed plans for each sector with proposed reforms to remove regulatory restrictions on competition.[120] Likewise, in October 1986, the *Commission de la Concurrence* dissolved SERFAAL and ARCI, two of the *supercentrales d'achat*.

While the DGCCRF was the main organization within the Ministry of the Economy to push for the eventual policy setup of the December *ordonnance*—split powers between the *Conseil de la Concurrence* and the DGCCRF and judicial authority over most final enforcement decision—it should be emphasized that this was contrary to the bureaucratic and organizational interests of the Ministry and the DGCCRF in particular. Prior to the 1986 *ordonnance*, the director general of the DGCCRF, Babusiaux, had near complete and total power—to change prices, to approve or deny a merger, to begin or end an investigation—to the point where the director general of industry would often come to the DGCCRF to ask favors or to approve certain actions.[121] The new policy removed nearly all of that discretion, giving final decision-making power to judicial authority.

However, there are two key reasons to doubt that these changes were driven by European influence or events, even beyond the direct evidence offered above. First of all, it was only in late 1987, after all of these events, that European Competition Commissioner Peter Sutherland proposed a reinvigoration of European competition rules. European merger regulations were introduced in 1989, after the new French law, and there is no record of any specific European discussions in French policy circles before this time. It was not until early 1988 that notes from Balladur's office discussed Commissioner Peter Sutherland's proposals from November 1987. The actual proposed text had been first examined in January 1988 and was to be discussed again in March and May.[122] Balladur's office also appears to have viewed the policy favorably on its own terms ("the new text includes significant improvements along the lines desired by several member states").[123]

[119] Lenöel to Balladur, "Plan de mesures de déreglementation de d'ouverture à la concurrence," August 29, 1986, 543AP/83, AN.

[120] Babusiaux to Balladur, "Réformes de structures pour développer la concurrence," January 7, 1987, B-0074074, CAEF; and see attached "Propositions de réformes d'ourvertur à la concurrence."

[121] Babusiaux Interview.

[122] "Le projet de règlement communautaire sur le contrôle des concentrations," undated document, B-0074076, CAEF.

[123] Ibid.

The European proposals from Brussels for expanded competition policy were put forth well after the French had already made most of their domestic reforms.

Second, despite many characterizations to the contrary, the institutional structure of French competition law and policy that formed out of these events does not resemble other European countries or the EU's Competition Authority, but rather has many features more akin to the United States. Whereas the German competition authority—the Cartel Office or *Bundeskartellamt*—is an independent bureaucratic authority, France developed a system of split authority for competition enforcement, with the DGCCRF responsible for investigations and direct enforcement, the *Conseil de la Concurrence* responsible for judgments, and appeals going through the normal judicial system via the Paris Appellate Court (*Cour d'appel de Paris*). This is much more akin to the American model of divided authority between the FTC, DOJ, and federal district courts. This model was, in fact, explicitly the goal of separating authority in this way, in order to "not put all your eggs in the same basket."[124]

Conclusion

This case has thus far shown just how significantly policy goals changed over the 1980s, based on the replacement of some overly committed policymakers, on learning among newer actors, and on the fact that the industrial policies of the early 1980s were directly at odds with the pro-competition policies undertaken thereafter. The diminishing returns to market power—domestic cartelization, poor investment choices and mobilization, and corporate malaise—led uncommitted policymakers to learn about the failures of the national champions policy, while established officials like Chevènement remained committed until they were removed. Policy change occurred after these actors moved up to positions of influence through bureaucratic turnover and pushed for policy change.

[124] Babusiaux Interview.

8
Conclusion

The primary claim of this book has been that policy regimes in favor of competition or market power face diminishing returns that lead to their internal undoing over time, through no external or exogenous shock. Competition—as a function of what it is and what it does—necessarily leads to diminishing returns over time if it is continuously pursued by policy. Competition works to improve economic efficiency precisely because it puts downward pressure on prices, and the greater that pressure, the lesser the profits. By the same token, market power contributes to the resources, investment, and competitiveness of lead firms, but this is precisely the result of removing the competitive pressures that otherwise push firms to lower prices, cut costs, and expand output. Pursuing market power alone will lead to stagnation and low investment in the long run.

As a matter of the political economy, these policy regimes endure so long, and eventually reverse course, as a result of commitment, learning, and turnover among the key policymakers who oversee and regulate policy areas like antitrust, intellectual property, trade, or industrial policy. Policymakers who have committed themselves to the current policy regime will push the regime to go further toward competition or market power, worsening the diminishing returns. Through chance, contingency, and mundane career paths, uncommitted policymakers—who are able and willing to learn and think differently about policy problems—are introduced to policymaking circles. As they push out and displace committed policymakers, policy begins to change.

The book has made this argument based on extensive, contextual archival evidence, providing a thick, descriptive account of how many individual policymakers navigated these policy problems, how various competing interests and perspectives were balanced or prioritized, and how those choices connected to the broader structural forces of diminishing returns in a national market.

Monopoly Politics. Erik Peinert, Oxford University Press. © Oxford University Press (2025).
DOI: 10.1093/oso/9780197789506.003.0008

In so doing, this book has sought to provide a clear, empirically testable, and theoretically generalizable approach to endogenous change. As elaborated in Chapter 2, it provides a general framework for understanding endogenous institutions and how they should be empirically assessed: (1) assert a mechanism for endogenous change *intrinsic* to the institution or policy, (2) derive detailed observable implications for the asserted mechanism or theory relative to alternatives, and (3) select cases as divergent parallel demonstrations (Skocpol and Somers 1980). In the context of this book, that mechanism is the diminishing returns to competition or market power, with the most important observable implications being the detailed process of commitment to simple mental models, material feedback from diminishing returns, turnover, and learning, with France and the United States selected as dissimilar parallel demonstrations. I now review these theoretical assertions in light of the evidence presented throughout the book.

Revisiting Findings

One foundational argument to explain why policymakers adopt policy regimes in the first place is that policymaking contexts push policymakers to latch onto simple *mental models* in favor of, respectively, competition or market power. Where policy contexts are defined by ambiguity, difficult trade-offs, low accountability, and the need for deductive categories, mental models allow all of that ambiguity to be dispensed in favor of clear decisions and rules of thumb. For instance, even with a more complex theory of administered prices and relative price inflexibility in the context of the Depression, New Deal policymakers shifted from the belief that, for example, "competition is essentially waste,"[1] to pushing for more competition in almost every arena during Thurman Arnold's antitrust campaign a few years later. Additionally, the Chicago school's framework "relieved judges of the burden of wrestling with complicated facts" (Leslie 2014, 934) by "assum[ing] away the troublesome points in the analysis" (Silkenat 1978). Likewise, postwar French policymakers shifted from mental models where competition and tariff reductions were the clear path to controlling inflation, to adopting converse mental models of market power, in which scale, profitability, and high levels of investment were the primary criteria for policy success.

[1] Robert Jackson, "An Economic Plan for America," 1932, Jackson Papers, Box 32.

The evidence for diminishing returns can only be indirectly observed through archival evidence, as the economic reports, data, and evidence that policymakers relied on at the time may not be entirely reliable in hindsight, even if they accurately represent their understanding of the material facts at the time. That notwithstanding, postwar France provides evidence of the diminishing returns to competition. After two decades of pro-competition policy, including trade liberalization, domestic and transnational competition rules, and anti-cartel procurement policies, France appears to have experienced a rapid decline in profits and the rate of private investment (*autofinancement*) in the late 1950s and early 1960s. And French policymakers in the Ministry of Finance clearly interpreted this as a the result of those pro-competition policies. Though less directly discussed in the same terms within the archival record, similar diminishing returns appear to have occurred in the 1970s and 1980s in the United States. After decades of free trade policy, stricter antitrust rules, and progressively weaker IP protections, international and domestic competition overtook American firms, which had no legal or economic mechanisms available to limit this competition. Policymakers across the Nixon, Ford, Carter, and Reagan administrations recognized problems at the intersection of trade, antitrust, and technology licensing, along with the decline in American competitiveness.

As for the diminishing returns to market power, during the New Deal in the United States, the National Recovery Administration (NRA) deepened and expanded many industrial self-government policies, in an attempt to quasi-cartelize the American economy and avoid destructive competition. The NRA, however, led to sustained higher prices, no notable increase in employment, and no substantial increase in output, as had been hoped, and researchers at the time understood this under the theory of "administered prices." In hindsight, Cole and Ohanian (2004, 813) provide a statistical analysis supporting the notion that the cartelizing effects of the NRA significantly prolonged the Depression in the United States "by creating rents and an inefficient insider-outsider friction that raised wages significantly and restricted employment," and C. D. Romer (1999) provides evidence that the NRA was responsible for rising prices despite an enduring recession. In France, similar diminishing returns to market power were seen in the 1980s, when the Socialists pushed the national champions policy to its extreme. By protecting the national champion firms from domestic competition to ensure their international competitiveness, their economy increasingly relied on perverse and anticompetitive practices, by price-gouging domestic consumers and dumping on foreign markets while avoiding making substantial investments or expansion into new markets.

Next, the cases have provided evidence of committed policymakers—those who expended resources or reputation in support of a policy regime—refusing to reconsider their views in light of contrary evidence and displaying cognitive dissonance to maintain or defend their preferred policy course. The architects of the NRA in the United States, such as Donald Richberg, Raymond Moley, or Hugh Johnson, never ceded that the NRA's economic policies were fundamentally flawed, even years later as others had taken that fact as granted. Committed pro-competition French policymakers in the 1960s, like Louis Franck, simply retired, as others, like Jacques Rueff, fell out of influence over time, but not before pro-competition tariff cuts were pushed even further. Nixon's first assistant attorney general of antitrust, William McLaren, fought the administration's reform proposals up to the point of his removal, and other administrations in the 1970s remained committed to pro-competition priorities they had laid out early in their tenure, despite each eventually facing similar policy problems. Under Mitterrand's presidency, Jean-Pierre Chevènement was removed from office as minister of research and industry in 1983 because of his continued opposition to any revision to anti-competition industrial policies.

However, this book has shown many cases of uncommitted policymakers changing their position over time as they are exposed to more information, even where they agreed with the policy regime at the outset. New researchers and advisers in the New Deal, such as Robert Jackson and Leon Henderson, had no stake in the existing policies but were in agreement with industrial self-government policies. They later led the anti-monopoly charge after a few years of learning. Nixon's inner circle saw the merit in antitrust policies from the beginning, but over time sought to revise them, and the Chicago school's views became prominent in part because of a number of converts to its perspective, in policy and in academia, rather than just by replacement. French policymakers, like Babusiaux (abnormally young for a senior post and not tied to particular policy priorities), were the most influential in reversing industrial policies, liberalizing prices, and implementing new competition policies in France.

Lastly, this book has also shown how many of these uncommitted policymakers were fired or appointed by contingent staff turnover. Leon Henderson got his job in the NRA by getting into a screaming match with Hugh Johnson. Robert Jackson was, by all accounts, given the antitrust portfolio for no particular reason. Peter Peterson, the first head of the Council on International Economic Policy (CIEP) under Nixon, appears to have been a last-minute substitute arranged within a week of when he started. Babusiaux, likewise, became the director general of the DGCC by chance after his predecessor took another job, and he kept that position despite an electoral promise by the conservatives to remove him. Whereas policy appointments are often made as a deliberate choice to place a committed ideologue in a position of power to change policy, most of the influential uncommitted policymakers here were appointed as a matter of course.

Alternative Theories

Having reviewed the evidence for the key claims of the argument, I now compare the evidence relative to the three alternative theories for policy and institutional change outlined at the outset of the book: interest-group theories, materialist or technological theories, and ideational theories. These generally view policy and institutional change as originating exogenously, either as the result of market shocks, new economic ideas, coalitional realignments, or new technologies. As many individual policy changes can be attributed to ideas, interest groups, or technology, these are compared as alternatives with respect to whether the theoretical framework can explain the broad shift in policy regimes.

First, *interest-group* arguments might see pro-competition policies as a conflict between consumers and small business on one hand and producer and big business on the other, with consumers favoring pro-competition policies and producers favoring anti-competition policies (Weymouth 2016; Rogowski and Kayser 2002). As an extension, the postwar golden era of American antitrust can be seen as a corollary of the political power of labor and consumers during that time, French postwar competition policies as the short-lived result of the temporary power of left-wing interests of smaller businesses and labor under the Fourth Republic, and later shifts as the result of these interest group shifts by big business.

However, interest groups appear to have been repeatedly pushed aside, or simply not involved, as broad policy changes were developed. On the other side, shifts to new policy regimes were often opposed—in substance or in detail—by the groups that most benefited from them. There was no significant interest group pushing for Roosevelt's trust-busting, and there were many business and labor groups opposed. France deepened its pro-competition policies in the early 1960s even as the *Conseil national du patronat français* (CNPF) and other business groups pleaded for assistance, but by the late 1960s when the government had changed course, French officials then complained that business was not sufficiently adopting its industrial policies. The process of American antitrust revision and the strengthening of intellectual property (IP) rights in the 1980s was inundated with industry lobbying. However, at the inception of these policies under Nixon, business was kept in the dark and deeply distrusted by Nixon's inner circle. And, the Reagan administration pushed for these policies, often more than industry groups wanted. Lastly, in the 1980s, the French Socialists pushed for competition policies separate from private lobbying, and business interests on no uncertain terms opposed any implementation of merger control.

Second, *materialist* theories suggest that technological changes or exogenous economic shocks lead to policy changes, such as where exposure to international trade or a new technology changes the relative advantages of policies for different groups. In this view, the Depression destabilized the industrial self-government policies of the 1920s, France's postwar experience was the result of exogenous increases in import competition, the Nixon and Reagan administrations were reacting to exogenous increases in international trade, and France's adaptations in the 1980s were either to match new technological requirements or the new European market.

Policymakers themselves usually argued that the material economic conditions were the result of prior decades of policy, not technology or a sudden economic shock. National Recovery Act (NRA) researchers in the New Deal clearly laid the blame on industrial self-government policies, even those that well preceded the NRA. The policy elite in 1960s France explicitly stated that it was financial considerations of profits and investment, not new technologies or material conditions, that motivated them to create national champions. Early Nixon administration revisionists and later Chicago school thinkers thought that antitrust policy *itself* was the problem, not just antitrust in light of exogenous material circumstances.

And even where there were clear material costs and effects, often these were the explicit result of policy rather than some exogenous change. One might object that rising international competition in postwar France and 1970s America were both exogenous. But France helped create of the European Community with strong pro-competition policies that were meant to limit the rents of domestic firms. The United States had been the main player in constructing the entire postwar free-trade order of progressively reduced tariffs. Furthermore, if exogenous shocks motivated the Nixon/Reagan antitrust revolution, they should have also been true for France, but at the moment France dismantled its national champions policy in favor of stronger competition rules. And, the dramatic divergence today between the pro-competition regulation of European as opposed to American markets suggests that materialist arguments are lacking.

Lastly, *ideational* theories suggest that new ideas about how the economy works, how economic variables relate to each other, and the causal beliefs of policymakers are central to understanding institutional and policy change. The Chicago school, developed outside of policy circles in academia, arguably shifted antitrust into an entirely different framework based on entirely different assumptions. Means's administered prices theory reoriented NRA researchers' understanding of the Depression and its causes, pushing them toward more competition. France's national champions policy had its intellectual foundations in works like Servan-Schreiber (1967) and Stoleru (1969), and the shift back to competition came at a time of rising neoliberal priorities along with deeper European integration.

However, whether through timing, the eventual form of policy, or how the ideas were used, these new ideas do not appear to be the main driver of policy change. NRA researchers were tracing real changes in prices, employment, and output that they did not previously know, and in fact distorted Means's original administered prices theory to reshape it as a pro-competition argument. In postwar France, the collapse in profits and *autofinancement* was a piece of information that was conveyed to the government and independently verified. The ideological foundations for the national champions policy came later, in the late 1960s, after the less-theorized choices earlier that decade to favor concentration. Chicago school antitrust arguments coexisted and thrived with broader anti-competition views that it formally detested. At the same time, some new archival evidence of this book aligns with existing arguments that the Chicago school was not entirely honest in its ideological foundations: it sought to strip back antitrust across the board, and some of its arguments were a political veneer over that fact.[2]

2 See Chapter 5 and Priest (2014).

Ideology, Partisanship, and Competition

One point of reflection is on the role of ideology and partisan interests in driving these changes. As presented, the theory has argued that these shifts are largely independent of policymakers' ideological orientation or party identification. The evidence would support this in most cases: policy changes were made most often within a given party or executive leadership team, such that conflict was often between adherents of each view within one political faction. There is, nonetheless, a necessary recognition that in these cases it was nonetheless right-wing governments that rethought policy to revive market power and left-wing governments that reconsidered their positions in order to reinvigorate competition. The anti-monopoly politics we see today in the United States follow this: while the Obama administration may have deepened the market power policy regime put in place in the 1980s, and Trump filed a number of cases against tech firms, the Biden administration's antitrust push still mostly falls along partisan lines, even if inconsistently, with Democrats being the driving force behind the Biden competition agenda.

While it remains the case that policy choices are not a function of party or ideology—many governments of all ideological orientations maintained policy regimes of each kind through their entire time in office—there are some reasons we might expect an ideological affinity. The left may be more ideologically capable of recognizing the problems caused by market power, as they entail high degrees of inequality, high levels of private and corporate power over the economy, and high prices for the working and middle classes. The right may be more ideologically predisposed to recognize the costs of competition, ruinous as it can be to business, profits, and the autonomy of private capital.

To elaborate, the motivating normative worldview of the political left is to eliminate unearned positions of privilege and private power, whether in terms of class, race, gender, education, or other categories. In terms of modern political theory, this position is succinctly captured and widely recognized in the work of Rawls (1973), who generated an entire theory of distributive justice on the basis that any and all advantages of race, class, gender, or any other inherited advantage are "morally arbitrary." While both broader and distinct, it bears a resemblance to non-normative economic understandings of what competition is and does in the market: competition arbitrages away advantaged market positions, allows newer entrants the opportunity to succeed on their own merits, and prevents the existence of continuous and unassailable market positions to creating an even playing field for all.

By contrast, at risk of essentializing diverse ideologies and movements, some theories of conservatism see the political right as primarily motivated to justify, legitimate, and defend the existing distribution of private economic and political power.[3] Nozick (1974), for example, is primarily concerned with justifying the permanence and indisputability of property rights, frequently over and above objections that such property was acquired in less-than-admirable ways. This again fits with a general understanding of what market power is: the establishment or maintenance of a private hierarchy of power within markets between firms and industries that have control over the distribution of income and those that do not. The normative belief that the capitalists or business leaders who are in these positions deserve to be in them fits with factual arguments that those in the positions of power to direct investment are responsible for economic dynamism and growth.

What these affinities mean is that policymakers from the right and left, respectively, might be eager to find interpretations of economic facts that align with their normative worldviews and eager to deflect from views that conflict with them. For example, a left-leaning policymaker may be predisposed to favor pro-competition policies for their equalizing effects; they will also be less likely to consider the possibility that the market would benefit from additional positions of privilege. By the same token, a conservative is likely to accept that the distribution of profits and market power reflect merit, but they are correspondingly unlikely to reach the conclusion that those advantages are harmful to market performance more broadly, in and of themselves. To do so may require accepting that the overall distribution of economic power, income, and profits are all unearned positions that bear no resemblance to merit or fairness.

Looking Forward

What are the implications of this research for politics and policy today? After all, this historical background is partly motivated by the scale of today's monopoly problem in the United States and the very recent resurgence

[3] This interpretation of conservatism follows that of Robin (2011), who argues that this belief binds all conservatives since the early modern period.

of anti-monopoly politics in the United States and elsewhere. Are we seeing the theory of diminishing returns, commitment, and learning play out again today? How much explanatory power does this theory have for today's world? I first reflect on recent developments in the United States, comment on the state of competition policy in Europe, and then briefly discuss the applicability of the theory more broadly.

The Return of the American Anti-Monopoly Movement

Since work on this book began, its primary prediction about the course of policy in the United States has largely come to pass. Against many expectations about the political influence of powerful technology companies, the Biden administration has adopted a strong anti-monopoly agenda, appointed aggressive antitrust enforcers in Lina Khan and Jonathan Kanter, and issued a broad executive order to reinvigorate competition in the American economy. A major antitrust action has been filed against each of the major American tech firms.[4] In the fall of 2022, the first notable enhancements of antitrust law were passed in the Merger Filing Fee Modernization Act of 2022 and the State Antitrust Enforcement Venue Act of 2022.

First, academic research and policy discussions in the past decade have provided an increasing amount of evidence for the diminishing returns to market power in the United States: extreme concentration (Grullon, Larkin, and Michaely 2019), very high profits with limited investment (Gutiérrez and Philippon 2017; Schwartz 2016), low growth (Teulings and Baldwin 2014), and that the declining share of income going to labor is linked to rising concentration (Autor et al. 2020; Barkai 2020). De Loecker, Eeckhout, and Unger (2020) first noted the dramatic rise in average markups—the gap between price and marginal cost—among top American firms since the early 1980s, increasing from 21 percent over marginal cost in 1980 to 61 percent over marginal cost by 2020.[5] Other sources of diminished competition have also gained attention. For example, the concentration of portfolio ownership under common institutional investors like Vanguard,

[4] *U.S. v. Google, LLC*, complaint filed October 20, 2020; *Federal Trade Commission v. Facebook, Inc.*, complaint filed December 9, 2020; *In the Matter of Microsoft, Inc. and Activision Blizzard, Inc.*, complaint filed December 8, 2022; *U.S. v. Google, Inc.*, complaint filed January 24, 2023; *Federal Trade Commission v. Amazon.com, Inc.*, complaint filed September 26, 2023; *U.S. v. Apple, Inc.*, complaint filed March 24, 2024.

[5] See also Kurz (2017), who uses a similar measure of "surplus wealth."

BlackRock, and State Street has significantly reduced companies' incentives to compete with other commonly owned firms (Antón et al. 2023; Azar, Schmalz, and Tecu 2018; Schmalz 2021). Additionally, the rise of powerful buyers—including big retailers like Walmart or manufacturing buyers like Apple—has been a significant contributor to wage stagnation in recent years (Wilmers 2018). Researchers and policymakers have likewise recently recognized that mergers and acquisitions activity often adopts tactics to intentionally skirt antitrust review, whether in the case of "killer acquisitions" by pharma to eliminate the development of competing drugs (Cunningham, Ederer, and Ma 2020) or "serial acquisitions" by tech firms (Commission et al. 2021) or private equity portfolio companies.

However, even as some of the problems became apparent and before the recent shift in policy, the policy choices of recent administrations showed a remarkable degree of commitment to existing policy approaches. Court decisions had for decades been further diminishing the ability to enforce against even direct price-fixing,[6] creating wider loopholes for monopolistic or "single-firm" conduct,[7] and making mergers progressively easier.[8] Even Obama, who had campaigned in 2008 as an outsider candidate to take on the outsized influence of corporations, largely installed adherents to the consumer welfare standard into enforcement positions and ended up bringing no monopoly cases and blocking very few mergers, even as his administration otherwise cheered on the rise of the American tech giants.[9] Yet by the end of Obama's tenure, his own administration was publishing reports about the rising monopoly problem, corporate concentration, and outsized profits (Council of Economic Advisers 2016).

Likewise, current political conflicts over American antitrust fall along lines between committed insider policymakers and previously uncommitted policymakers and advocates without prior careers in antitrust. Some of the most influential Biden policymakers to push the Biden competition agenda, such as Brian Deese, had previously worked in economic policy

[6] See, in particular, *Matsushita Electrical Industrial Co., Ltd. v. Zenith Radio Corp.*, 475 U.S. 574 (1986); *Bell Atlantic Corp. v. Twombly*, 550 U.S. 544 (2007), both of which raised pleading standards in price-fixing cases.

[7] See, for example, *Ohio v. American Express Co.*, 138 S.Ct. 2274 (2018). American Express had a gag policy to prevent merchants from directing customers to lower-cost card issuers—straightforward restraint on competition, but the Supreme Court found it justifiable based on ostensible efficiencies.

[8] See, for example, *U.S. v. Baker Hughes Inc.*, 908 F.2d 981 (D.C. Cir. 1990); *New York v. Deutsche Telekom AG.*, 439 F. Supp. 3d 179 (S.D.N.Y. 2020).

[9] For more context, see Brown et al. (2021).

in the Obama administration. Others, such as Bharat Ramamurti, come from the staff of outsider politicians like Elizabeth Warren. The top positions for antitrust and competition specifically—Lina Khan (Federal Trade Commission), Jonathan Kanter (Department of Justice), or the White House (Tim Wu)—either entered government through academia or sat outside the mainstream antitrust bar. While not directly related to the commitment of policymakers, it is also worth noting that the academics to first recognize the modern monopoly problem are not mainstream antitrust scholars or industrial organization economists. Instead, they come from orthodox legal academia, non-economics social sciences, or other subfields of economics such as labor or financial economics.

The political conflict over antitrust likewise is occurring more within political parties than across them, somewhat downplaying the relative importance of electoral politics, even though the Biden administration is running for reelection on an anti-monopoly platform. The Trump administration filed the first antitrust cases against Google and Facebook, which the Biden administration has simply continued. Legislative proposals both for and against stronger antitrust policy are usually brought and opposed in a broadly bipartisan fashion. Federal enforcement actions against major technology firms have been joined by a large number of conservative state governments.

While there are thus reasons to believe this pattern is playing out again, there are plausible counterarguments. While the mechanisms of the theory appear to be playing out, at a practical level the potential political turmoil of a second Trump administration could undo or halt any policy changes brought by the Biden presidency, or by Trump's original term in office. At the same time, when many policy moves are made at once, they can take on their own momentum, and the Biden administration has initiated dozens of competition-related rule-makings and dozens of enforcement actions. While some of these can and might be halted with a shift in power, enforcement actions in particular rarely are.

European Champions?

Meanwhile, across the Atlantic, events of recent years indicate that the European Union may be shifting back to favor anti-competition industrial policies, after decades of substantially stronger competition rules, following a decade of lower profits in the 2010s as a result of a continuous recession with the Eurocrisis, as well as low profitability relative to the United States more generally (Philippon 2019). While it is unclear the direction that European competition and industrial policies will go, the perceived threat of unfair competition from Chinese multinationals, backed as they are by the Chinese state, has led several national governments to push for certain clawbacks of European competition rules in order to successfully compete at scale in international markets.

While this book has focused more on France than on European competition policy, European policy has become strongly pro-competition and has subsumed much of the responsibility and authority for competition rules into the broader European regime, as explored in Chapter 7. Discussed peripherally in Chapter 4, the European Union's competition policy had its origins first in the European Coal and Steel Community (ECSC) in 1950, but especially the Treaty of Rome in 1957. These rules were relatively weak for their first several decades in operation, however, as they completely ignored questions about merger control, monopolization, and abuse by dominant firms, and only had an ineffective anti-cartel policy in Regulation 17/62. Merger controls were added in 1989, and in 2003, Regulation 1/2003 resolved many of the weaknesses in the anti-cartel rules, removing the preregistration requirements and implementing incentives for cartel participants to defect and report to the authorities. Regulation 1/2003 likewise formally moved authority over competition law up to the European level.

As a result, European competition policy has become particularly aggressive and pro-competition, resulting in a significant "Atlantic divide in antitrust" (Gifford and Kudrle 2015). It includes an "abuse of dominance" standard for single-firm conduct that proscribes broader forms of anticompetitive conduct than America's Sherman Act. Europe's enforcement body, the Department for Competition (DG Comp), is likewise substantially more independent than the equivalent authorities in the United States. Thus, in the early 2010s, while the United States opted to either ignore or refuse to pursue enforcement actions against anticompetitive or monopolistic conduct by its tech firms, the EU showed no such restraint, levying record fines against Google (2.42 billion euros in 2017 and 4.3 euros in 2018 and billion-euro fines against a plethora of European and multinational firms: Intel (2009), Daimler (2016), Qualcomm (2018), Microsoft (2009), Scania (2017), and others. The European competition authority, DG Comp, is independent from political pressures from member states and has a proven record of blocking mergers above the loud objections of the member states in question for a given merger (Büthe 2007; Ergen and Kohl 2019; Foster 2022, 2024). Additionally, whereas in the United States the conflict between IP and antitrust is a continuous battle, the way that each was institutionalized into the European Union gave competition policy almost total preeminence over IP concerns (Czapracka 2010; Käseberg 2012).

As emphasized by scholars of antitrust and competition, Europe's institutional structure in some ways lends itself to stronger enforcement. Namely, the European competition regime and the European Union emerged from multiple rounds of intergovernmental bargaining and negotiation (Moravcsik 1998; Jabko 2006). The process of European unification was fraught with distributional disputes between states about the fairness of the contents of different arrangements, so member states were vigilant to ensure that others would not have loopholes to gain unfair advantages (Moravcsik 1998). Therefore, rules on "state aid"—direct support for firms from one member state—are relatively strong, particularly as the common market has become more integrated in recent decades, because such aid distorts competition and provides specific advantages for some members at the expense of others. Second, the DG Comp is political and institutionally independent from both individual member states and the government in Brussels, in part because the smaller of the original European Community members, like Belgium and the Netherlands, wanted strong and independent authorities in Brussels to limit the influence of larger member states. Philippon (2019) argues that this is the primary reason why European competition enforcement has performed so well, particularly because there are very few entry points for corporate or lobbying interests.

There is, however, increasing talk of changing competition and industrial policy at the European level, in order to create "European champion" multinational firms that would be able to compete and win against otherwise more successful American and Chinese firms. In tandem with the revival of climate and industrial policy in Europe generally (Di Carlo and Schmitz 2023), many viewpoints contend that this is partly in response to the wave of industrial policies recently passed in the United States; in particular, the Inflation Reduction Act (IRA) will provide $369 billion in subsidies for clean technologies manufactured domestically, and the CHIPS Act provided over

$40 billion to re-shore silicon chip fabrication. Europe's revived industrial policy is often rhetorically wrapped up with its own climate policies, such as the Green Deal Industrial Plan passed in February 2023, which simplified regulations and expanded block grant exceptions to state aid rules in order to encourage the uptake of renewable technologies.

However, these debates began prior to the passage of any of these industrial policies, and more than climate policy or the IRA, international competitiveness relative to Chinese and American companies loomed heavily over the conversation. At a time when American technology giants have long been dominant in the cutting-edge industries and Chinese multinationals are expanding internationally through both acquisitions and internal growth, there is a sense among European policymakers that more is needed to put European business on an even playing field with its international competitors. So, in February 2019, when the European Commission blocked the merger between Siemens and Alstom, this angered both the French and German governments, which had both lauded the deal as a necessary European champion. A few weeks later, the two governments released a joint manifesto for European industrial policy.[10] It suggested revising European merger control to take greater consideration of foreign state subsidies (i.e., Chinese), consider dynamic global competition over domestic market shares, and allow the European Council to override the Commission's competition decisions.

While these proposals faced significant pushback from DG Comp, the European Commission, and smaller member states, the debate continues today. On one hand, in 2022 the EU passed the Digital Markets Act, an antitrust-esque regulatory policy to bar "gatekeeper" tech firms from abusing their market position to preference their own products or block new entrants from the market. On the other hand, with Chinese manufacturers of renewable technologies, particularly electric vehicles (EVs), making rapid inroads into European markets—following years of their own subsidies and implicit state supports—Europe in July 2024 imposed a 38 percent tariff on Chinese EVs. Likewise, in April 2023, the Commission simplified its merger process to allow legal mergers to be cleared faster. It remains to be seen what direction, if any, Europe will go.

[10] Bundesmisterium für Wirtschaft und Energie and Ministère de l'Économie et des Finances, "A Franco-German Manifesto for a European Industrial Policy Fit for the 21st Century,"

A Universal Pattern?

Beyond the questions of its applicability today, to what degree are the alternations between policy regimes of competition and market power, and the theory of diminishing returns, commitment, and learning, universal across economies and countries? As discussed in the introduction, several other countries displayed similar patterns of shifts back and forth between favoring competition and market power. Japan, while forced to adopt antitrust policies following World War II, turned shortly thereafter to national champion–style industrial policies, before turning back to reinvigorated antitrust policies in the 1980s. Australia, unlike most of the Anglo-American world at the time, had a permissive or outright supportive view toward cartels and corporate concentration during most of the postwar period, but then reinvigorated its antitrust laws in the 1970s and 1980s in light of declining competitiveness and corporate concentration in the hands of foreign owners (Freyer 2006, 315–392). The United Kingdom and Canada, in contrast, largely followed the United States' pattern: favoring various forms of cartelization in the interwar period; enhancing antitrust, free trade, and competition in the postwar period; and then weakening those policies with the adoption of Chicago school thinking or similar approaches in the 1980s. The exact degree to which these changes do or do not follow the contours of this theory, however, requires further study.

Conversely, the theory does not appear to apply to certain other types of countries: countries that run consistent trade surpluses, referring primarily to Germany in the 20th century and China today. Called "export-led" models by the burgeoning literature on growth models (Baccaro and Pontusson 2016; Baccaro, Blyth, and Pontusson 2022), these governments maintain consistent trade surpluses through some combination of directed subsidies, systematic undervaluation of domestic prices (Höpner 2019), wage suppression to force excess savings for investment (Klein and Pettis 2020), and other export aids. As long as the rest of the world is willing to provide the consumption to absorb their excess output, there wouldn't be diminishing returns in the domestic context. Investment would be plentiful with high savings, prices would be low as a result of systematic undervaluation, and growth would continue as long consumption abroad continues to expand.

A cursory look at current patterns of Chinese competition illustrates the point. While it has been shown that China's antitrust policies and enforcement have grown into a force of their own with independent authorities

(Zhang 2021), export subsidies and industrial support still loom over the state of competition and market power in China. Because many of China's producers are so heavily subsidized, they face the risk of facing trade sanctions abroad from dumping (exporting below cost). However, as domestic Chinese markets remain highly competitive with these subsidies, Chinese industries that have attempted to avoid these trade sanctions by coordinating their export policies end up facing antitrust sanctions abroad for price-fixing (Zhang 2021, 163–199). Because the government continues supporting investment so directly and ensures the survival of a number of firms, the diminishing returns to competition are limited despite highly competitive markets.

In that light, it is quite possible that this theory broadly continues to only apply to the three remaining jurisdictions in the world that have both a coherent internal market as well as economic and policy autonomy over that market: the United States, the European Union, and China. The United States is already moving toward a competition policy regime, the European Union is experiencing internal debates over competition and industrial policies, and though only briefly considered here, China continues to maintain a large export surplus with suppressed domestic consumption, arguably avoiding the diminishing returns through which it might fall into this pattern.

Implications for Political Science

Even if an increasingly globalized world does narrow the number of jurisdictions or cases to which this exact theory might apply, it carries broader implications for political economy and political science more generally. The first is to emphasize the central importance of antitrust and competition policies to our understanding of political economy and popular politics. Often relegated as a corner of obtuse technical policy (both in scholarship and policy circles), at a high level antitrust is the policy area meant to ensure that capitalism does what we want capitalism to do.[11] Further, differences in the details of antitrust and competition policies are in many ways the defining institutional features that distinguish different national models of

[11] Credit to Rawi Abdelal for this phrasing.

capitalism,[12] determining which types of firms are allowed to exist, in what organizational forms, and with what relationships with other firms (Paul 2020), meaning that many of the categories taken for granted as natural in political economy are subject to potential change at the moments when antitrust and competition policies do as well.

With respect to popular politics, antitrust and related policies are often the locus point of popular backlash against corporate and business power. As one of the key policy locus points for ideological contestation over what capitalism and markets are and what they mean, antitrust is also one of the policy areas where discontents across the ideological spectrum can find unlikely agreement, with Trump-aligned conservatives finding themselves in unlikely alliances with progressive left-wing leaders like Elizabeth Warren. And while antitrust and anti-monopoly issues have usually remained far from the public eye during elections (the 1912 American presidential election was the last time it was a core campaign issue), president Biden had clearly planned to run on these issues, highlighting his crackdown on tech giants, antitrust enforcement against pharmaceutical companies for patent violations, banning anticompetitive corporate pricing tactics, and banning the imposition of noncompete agreements on workers.

Second, by emphasizing endogenous diminishing returns, this argument has presented a contrasting alternative to longstanding arguments about path dependence and increasing returns. Many historical institutionalist and related accounts rely on some form of a "punctuated equilibrium" model to explain change, wherein institutions are path dependent and characterized by increasing returns (Pierson 2000), unless external shocks destabilize them to generate "critical junctures" (Capoccia and Kelemen 2007). However, this theory has shown how the interaction of the same variables over time can generate both policy stability at first and policy change later on. Initially, a policy regime reinforces itself through the adoption and commitment to certain mental models, and presumably also because it is at least partially resolving some of the problems of the previous regime. By contrast, the regime generates diminishing returns that undermine it, precisely because that policy trajectory was locked in at an earlier time. Scholars of

[12] See Berk (2009), Foster (2024), and Prasad (2012) for versions of the argument that antitrust was the defining difference between "liberal market economies" and "coordinated market economies" in the varieties of capitalism theory. See Arslan (2023) and Peinert (2020) for discussions of how the introduction and diffusion of antitrust policies have arguably restructured transnational markets.

institutional and policy change should consider that some policy and institutional areas might lend themselves to continuous instability and change over time, rather than patterns of institutional lock-in and path dependence.

Third and building on this, the extensive archival research conducted highlights the importance of viewing bureaucrats, policy staff, and other mid- and low-level government personnel as agents. Institutions like government bureaucracies, agencies, and ministries are not simply maintaining a stable structure when they write memos and reports, share information, pass along recommendations, oppose policy changes, request additional funding, and the like. These bureaucratic actions, in many ways mundane and uninteresting in and of themselves, can nonetheless be actions to persuade, move the Overton window, make coordinated and unseen adjustments to policy, redirect resources or public attention, or set the policy and political agenda. These actions can seem (and be) symbolic in the moment, but they likewise usually can go unseen and unrecognized for their importance until well after they have accumulated into major shifts in policy.

Lastly, the joint mechanisms of commitment and turnover highlight a potentially ubiquitous mechanism shaping politics across political issues, policy domains, and countries. While the argument here builds on prior arguments about the removal of adherents to prior paradigms (Hall 1993; Kuhn 1962), the evidence present does show how policy can often move principally through the removal of the committed adherents and their replacement by newer agents. Crucially, the theory and evidence suggest that these newer agents do not necessarily need to have contrasting interests, preferences, or beliefs; rather, the fact that they they have not sunk their careers, reputations, pride, or identity into a certain viewpoint can be enough to introduce doubt and encourage rethinking. This same chain of mechanisms could plausibly be decisive in other areas of policy as varied as immigration, welfare, or minority rights, and could also apply to social movements and electoral politics, where movement or campaign tactics shift primarily through turnover and learning rather than through process of rational updating.

Policy Implications: A Stable Balance?

Lastly, there are several implications for poliymakers, some of which are likely intuitively known to practitioners. First is that in technical policy areas such as this, replacing longstanding staff, bureaucrats, or policy elites is likely central to effecting policy change, even independently of the specific beliefs of those who replace them. To the degree that commitment is a powerful constraint on policy and political reconsideration, installing ambitious but unaligned policymakers might permit more space for change than to staff key roles with leaders with any prior commitments to which they may be or feel obligated.

Centrally, however, the book has left open the question of how one could build a stable policy balance between competition and market power in the long run. After all, most of the implementers of the policy regimes studied here believed that their own version of policy represented an appropriate and stable balance between competitive pressures and protections from the vicissitudes of the market, even as each subsequently reached its own limits decades later. Is there a stable policy regime that can strike the right balance?

The neo-Brandeisians pushing Biden's competition agenda tend to reject simple categories like competition and market power as sufficient descriptors, presenting a possible way forward for a more measured balance between the two. Paul (2020), for example, generally rejects the view of antitrust as a question of competition versus monopoly, instead seeing antitrust as an allocator of "coordination rights," conferring certain favored groups and organizations the rights to organize and avoid the turmoil of direct competition, while subjecting others to it. Others have highlighted values of "fair competition" or "regulated competition," rejecting universal categories of competition and monopoly in favor of certain forms of competition or protections from the market as being beneficial or not (Berk 2009; Sawyer 2018; Vaheesan 2022). This has also expanded to explore how antitrust, by allowing central firms to coordinate restrictively with subcontractors while prohibiting weaker groups from collectively coordinating, has contributed to the "fissuring" of the American workplace (Callaci 2021; Hafiz 2022; Paul 2019).

However, this book would suggest that a balanced and nuanced approach between the two may be politically unstable, almost regardless of its economic merits. Simple mental models and framings—that competition is beneficial and that corporate concentration is harmful—have a political power of their own, precisely because of their lack of nuance and their ability to dispense with complexity. A need for cognitive closure does not just mean that policymakers—judges, enforcers, and regulators—are committed to certain policy regimes, it means that they want that policy regime to be reducible to simple rules of thumb, presumptions, and decision rules. This bodes poorly for the political project of counterbalancing simple mental models with the nuance, ambiguity, and uncertainties of which coordination rights should be permitted, what is fair versus unfair competition, and so on.

So now, as the Biden administration has attempted to restore competition in the American economy, a tension exists between those among the neo-Brandeisian camp who wish to emphasize *fair* competition and those who advocate to simply increase competition. For example, the Biden executive order on competition broadly framed its goal as simply increasing competition in every instance it mentioned. And despite well-thought objections from neo-Brandeisian thinkers that such an approach is flawed, both the Biden administration and the broader anti-monopoly agenda continue on with simple arguments that concentration is bad and competition is good.

Bibliography

Abdelal, Rawi. 2007. *Capital Rules: The Construction of Global Finance.* Cambridge, MA: Harvard University Press.

Adams, William James. 1989. *Restructuring the French Economy: Government and the Rise of Market Competition since World War II.* Washington, DC: Brookings Institution Press.

Aghion, Philippe, Nick Bloom, Richard Blundell, Rachel Griffith, and Peter Howitt. 2005. "Competition and Innovation: An Inverted-U Relationship." *The Quarterly Journal of Economics* 120 (2): 701–728. https://doi.org/10.1093/qje/120.2.701.

Aghion, Philippe, Peter Howitt, and Susanne Prantl. 2015. "Patent Rights, Product Market Reforms, and Innovation." *Journal of Economic Growth* 20: 223–262.

Aglietta, Michel. 2000. *A Theory of Capitalist Regulation: The US Experience.* New York, NY: Verso.

ALA Schechter Poultry Corp. v. United States, 295 U.S. 495 (1935).

Antón, Miguel, Florian Ederer, Mireia Giné, and Martin Schmalz. 2023. "Common Ownership, Competition, and Top Management Incentives." *Journal of Political Economy* 131 (5): 1294–1355.

Arkes, Hal R., and Catherine Blumer. 1985. "The Psychology of Sunk Cost." *Organizational Behavior and Human Decision Processes* 35 (1): 124–140. https://doi.org/10.1016/0749-5978(85)90049-4.

Arrighi, Giovanni. 1994. *The Long Twentieth Ccentury: Money, Power, and the Origins of our Times.* New York, NY: Verso.

Arrighi, Giovanni, and Beverly Silver. 1999. *Chaos and Governance in the Modern World System.* Minneapolis, MN: University of Minnesota Press.

Arrow, Kenneth. 1962. "Economic Welfare and the Allocation of Resources to Invention." In *The Rate and Direction of Inventive Activity: Economic and Social Factors*, edited by National Bureau Committee for Economic Research and the Committee on Economic Growth of the Social Science Research Councils, 609–626. Princeton, NJ: Princeton University Press.

Arslan, Melike. 2023. "Legal Diffusion as Protectionism: The Case of the US Promotion of Antitrust Laws." *Review of International Political Economy* 30 (6): 2285–2308.

Askenazy, Philippe. 2015. *The Blind Decades: Employment and Growth in France, 1974–2014.* Oakland, CA: University of California Press.

Autor, David, David Dorn, Lawrence F. Katz, Christina Patterson, and John Van Reenen. 2020. "The Fall of the Labor Share and the Rise of Superstar Firms." *The Quarterly Journal of Economics* 135 (2): 645–709. https://doi.org/10.1093/qje/qjaa004.

Azar, José, Martin C. Schmalz, and Isabel Tecu. 2018. "Anticompetitive Effects of Common Ownership." *The Journal of Finance* 73 (4): 1513–1565.

Baccaro, Lucio, Mark Blyth, and Jonas Pontusson. 2022. *Diminishing Returns: The New Politics of Growth and Stagnation.* Oxford: Oxford University Press.

Baccaro, Lucio, and Jonas Pontusson. 2016. "Rethinking Comparative Political Economy: The Growth Model Perspective." *Politics & Society* 44 (2): 175–207.

Baccini, Leonardo, Pablo M. Pinto, and Stephen Weymouth. 2017. "The Distributional Consequences of Preferential Trade Liberalization: Firm-Level Evidence." *International Organization* 71 (2): 373–395.

Baer, William J. 1988. "At the Turning Point: The Commission in 1978." *Journal of Public Policy & Marketing* 7 (1): 11–20.

Baran, Paul A., and Paul M. Sweezy. 1966. *Monopoly Capital: An Essay on the American Economic and Social Order.* New York, NY: Monthly Review Press.

Barber, William J. 1996. *Designs within Disorder: Franklin D. Roosevelt, the Economists, and the Shaping of American Economic Policy, 1933–1945.* Cambridge, UK: Cambridge University Press.

Barjot, Dominique. 2013. "Les cartels, une voie vers l'intégration européenne?" *Revue économique* 64 (6): 1043–1066.

Barjot, Dominique. 2014. "Cartels et cartellisation: des instruments contre les crises?" *Entreprises et histoire*, no. 3: 5–19.

Barkai, Simcha. 2020. "Declining Labor and Capital Shares." *The Journal of Finance* 75 (5): 2421–2463.

Barth, Erling, Alex Bryson, James C. Davis, and Richard Freeman. 2016. "It's Where You Work: Increases in the Dispersion of Earnings across Establishments and Individuals in the United States." *Journal of Labor Economics* 34 (S2): S67–S97. https://doi.org/10.1086/684045.

Bawn, Kathleen, Martin Cohen, David Karol, Seth Masket, Hans Noel, and John Zaller. 2012. "A Theory of Political Parties: Groups, Policy Demands and Nominations in American Politics." *Perspectives on Politics* 10 (3): 571–597.

Baxter, William F. 1966. "Legal Restrictions on Exploitation of the Patent Monopoly: An Economic Analysis." *Yale Law Journal* 76: 267.

Beckert, Jens. 1996. "What Is Sociological about Economic Sociology? Uncertainty and the Embeddedness of Economic Action." *Theory and Society* 25 (6): 803–840.

Bennett, Andrew. 2008. "Process Tracing: A Bayesian Approach." In *Oxford Handbook of Political Methodology*, edited by Janet M. Box-Steffensmeier, Henry E. Brady, David Collier, 702–721. Oxford, UK: Oxford University Press.

Bennett, Andrew, and Jeffrey T. Checkel. 2015. *Process Tracing.* Cambridge, UK: Cambridge University Press.

Berge, Wendell. 1944. *Cartels: Challenge to a Free World.* Washington, DC: Public Affairs Press.

Berger, Suzanne. 1981. "Lame Ducks and National Champions: Industrial Policy in the Fifth Republic." In *The Fifth Republic at Twenty*, edited by William G. Andrews & Stanley Hoffmann, 160–178. Albany, NY: State University of New York Press.

Berk, Gerald. 2009. *Louis D. Brandeis and the Making of Regulated Competition, 1900–1932.* Cambridge, UK: Cambridge University Press.

Berle, Adolf, and Gardner Means. 1932. *The Modern Corporation and Private Property*. New York, NY: Harcourt.

Berman, Elizabeth Popp. 2022. *Thinking Like an Economist: How Efficiency Replaced Equality in U.S. Public Policy*. Princeton, NJ: Princeton University Press.

Billows, Sebastian. 2016. "À qui profite la concurrence?" *Gouvernement et action publique*, no. 4: 69–91.

Billows, Sebastian. 2017. "Le marché et la règle: l'encadrement juridique des relations entre la grande distribution et ses fournisseurs." PhD diss., Paris, Institut d'études politiques.

Blyth, Mark. 2002. *Great Transformations: Economic Ideas and Institutional Change in the Twentieth Century*. Cambridge, UK: Cambridge University Press.

Bork, Robert H. 1965a. "Contrasts in Antitrust Theory: I." *Columbia Law Review* 65 (3): 401–416.

Bork, Robert H. 1965b. "The Rule of Reason and the Per Se Concept: Price Fixing and Market Division." *The Yale Law Journal* 74 (5): 775–847.

Bork, Robert H. 1967. "The Goals of Antitrust Policy." *The American Economic Review* 57 (2): 242–253.

Bork, Robert H. 1978. *The Antitrust Paradox: A Policy at War with Itself*. New York, NY: Basic Books.

Bork, Robert H., and Ward S. Bowman. 1965. "The Crisis in Antitrust." *Columbia Law Review* 65 (3): 363–376.

Borkin, Joseph, and Charles A. Welsh. 1943. *Germany's Master Plan: The Story of Industrial Offensive*. New York, NY: Duell, Sloan / Pearce.

Boublil, Alain. 1977. *Le socialisme industriel*. Paris, France: Presses universitaires de France.

Boyer, Robert. 1990. *The Regulation School: A Critical Introduction*. New York, NY: Columbia University Press.

Brady, Robert A. 1937. *The Spirit and Structure of German Fascism*. London, UK: Gollancz.

Brault, Dominique. 1987. *L'État et l'ésprit de concurrence en France*. Paris, France: Economica.

Brenner, Robert. 2006. *The Economics of Global Turbulence: The Advanced Capitalist Economies from Long Boom to Long Downturn, 1945–2005*. New York, NY: Verso.

Brinkley, Alan. 1995. *The End of Reform: New Deal Liberalism in Recession and War*. New York, NY: Vintage.

Brown, Krista, Matt Buck, Pat Garofalo, Lucas Kunce, Sarah Miller, Kalen Pruss, Reed Showalter, Matt Stoller, and Olivia Webb. 2021. "The Courage to Learn: A Retrospective on Antitrust and Competition Policy during the Obama Administration and Framework for a New, Structuralist Approach."

Brown Shoe Co., Inc. v. United States, 370 U.S. 294 (1962).

Brunswick Corp. v. Pueblo Bowl-O-Mat, Inc., 429 U.S. 477 (1977).

Büthe, Tim. 2007. "The Politics of Competition and Institutional Change in European Union: The First Fifty Years." In *Making History: European Integration and*

Institutional Change at Fifty, edited by Sophie Meunier and Kathleen McNamara, 8:175–193. Oxford, UK: Oxford University Press.

Callaci, Brian. 2021. "Control Without Responsibility: The Legal Creation of Franchising, 1960–1980." *Enterprise & Society* 22(1): 156–82. https://doi.org/10.1017/eso.2019.58.

Callaci, Brian. 2021. "What Do Franchisees Do? Vertical Restraints as Workplace Fissuring and Labor Discipline Devices." *Journal of Law and Political Economy* 1 (3): 397–444.

Capoccia, Giovanni, and R. Daniel Kelemen. 2007. "The Study of Critical Junctures: Theory, Narrative, and Counterfactuals in Historical Institutionalism." *World Politics* 59 (3): 341–369.

Chamberlin, Edward. 1933. *The Theory of Monopolistic Competition*. Cambridge, MA: Harvard University Press.

Chandler, Alfred Dupont. 1977. *The Visible Hand: The Managerial Revolution in American Business*. Cambridge, MA: Harvard University Press.

Chandler, Alfred Dupont. 2001. *Inventing the Electronic Century: The Epic Story of the Consumer Electronics and Computer Industries*. Cambridge, MA: Harvard University Press.

Chatriot, Alain. 2008. "Les ententes: débats juridiques et dispositifs législatifs (1923–1953) La genèse de la politique de la concurrence en France." *Histoire, économie & societé* 27 (1): 7–22.

Chorev, Nitsan. 2007. *Remaking U.S. Trade Policy: From Protectionism to Globalization*. Ithaca, NY: Cornell University Press.

Christophers, Brett. 2016. *The Great Leveler: Capitalism and Competition in the Court of Law*. Cambridge, MA: Harvard University Press.

Christophers, Brett. 2020. *Rentier Capitalism: Who Owns the Economy, and Who Pays for It?* London, UK: Verso Books.

Cohen, Elie. 1989. *L'État brancardier: Politiques du déclin industriel (1974–1984)*. Paris, France: Calmann-Lévy.

Cole, Harold L, and Lee E Ohanian. 2004. "New Deal Policies and the Persistence of the Great Depression: A General Equilibrium Analysis." *Journal of political Economy* 112 (4): 779–816.

Commission, Federal Trade, et al. 2021. "Non-HSR Reported Acquisitions by Select Technology Platforms, 2010-2019-A report of the FTC (2021)."

Consten SaRL and Grundig GmbH v Commission. 1966. *Cases 56/64 and 58/64, ECR 299*.

Continental T.V. Inc. v. GTE Sylvania Inc., 433 U.S. 36. 1977.

Council of Economic Advisers. 2016. *Benefits of Competition and Indicators of Market Power*. Technical report. White House.

Cuff, Robert D. 1973. *The War Industries Board: Business-Government Relations during World War I*. Baltimore, MD: Johns Hopkins University Press.

Culpepper, Pepper D. 2010. *Quiet Politics and Business Power: Corporate Control in Europe and Japan*. Cambridge, UK: Cambridge University Press.

Culpepper, Pepper D., and Kathleen Thelen. 2020. "Are We All Amazon Primed? Consumers and the Politics of Platform Power." *Comparative Political Studies* 53 (2): 288–318.

Cunningham, Colleen, Florian Ederer, and Song Ma. 2020. "Killer Acquisitions." *Journal of Political Economy* (forthcoming), *available at SSRN 3241707.*

Czapracka, Katarzyna. 2010. *Intellectual Property and the Limits of Antitrust: A Comparative Study of US and EU Approaches.* Northampton, MA: Edward Elgar Publishing.

Dafermos, Yannis, Daniela Gabor, and Jo Michell. 2023. Institutional supercycles: an evolutionary macro-finance approach. *New Political Economy, 28*(5), 693–712. https://doi.org/10.1080/13563467.2022.2161497

Davies, William. 2010. "Economics and the 'Nonsense' of Law: The Case of the Chicago Antitrust Revolution." *Economy and Society* 39 (1): 64–83.

De Loecker, Jan, Jan Eeckhout, and Gabriel Unger. 2020. "The Rise of Market Power and the Macroeconomic Implications." *The Quarterly Journal of Economics* 135 (2): 561–644.

Denzau, Arthur T., and Douglass C. North. 1994. "Shared Mental Models: Ideologies and Institutions." *Kyklos* 47 (1): 3–31.

Derthick, Martha, and Paul J. Quirk. 1985. *The Politics of Deregulation.* Washington, DC: Brookings Institution Press.

Di Carlo, Donato, and Luuk Schmitz. 2023. "Europe First? The Rise of EU Industrial Policy Promoting and Protecting the Single Market." *Journal of European Public Policy* 30 (10): 2063–2096.

Didry, Claude, and Frédéric Marty. 2016. "La politique de concurrence comme levier de la politique industrielle dans la France de l'après-guerre." Available at https://www.cairn.info/revue-gouvernement-et-action-publique-2016-4-page-23.htm, *Gouvernement et action publique* 4 (4): 23–45.

DiMaggio, Paul J., and Walter W. Powell. 1983. "The Iron Cage Revisited: Institutional Isomorphism and Collective Rationality in Organizational Fields." *American Sociological Review* 48 (2): 147–160.

Djelic, Marie-Laure. 1998. *Exporting the American Model: The Post-War Transformation of European Business.* Oxford, UK: Oxford University Press.

Dobbin, Frank. 1994. *Forging Industrial Policy: The United States, Britain, and France in the Railway Age.* Cambridge, UK: Cambridge University Press.

Dobbin, Frank, and Timothy J. Dowd. 2000. "The Market That Antitrust Built: Public Policy, Private Coercion, and Railroad Acquisitions, 1825 to 1922." *American Sociological Review* 5 (65): 631–657.

Drahos, Peter, and John Braithwaite. 2002. *Information Feudalism: Who Owns the Knowledge Economy.* London, UK: Routledge.

Duchêne, François. 1994. *Jean Monnet: The First Statesman of Interdependence.* New York, NY: Norton.

Dumez, Hervé, and Alain Jeunemaitre. 1989. *Diriger l'économie: l'État et les prix en France 1936-1986.* Paris, France: Harmattan.

Easterbrook, Frank H. 1984. "Limits of Antitrust." *Texas Law Review* 63 (1): 1–40.

Eddy, Arthur J. 1912. *The New Competition: An Examination of the Conditions Underlying the Radical Change That IIs Taking Place in the Commercial and Industrial World; The Change from a Competitive to a Cooperative Basis.* New York, NY: D. Appleton & Co.

Edwards, Corwin D. 1943. "Thurman Arnold and the Antitrust Laws." *Political Science Quarterly* 58 (3): 338–355. https://doi.org/10.2307/2144489.

Eisner, Marc Allen. 1991. *Antitrust and the Triumph of Economics: Institutions, Expertise, and Policy Change.* Chapel Hill, NC: University of North Carolina Press.

Elinson, Gregory. 2015. "Shifting Coalitions: Business Power, Partisan Politics, and the Rise of the Regulatory State." PhD diss., University of California, Berkeley.

Elzinga, Kenneth G, and David E Mills. 2011. "The Lerner Index of Monopoly Power: Origins and Uses." *American Economic Review* 101 (3): 558–564.

Ergen, Timur, and Sebastian Kohl. 2019. "Varieties of Economization in Competition Policy: Institutional Change in German and American Antitrust, 1960–2000." *Review of International Political Economy* 26 (2): 256–286.

Esping-Andersen, Gosta. 1990. *The Three Worlds of Welfare Capitalism.* Princeton, NJ: Princeton University Press.

Fairfield, Tasha, and Andrew E. Charman. 2017. "Explicit Bayesian Analysis for Process Tracing: Guidelines, Opportunities, and Caveats." *Political Analysis* 25 (3): 363–380.

Federal Trade Commission v. Arch Coal, Inc., 329 F. Supp. 2d 109. D.D.C (2004).

Fligstein, Neil. 1990. *The Transformation of Corporate Control.* Cambridge, MA: Harvard University Press.

Fligstein, Neil. 2002. *The Architecture of Markets: An Economic Sociology of Twenty-First-Century Capitalist Societies.* Princeton, NJ: Princeton University Press.

Foster, Chase. 2022. "Varieties of Neoliberalism: Courts, Competition Paradigms and the Atlantic Divide in Anti-Trust." *Socio-Economic Review* 20 (4): 1653–1678.

Foster, Chase. 2024. "Legalism without Adversarialism?: Bureaucratic Legalism and the Politics of Regulatory Implementation in the European Union." *Regulation & Governance* 18 (1): 53–72.

Fox, Eleanor M., and Lawrence A. Sullivan. 1987. "Antitrust–Retrospective and Prospective: Where Are We Coming from—Where Are We Going." *NYUL Rev.* 62: 936.

Franck, Louis. 1958. *Les Prix.* Paris, France: Presses Universitaires de France.

Franck, Louis. 1963. *La Libre Concurrence.* Paris, France: Presses Universitaires de France.

Freyer, Tony. 1992. *Regulating Big Business: Antitrust in Great Britain and America, 1880—1990.* Cambridge, UK: Cambridge University Press.

Freyer, Tony. 2006. *Antitrust and Global Capitalism, 1930–2004.* Cambridge, UK: Cambridge University Press.

Frieden, Jeffry A., and Ronald Rogowski. 1996. "The Impact of the International Economy on National Policies: An Analytical Overview." In *Internationalization and Domestic Politics*, edited by Robert Keohane, and Helen V. Milner, 25–47. Cambridge, UK: Cambridge University Press.

Fugate, Wilbur L. 1958. *Foreign Commerce and the Antitrust Laws.* Boston, MA: Little, Brown & Co.

Furman, Jason, and Peter Orszag. 2018. "A Firm-Level Perspective on the Role of Rents in the Rise in Inequality." In *Toward a Just Society*, 19–47. Columbia University Press.

Galbraith, John Kenneth. 1952a. *A Theory of Price Control.* Cambridge, MA: Harvard University Press.

Galbraith, John Kenneth. 1952b. "*American Capitalism: The Concept of Countervailing Power." London, UK: Penguin.*

Gerber, David J. 1998. *Law and Competition in Twentieth Century Europe: Protecting Prometheus.* Oxford, UK: Oxford University Press.

Gerschenkron, Alexander. 1962. *Economic Backwardness in Historical Perspective.* Cambridge, MA: Harvard University Press.

Gertner, Jon. 2012. *The Idea Factory: Bell Labs and the Great Age of American Innovation.* London, UK: Penguin.

Gifford, Daniel J., and Robert T. Kudrle. 2015. *The Atlantic Divide in Antitrust: An Examination of US and EU Competition Policy.* Chicago, IL: University of Chicago Press.

Goldgeier, James M., and Philip E. Tetlock. 2001. "Psychology and International Relations Theory." *Annual Review of Political Science* 4 (1): 67–92. https://doi.org/10.1146/annurev.polisci.4.1.67.

Golec de Zavala, Agnieszka, Aleksandra Cislak, and Elzbieta Wesolowska. 2010. "Political Conservatism, Need for Cognitive Closure, and Intergroup Hostility." *Political Psychology* 31 (4): 521–541.

Golec de Zavala, Agnieszka, and Agnieszka Van Bergh. 2007. "Need for Cognitive Closure and Conservative Political Beliefs: Differential Mediation by Personal Worldviews." *Political Psychology* 28 (5): 587–608.

Gordon, David M. 1978. "Up and Down the Long Roller Coaster." In *US Capitalism in Crisis*, 22–34. New York, NY: Union for Radical Political Economics.

Gordon, David M., Richard Edwards, and Michael Reich. 1982. *Segmented Work, Divided Workers: The Historical Transformation of Labor in the United States.* Cambridge, UK: Cambridge University Press.

Gourevitch, Peter. 1986. *Politics in Hard Times: Comparative Responses to International Economic Crises.* Ithaca, NY: Cornell University Press.

Gowan, Peter. 1999. *The Global Gamble: Washington's Faustian Bid for World Dominance.* New York, NY: Verso.

Greif, Avner, and David D. Laitin. 2004. "A Theory of Endogenous Institutional Change." *American Political Science Review* 98 (4): 633–652.

Grullon, Gustavo, Yelena Larkin, and Roni Michaely. 2019. "Are US Industries Becoming More Concentrated?"." *Review of Finance* 23 (4): 697–743.

Gutiérrez, Germán, and Thomas Philippon. 2017. *Investmentless Growth: An Empirical Investigation.* Technical report. Brookings Papers on Economic Activity.

Gutiérrez, Germán, and Thomas Philippon. 2018. "Ownership, Concentration, and Investment." *AEA Papers and Proceedings* 108: 432–37.

Gutiérrez, Germán, and Thomas Philippon. 2019. *The Failure of Free Entry.* Technical report. National Bureau of Economic Research.

Gutiérrez, Germán, and Thomas Philippon. 2020. *Some Facts about Dominant Firms.* Technical report. National Bureau of Economic Research.

Hacker, Jacob S. 2004. "Privatizing Risk without Privatizing the Welfare State: The Hidden Politics of Social Policy Retrenchment in the United States." *American Political Science Review* 98 (2): 243–260.

Hacker, Jacob S., and Paul Pierson. 2010. *Winner-Take-All Politics: How Washington Made the Rich Richer—And Turned Its Back on the Middle Class.* New York, NY: Simon / Schuster.

Hafiz, Hiba. 2022. "The Brand Defense." *Berkeley Journal of Employment and Labor Law* 43 (1): 1–78.

Haley, John O. 2001. *Antitrust in Germany and Japan: The First Fifty Years, 1947–1998.* Seattle, WA: University of Washington Press.

Hall, Peter A. 1986. *Governing the Economy: The Politics of State Intervention in Britain and France.* Oxford, UK: Oxford University Press.

Hall, Peter A. 1989. *The Political Power of Economic Ideas: Keynesianism across Nations.* Princeton, NJ: Princeton University Press.

Hall, Peter A. 1993. "Policy Paradigms, Social Learning, and the State: The Case of Economic Policymaking in Britain." *Comparative Politics* 25 (3): 275–296. https://doi.org/10.2307/422246.

Hall, Peter A. 2003. "Aligning Ontology and Methodology in Comparative Research." In *Comparative Historical Analysis in the Social Sciences*, edited by James Mahoney and Dietrich Rueschemeyer, 373–404. Cambridge, UK: Cambridge University Press.

Hall, Peter A. 2006. "Systematic Process Analysis: When and How to Use it." *European Management Review* 3 (1): 24–31.

Hall, Peter A., and David Soskice. 2001. *Varieties of Capitalism: The Institutional Foundations of Comparative Advantage.* Oxford, UK: Oxford University Press.

Hawley, Ellis Wayne. 1966. *The New Deal and the Problem of Monopoly.* Princeton, NJ: Princeton University Press.

Hayward, Jack. 1986. *The State and the Market Economy: Industrial Patriotism and Economic Intervention in France.* Brighton, UK: Wheatsheaf Books.

Heath, Chip. 1995. "Escalation and De-Escalation of Commitment in Response to Sunk Costs: The Role of Budgeting in Mental Accounting." *Organizational Behavior and Human Decision Processes* 62 (1): 38–54. https://doi.org/10.1006/obhd.1995.1029.

Helleiner, Eric. 1996. *States and the Reemergence of Global Finance: From Bretton Woods to the 1990s.* Ithaca, NY: Cornell University Press.

Himmelberg, Robert F. 1965. "The War Industries Board and the Antitrust Question in November 1918." *The Journal of American History* 52 (1): 59–74.

Himmelberg, Robert F. 1968. "Business, Antitrust Policy, and the Industrial Board of the Department of Commerce, 1919." *Business History Review* 42 (1): 1–23.

Himmelberg, Robert F. 1976. *The Origins of the National Recovery Administration: Business, Government, and the Trade Association Issue, 1921–1933.* New York, NY: Fordham University Press.

Hofstadter, Richard. 1965. "What Happened to the Antitrust Movement?" In *The Paranoid Style in American Politics and Other Essays*, 188–237. New York: Alfred A. Knopf.

Hope, David, and David Soskice. 2016. "Growth Models, Varieties of Capitalism, and Macroeconomics." *Politics & Society* 44 (2): 209–226.

Höpner, Martin. 2019. "The German Undervaluation Regime under Bretton Woods: How Germany Became the Nightmare of the World Economy." *Available at SSRN 3333760.*

Hovenkamp, Herbert. 1985. "Antitrust Policy after Chicago." *Michigan Law Review*: 213–284.

Hovenkamp, Herbert. 2009. *The Neal Report and the Crisis in Antitrust.* Technical report. University of Pennsylvania Faculty Scholarship.

Hudson, Michael. 2003. *Super Imperialism: The Origin and Fundamentals of U.S. World Dominance.* New York, NY: Pluto Press.

Illinois Brick Co. v. Illinois, 431 U.S. 720 (1977).

International Salt Co. v. United States, 332 U.S. 392 (1947).

Iversen, Torben. 1996. "Power, Flexibility, and the Breakdown of Centralized Wage Bargaining: Denmark and Sweden in Comparative Perspective." *Comparative Politics* 28 (4): 399–436. https://doi.org/10.2307/422051.

Iversen, Torben, and Anne Wren. 1998. "Equality, Employment, and Budgetary Restraint: The Trilemma of the Service Economy." *World Politics* 50 (4): 507–546. https://doi.org/10.1017/S0043887100007358.

Jabko, Nicolas. 2006. *Playing the Market: A Political Strategy for Uniting Europe, 1985–2005.* Ithaca, NY: Cornell University Press.

Jacques, Tristan. 2016. "Refus de vente interdit!" *Gouvernement et action publique*, no. 4: 47–67.

Jervis, Robert. 1976. *Perception and Misperception in International Politics.* Princeton, NJ: Princeton University Press.

Johnson, Chalmers. 1982. *MITI and the Japanese Miracle: The Growth of Industrial Policy: 1925–1975.* Stanford, CA: Stanford University Press.

Kaiser Aluminum Chemical Corp. v. F.T.C., 652 F.2d 1324 (7th Cir. 1981).

Käseberg, Thorsten. 2012. *Intellectual Property, Antitrust and Cumulative Innovation in the EU and the US.* Oxford, UK: Bloomsbury Publishing.

Khan, Lina M. 2017. "Amazon's Antitrust Paradox." *Yale Law Journal* 126 (3): 564–907.

Khan, Lina M. 2018. "The Ideological Roots of America's Market Power Problem." *Yale LJF* 127: 960.

King, Gary, Robert O Keohane, and Sidney Verba. 1994. *Designing Social Inquiry: Scientific Inference in Qualitative Research.* Princeton, NJ: Princeton University Press.

Kipping, Matthias. 2001. "Les relations gouvernement-monde des affaires dans la France de l'après-guerre: adaptations et adaptabilité d'un système original." Available at https://www.persee.fr/doc/hes_0752-5702_2001_num_20_4_2247, *Histoire Économie et Société* 20 (4): 577–596.

Kipping, Matthias. 2002. *La France et les origines de l'Union européenne: intégration économique et compétitivité internationale.* Vincennes, France: Comité pour l'histoire économique et financière.

Klein, Matthew C., and Michael Pettis. 2020. *Trade Wars Are Class Wars: How Rising Inequality Distorts the Global Economy and Threatens International Peace.* New Haven, CT: Yale University Press.

Knight, Jack. 1992. *Institutions and Social Conflict.* Cambridge, UK: Cambridge University Press.

Kondratieff, N. D., and W. F. Stolper. 1935. "The Long Waves in Economic Life." *The Review of Economics and Statistics* 17 (6): 105–115.

Kotz, David M., Terrence McDonough, and Michael Reich. 1994. *Social Structures of Accumulation: The Political Economy of Growth and Crisis.* Cambridge, UK: Cambridge University Press.

Kovacic, William E., and Carl Shapiro. 2000. "Antitrust Policy: A Century of Economic and Legal Thinking." *Journal of Economic Perspectives* 14 (1): 43–60.

Krasner, Stephen. 1984. "Approaches to the State: Alternative Conceptions and Historical Dynamics." *Comparative Politics* 16 (2): 223–246.

Kruglanski, Arie W., and Donna M. Webster. 1996. "Motivated Closing of the Mind: 'Seizing' and 'Freezing.'" *Psychological Review*, 263–283. https://doi.org/10.1037/0033-295x.103.2.263.

Kuhn, Thomas S. 1962. *The Structure of Scientific Revolutions.* Chicago, IL: University of Chicago Press.

Kuisel, Richard F. 1981. *Capitalism and the State in Modern France: Renovation and Economic Management in the Twentieth Century.* Cambridge, UK: Cambridge University Press.

Kurz, Mordecai. 2017. *On the Formation of Capital and Wealth.* Technical report. University of Chicago, Working Paper.

Kurz, Mordecai. 2023. *The Market Power of Technology: Understanding the Second Gilded Age.* New York, NY: Columbia University Press.

Lancieri, Filippo, Eric A. Posner, and Luigi Zingales. 2024. "The Political Economy of the Decline of Antitrust Enforcement in the United States." *Antitrust Law Journal* 85 (2): 441–519.

Lande, Robert H. 1982. "Wealth Transfers as the Original and Primary Concern of Antitrust: The Efficiency Interpretation Challenged." *Hastings Lj* 34: 65.

Lee, Frederic S. 1998. *Post Keynesian Price Theory.* Cambridge, UK: Cambridge University Press.

Leegin Creative Leather Products Inc. v. PSKS Inc., 551 U.S. 877 (2007).

Lerner, A. P. 1934. "The Concept of Monopoly and the Measurement of Monopoly Power." *The Review of Economic Studies* 1 (3): 157–175.

Leslie, Christopher R. 2014. "Antitrust Made (Too) Simple." *Antitrust Law Journal* 79: 917.

Lester, Richard K., and Michael J. Piore. 2004. *Innovation: The Missing Dimension.* Cambridge, MA: Harvard University Press.

Levy, Jonah D. 1999. *Tocqueville's Revenge: State, Society, and Economy in Contemporary France.* Cambridge, MA: Harvard University Press.

Li, Wendy Y. 2023. "Regulatory Capture's Third Face of Power." *Socio-Economic Review* 21 (2): 1217–1245.

Lord, Charles G., Lee Ross, and Mark R. Lepper. 1979. "Biased Assimilation and Attitude Polarization: The Effects of Prior Theories on Subsequently Considered Evidence." *Journal of Personality and Social Psychology* 37 (11): 2098–2108. https://doi.org/10.1037/0022-3514.37.11.2098.

Loriaux, Michael Maurice. 1991. *France after Hegemony: International Change and Financial Reform.* Ithaca, NY: Cornell University Press.

Mahoney, James. 2000. "Path Dependence in Historical Sociology." *Theory and Society* 29 (4): 507–548. https://doi.org/10.1023/A:1007113830879.

Mahoney, James, and Kathleen Thelen. 2010. *Explaining Institutional Change: Ambiguity, Agency, and Power.* Cambridge, UK: Cambridge University Press.

Maier, Charles S. 1977. "The Politics of Productivity: Foundations of American International Economic Policy after World War II." *International Organization* 31 (4): 607–633.

Marty, Frédéric. 1999. "Électricité de France et les constructeurs de matériels électromécaniques. La construction d'un cercle vertueux de coopération (1946–1955)." *Bulletin d'histoire de l'électricité* 34: 51–98.

Mason, Paul. 2015. *Postcapitalism: A Guide to Our Future.* New York, NY: Farrar, Straus, / Giroux.

Matsushita Electrical Industrial Co., Ltd. v. Zenith Radio Corp., 475 U.S. 574 (1986).

Means, Gardiner Coit. 1935. *Senate Document 13: Industrial Prices and their Relative Inflexibility.* Available at https://archive.org/details/CAT10505731. Washington, DC: US Government Printing Office.

Melitz, Marc J. 2003. "The Impact of Trade on Intra-Industry Reallocations and Aggregate Industry Productivity." *Econometrica* 71 (6): 1695–1725.

Meyer, John W., and Brian Rowan. 1977. "Institutionalized Organizations: Formal Structure as Myth and Ceremony." *American Journal of Sociology* 83 (2): 340–363.

Milanovic, Branko. 2016. *Global Inequality: A New Approach for the Age of Globalization.* Cambridge, MA: Harvard University Press.

Milward, Alan S. 1984. *The Reconstruction of Western Europe, 1945–1951.* Berkeley, CA: University of California Press.

Monnet, Eric. 2018. *Controlling Credit: Central Banking and the Planned Economy in Postwar France, 1948–1973.* Cambridge, UK: Cambridge University Press.

Monsanto Co. v. Spray-Rite Svc. Corp., 465 U.S. 752 (1984).

Montalban, Matthieu, Sigfrido Ramirez-Perez, and Andy Smith. 2011. *EU Competition Policy Revisited: Economic Doctrines within European Political Work.* Technical report. Available at https://www.researchgate.net/publication/254417941_EU_Competition_Policy_Revisited_Economic_Doctrines_Within_European_Political_Work. GREThA, Working Paper.

Moravcsik, Andrew. 1998. *The Choice for Europe: Social Purpose and State Power from Messina to Maastricht.* Ithaca, NY: Cornell University Press.

Neumann, Franz Leopold. 1942. *Behemoth: The Structure and Practice of National Socialism, 1933–1944.* London, UK: Viktor Gollancz.

New York v. Deutsche Telekom AG., 439 F. Supp. 3d 179 (S.D.N.Y. 2020).

Nisbett, Richard E., and Lee Ross. 1980. *Human Inference: Strategies and Shortcomings of Social Judgment.* Englewood Cliffs, NJ: Prentice-Hall.

Nord, Philip. 2010. *France's New Deal: From the Thirties to the Postwar Era.* Princeton, NJ: Princeton University Press.

Nordhaus, William D. 1974. "The Falling Share of Profits." *Brookings Papers on Economic Activity* 1974 (1): 169–217.

Nozick, Robert. 1974. *Anarchy, State, and Utopia.* Vol. 5038. New York, NY: Basic Books.

Ohio v. American Express Co., 138 S.Ct. 2274 (2018).

Olson, Mancur. 1965. *The Logic of Collective Action.* Cambridge, MA: Harvard University Press.

Owen, John M. 2010. *The Clash of Ideas in World Politics: Transnational Networks, States, and Regime Change, 1510–2010.* Princeton, NJ: Princeton University Press.

Paul, Sanjukta. 2019. "Fissuring and the Firm Exemption." *Law & Contemporary Problems* 82: 65.

Paul, Sanjukta. 2020. "Antitrust as Allocator of Coordination Rights." *UCLA Law Review* 67 (2): 1–64.

Peinert, Erik. 2020. "Cartels, Competition, and Coalitions: The Domestic Drivers of International Orders." *Review of International Political Economy*, 1–25.

Peinert, Erik. 2023. "Intellectual Property and the Fissured Economy." *American Affairs* 7 (2): 3–22.

Perlstein, Rick. 2014. *The Invisible Bridge: The Fall of Nixon and the Rise of Reagan.* Simon / Schuster.

Pertschuk, Michael. 1982. *Revolt against Regulation: The Rise and Pause of the Consumer Movement.* University of California Press.

Peterson, Peter G. 1971a. *The United States in the Changing World Economy.* Vol. 1. Washington, DC: US Government Printing Office.

Peterson, Peter G. 1971b. *The United States in the Changing World Economy.* Vol. 2. Washington, DC: US Government Printing Office.

Peterson, Peter G. 2009. *The Education of an American Dreamer: How a Son of Greek Immigrants Learned His Way from a Nebraska Diner to Washington, Wall Street, and Beyond.* New York, NY: Twelve.

Philippon, Thomas. 2019. *The Great Reversal: How America Gave Up on Free Markets.* Cambridge, MA: Harvard University Press.

Pierson, Paul. 2000. "Increasing Returns, Path Dependence, and the Study of Politics." *American Political Science Review* 94 (2): 251–267. https://doi.org/10.2307/2586011.

Piore, Michael J, and Charles Sabel. 1984. *The Second Industrial Divide: Possibilities for Prosperity.* New York, NY: Basic Books.

Pitofsky, Robert. 2008. *How the Chicago School Overshot the Mark: The Effect of Conservative Economic Analysis on US Antitrust.* Oxford University Press.

Posner, Richard A. 1971. "A Program for the Antitrust Division." *The University of Chicago Law Review* 38 (3): 500–536.

Posner, Richard A. 1974. "Exclusionary Practices and the Antitrust Laws." *The University of Chicago Law Review* 41 (3): 506–535.

Posner, Richard A. 1979. "The Chicago School of Antitrust Analysis." *University of Pennsylvania Law Review* 127 (4): 925–948.

Posner, Richard A. 1976. *Antitrust Law: An Economic Perspective.* Chicago, IL: University of Chicago Press.

Powell, Lewis F. 1971. "Attack on American Free Enterprise System." *Memo from Lewis Powell to Eugene Sydnor, Jr.*

Prasad, Monica. 2012. *The Land of Too Much: American Abundance and the Paradox of Poverty.* Cambridge, MA: Harvard University Press.

Priest, George L. 2014. "Bork's Strategy and the Influence of the Chicago School on Modern Antitrust Law." *The Journal of Law and Economics* 57 (S3): S1–S17.

Quennouëlle-Corre, Laure. 2000. *La Direction du Trésor 1947-1967: L'État-banquier et la croissance.* Vincennes, France: Comité pour l'histoire économique et financière.

Rahman, K. Sabeel, and Kathleen Thelen. 2019. "The Rise of the Platform Business Model and the Transformation of Twenty-First-Century Capitalism." *Politics & Society* 47 (2): 177–204.

Rawls, John. 1973. *A Theory of Justice.* Cambridge, MA: Harvard University Press.

Reiter v. Sonotone Corp., 442 U.S. 330 (1979).

Rikap, Cecilia. 2022. "Amazon: A Story of Accumulation through Intellectual Rentiership and Predation." *Competition & Change* 26 (3–4): 436–466.

Robin, Corey. 2011. *The Reactionary Mind: Conservatism from Edmund Burke to Sarah Palin.* Oxford, UK: Oxford University Press.

Robinson, Joan. 1933. *The Economics of Imperfect Competition.* New York, NY: Macmillan.

Rogowski, Ronald, and Mark Andreas Kayser. 2002. "Majoritarian Electoral Systems and Consumer Power: Price-Level Evidence from the OECD Countries." *American Journal of Political Science*: 526–539.

Romer, Christina D. 1999. "Why Did Prices Rise in the 1930s?" *The Journal of Economic History* 59 (1): 167–199.

Romer, Paul M. 1990. "Endogenous Technological Change." *Journal of Political Economy* 98 (5): S71–S102.

Ross, Lee, Mark R. Lepper, and Michael Hubbard. 1975. "Perseverance in Self-Perception and Social Perception: Biased Attributional Processes in the Debriefing Paradigm." *Journal of Personality and Social Psychology* 32 (5): 880.

Safire, William. 1975. *Before the Fall: An Inside vVew of the Pre-Watergate White House.* New York, NY: Doubleday & Co.

Sanders, Elizabeth. 1999. *Roots of Reform: Farmers, Workers, and the American State, 1877–1917.* University of Chicago Press.

Saunders, Elizabeth N. 2011. *Leaders at War: How Presidents Shape Military Interventions.* Ithaca, NY: Cornell University Press.

Sawyer, Laura Phillips. 2018. *American Fair Trade: Proprietary Capitalism, Corporatism, and the 'New Competition,' 1890–1940.* Cambridge University Press.

Schickler, Eric. 2001. *Disjointed Pluralism: Institutional Innovation and the Development of the U.S. Congress.* Princeton, NJ: Princeton University Press.

Schlesinger, Arthur M. 1957. *The Crisis of the Old Order, The Age of Roosevelt.* Vol. 1. New York, NY: Houghton Mifflin Harcourt.

Schlesinger, Arthur M. 1958. *The Coming of the New Deal: 1933–1935, The Age of Roosevelt.* Vol. 2. New York, NY: Houghton Mifflin Harcourt.

Schlesinger, Arthur M. 1960. *The Politics of Upheaval: 1935–1936, The Age of Roosevelt.* Vol. 3. New York, NY: Houghton Mifflin Harcourt.

Schmalensee, Richard. 1998. "Bill Baxter in the Antitrust Arena: An Economist's Appreciation." *Stanford Law Review* 51: 1317.

Schmalz, Martin C. 2021. "Recent Studies on Common Ownership, Firm Behavior, and Market Outcomes." *The Antitrust Bulletin* 66 (1): 12–38.

Schmidt, Vivien A. 1996. *From State to Market?: The Transformation of French Business and Government.* Cambridge, UK: Cambridge University Press.

Schmidt, Vivien A. 2002. *The Futures of European Capitalism.* Oxford, UK: Oxford University Press.

Schonfield, Andrew. 1965. *Modern Capitalism: The Changing Balance of Public and Private Power.* London, UK: Oxford University.

Schumpeter, Joseph A. 1942. *Capitalism, Socialism, and Democracy.* New York, NY: Harper / Brothers.

Schumpeter, Joseph Alois. 1939. *Business Cycles: A Theoretical, Historical, and Statistical Analysis of the Capitalist Process.* New York, NY: McGraw-Hill.

Schwartz, Herman Mark. 2016. "Wealth and Secular Stagnation: The Role of Industrial Organization and Intellectual Property Rights." *Russel Sage Foundation Journal* 2 (6): 226–249.

Schwartz, Herman Mark. 2020. "Intellectual Property, Technorents and the Labour Share of Production." *Competition & Change* (*available online*):1–21.

Schwartz, H. M. (2021). Global secular stagnation and the rise of intellectual property monopoly. *Review of International Political Economy, 29*(5), 1448–1476. https://doi.org/10.1080/09692290.2021.1918745

Sell, Susan K. 1998. *Power and Ideas: North-South Politics of Intellectual Property and Antitrust.* Albany, NY: SUNY Press.

Sell, Susan K. 2003. *Private Power, Public Law: The Globalization of Intellectual Property Rights.* Cambridge, UK: Cambridge University Press.

Servan-Schreiber, Jean-Jacques. 1967. *Le défi américain.* Paris, France: Denoël.

Silkenat, James R. 1978. "Book Review: The Antitrust Paradox: A Policy at War with Itself." *University of Pennsylvania Law Review* 127 (1): 273–282.

Skocpol, Theda, and Margaret Somers. 1980. "The Uses of Comparative History in Macrosocial Inquiry." *Comparative Studies in Society and History* 22 (2): 174–197.

Song, Jae, David J. Price, Fatih Guvenen, Nicholas Bloom, and Till Von Wachter. 2019. "Firming Up Inequality." *The Quarterly Journal of Economics* 134 (1): 1–50. https://doi.org/10.1093/qje/qjy025.

Standard Oil Co. of California and Standard Stations, Inc. v. United States, 337 U.S. 293 (1949).

State Oil Co. v. Khan, 522 U.S. 3 (1997).

Staw, Barry M. 1976. "Knee-Deep in the Big Muddy: A Study of Escalating Commitment to a Chosen Course of Action." *Organizational Behavior and Human Performance* 16 (1): 27–44. https://doi.org/10.1016/0030-5073(76)90005-2.

Steinmo, Sven. 2010. *The Evolution of Modern States: Sweden, Japan, and the United States*. Cambridge, UK: Cambridge University Press.

Stevens, Ashley J. 2004. "The Enactment of Bayh-Dole." *The Journal of Technology Transfer* 29 (1): 93–99.

Stoleru, Lionel. 1969. *L'impératif industriel*. Paris, France: Seuil.

Stoller, Matt. 2019. *Goliath: The 100-Year War between Monopoly Power and Democracy*. New York, NY: Simon & Schuster.

Streeck, Wolfgang, and Kathleen Ann Thelen. 2005. *Beyond Continuity: Institutional Change in Advanced Political Economies*. Oxford, UK: Oxford University Press.

Summers, Anthony. 2000. *The Arrogance of Power: The Secret World of Richard Nixon*. New York, NY: Penguin Books.

Tetlock, Philip E. 1999. "Theory-Driven Reasoning about Plausible Pasts and Probable Futures in World Politics: Are We Prisoners of Our Preconceptions?" *American Journal of Political Science* 43 (2): 335–366. https://doi.org/10.2307/2991798.

Tetlock, Philip E. 2005. *Expert Political Judgment: How Good Is It? How Can We Know?* Princeton, NJ: Princeton University Press.

Teulings, Coen, and Richard Baldwin. 2014. "Secular Stagnation: Facts, Causes and Cures." *London: Centre for Economic Policy Research-CEPR*.

Thelen, Kathleen. 1999. "Historical Institutionalism in Comparative Politics." *Annual Review of Political Science* 2 (1): 369–404.

Thelen, Kathleen. 2014. *Varieties of Liberalization and the New Politics of Social Solidarity*. Cambridge, UK: Cambridge University Press.

Timken Roller Bearing Co. v. United States, 341 U.S. 593 (1951).

Townsend, James B. 1980. *Extraterritorial Antitrust: The Sherman Antitrust Act Versus US Business Abroad*. Boulder, CO: Westview Press.

United States v. Baker Hughes Inc., 908 F.2d 981 (D.C. Cir. 1990).

United States v. Alcoa, 148 F.2d 416 (2d Cir. 1945).

United States v. Arnold, Schwinn & Co., 388 U.S. 365 (1967).

United States v. General Dynamics Corp., 415 U.S. 486 (1974).

United States v. General Elec. Co., 272 U.S. 476 (1926).

United States v. General Electric Co., 80 F. Supp. 989 (S.D.N.Y. 1948).

United States v. General Electric Co., 82 F. Supp. 753 (D.N.J. 1949).

United States v. International Harvester Co., 564 F.2d 769 (7th Cir. 1977).

United States v. Minnesota Mining & Mfg. Co., 92 F. Supp. 947 (D. Mass. 1950).

United States v. National Lead Co., 332 U.S. 319 (1947).

United States v. Philadelphia Nat'l Bank, 374 U.S. 321 (1963).

United States v. Socony-Vacuum Oil Co., 310 U.S. 150 (1940).

United States v. Trans-Missouri Freight Assn., 166 U.S. 290 (1897).

United States v. United States Steel Corp., 251 U.S. 417 (1920).

United States v. Von's Grocery Co., 384 U.S. 270 (1966).

Vaheesan, Sandeep. 2022. “The Morality of Monopolization Law.” *Wm. & Mary L. Rev. Online* 63:119.

Vail, Mark I. 2017. *Liberalism in Illiberal States: Ideas and Economic Adjustment in Contemporary Europe.* Oxford, UK: Oxford University Press.

Van Bavel, and Bas. 2016. *The Invisible Hand?: How Market Economies Have Emerged and Declined since AD 500.* Oxford, UK: Oxford University Press.

Van Evera, Stephen. 1997. *Guide to Methods for Students of Political Science.* Ithaca, NY: Cornell University Press.

Verdier, Daniel. 2002. *Moving Money: Banking and Finance in the Industrialized World.* Cambridge, UK: Cambridge University Press.

Vogel, David. 1989. *Fluctuating Fortunes: The Political Power of Business in America.* Beard Books.

Wade, Nicholas. 1979. “Carter Plan to Spur Industrial Innovation: Elaborate Bureaucratic Exercise Produces Small-Scale Program to Revitalize US Industry.” *Science* 206 (4420): 800–801.

Waller, Spencer Weber. 2006. *Thurman Arnold: A Biography.* New York University Press.

Warlouzet, Laurent. 2011. *Le choix de la CEE par la France: L'Europe économique en débat de Mendès France à de Gaulle (1955–1969).* Vincennes, France: Comité pour l'histoire économique et financière.

Warlouzet, Laurent. 2018. *Governing Europe in a Globalizing World: Neoliberalism and its Alternatives following the 1973 Oil Crisis.* London, UK: Routledge.

Waterhouse, Benjamin C. 2013. *Lobbying America: The Politics of Business from Nixon to NAFTA.* Princeton, NJ: Princeton University Press.

Webster, Donna M., and Arie W. Kruglanski. 1994. “Individual Differences in Need for Cognitive Closure.” *Journal of Personality and Social Psychology* 67 (6): 1049. https://doi.org/10.1037//0022-3514.67.6.1049.

Weil, David. 2014. *The Fissured Workplace: Why Work Became So Bad for So Many and What Can Be Done to Improve It.* Cambridge, MA: Harvard University Press.

Wells, Wyatt C. 2002. *Antitrust and the Formation of the Postwar World.* New York, NY: Columbia University Press.

Weymouth, Stephen. 2016. “Competition Politics: Interest Groups, Democracy, and Antitrust Reform in Developing Countries.” *The Antitrust Bulletin* 61 (2): 296–316.

Widmaier, Wesley. 2016. *Economic Ideas in Political Time.* Cambridge, UK: Cambridge University Press.

Williams, Philip M. 1964. *Crisis and Compromise: Politics and the Fourth Republic.* London, UK: Longmans.

Wilmers, Nathan. 2018. “Wage Stagnation and Buyer Power: How Buyer-Supplier Relations Affect US Workers' Wages, 1978 to 2014.” *American Sociological Review* 83 (2): 213–242.

Zhang, Angela. 2021. *Chinese Antitrust Exceptionalism: How the Rise of China Challenges Global Regulation.* Oxford, UK: Oxford University Press.

Zysman, John. 1983. *Governments, Markets, and Growth: Financial Systems and the Politics of Industrial Change.* Ithaca, NY: Cornell University Press.

Index

Page references in *italics* indicate a figure; page references in **bold** indicate a table.